# Adobe® Illustrator® CC
# Digital Classroom®

Jennifer Smith and the AGI Creative Team

WILEY |

# Adobe® Illustrator® CC Digital Classroom®

Published by
John Wiley & Sons, Inc.
10475 Crosspoint Blvd.
Indianapolis, IN 46256

Copyright © 2013 by John Wiley & Sons, Inc., Indianapolis, Indiana
Published simultaneously in Canada
ISBN: 978-1-118-63971-9
Manufactured in the United States of America
10 9 8 7 6 5 4 3 2 1

For general information on our other products and services or to obtain technical support, please contact our Customer Care Department within the U.S. at (877) 762-2974, outside the U.S. at (317) 572-3993 or fax (317) 572-4002.

Wiley publishes in a variety of print and electronic formats and by print-on-demand. Some material included with standard print versions of this book may not be included in e-books or in print-on-demand. If this book refers to media such as a CD or DVD that is not included in the version you purchased, you may download this material after registering your book at www.digitalclassroombooks.com/CC/Illustrator. For more information about Wiley products, visit www.wiley.com.

Please report any errors by sending a message to errata@agitraining.com

Library of Congress Control Number: 2013948014

## Credits

**Revisions and Writing**
Bill Carberry

**President, American Graphics Institute and Digital Classroom Series Publisher**
Christopher Smith

**Executive Editor**
Jody Lefevere

**Technical Editors**
Haziel Olivera, Lauren Mickol

**Editor**
Karla E. Melendez

**Editorial Director**
Robyn Siesky

**Business Manager**
Amy Knies

**Senior Marketing Manager**
Sandy Smith

**Vice President and Executive Group Publisher**
Richard Swadley

**Vice President and Executive Publisher**
Barry Pruett

**Senior Project Coordinator**
Katherine Crocker

**Project Manager**
Cheri White

**Graphics and Production Specialist**
Jason Miranda, Spoke & Wheel

**Media Development Project Supervisor**
Chris Leavey

**Proofreading**
Karla E. Melendez

**Indexing**
Michael Ferreira

## About the Authors

**Jennifer Smith** is a designer, educator, and author. She has authored more than 20 books on digital design and creative software tools. She provides consulting and training services across a wide range of industries, including working with software developers, magazine publishers, catalog and online retailers, as well as some of the biggest names in fashion, apparel, and footwear design. When not writing or consulting, you'll find her delivering professional development workshops for colleges and universities.

Jennifer also works extensively in the field of web usability and user experience design. Jennifer works alongside application developers and web developers to create engaging and authentic experiences for users on mobile devices, tablets, and traditional computers. She has twice been named a Most Valuable Professional by Microsoft for her work in user experience (UX), user interface (UI) design fields, and her leadership in educating users on how to integrate design and development skills.

Jennifer Smith's books on Photoshop, Illustrator, and the Creative Suite tools include the *Photoshop Digital Classroom*, the *Illustrator Digital Classroom*, and the *Adobe Creative Suite for Dummies*, all published by Wiley. She has also authored *Wireframing and Prototyping with Expression Blend & Sketchflow*.

Jennifer is the cofounder of the American Graphics Institute (AGI). You can find her blog and contact her at *JenniferSmith.com* and follow her on Twitter @jsmithers.

The **AGI Creative Team** is composed of Adobe Certified Experts and Instructors from AGI. The AGI Creative Team has authored more than 25 Digital Classroom books and has created many of Adobe's official training guides. The AGI Creative Team works with many of the world's most prominent companies, helping them use creative software to communicate more effectively and creatively. They work with design, creative, and marketing teams around the world, delivering private customized training programs, while teaching regularly scheduled classes at AGI's locations. The AGI Creative Team is available for professional development sessions at companies, schools, and universities. Get more information at *agitraining.com*.

## Acknowledgments

Thanks to our many friends at Adobe Systems, Inc. who made this book possible and assisted with questions and feedback during the writing process. To the many clients of AGI who have helped us better understand how they use Illustrator and provided us with many of the tips and suggestions found in this book. A special thanks to the instructional team at AGI for their input and assistance in the review process and for making this book such a team effort.

# Register your Digital Classroom book for exclusive benefits

Registered owners receive access to:

 The most current lesson files

 Technical resources and customer support

 Notifications of updates

 Online access to video tutorials

 Downloadable lesson files

 Samples from other Digital Classroom books

Register at *DigitalClassroomBooks.com/CC/Illustrator*

# DigitalClassroom

Register your book today at
DigitalClassroomBooks.com/CC/Illustrator

# Contents

## Starting up

## Lesson 1: Adobe Illustrator CC Jumpstart

## Lesson 2: Getting to Know the Workspace

## Lesson 3: Illustrator CC Essentials

## Lesson 4: Adding Color

## Lesson 5: Working with the Drawing Tools

## Lesson 6: Exploring Additional Color Options

## Lesson 7: Using Patterns

## Lesson 8: Working with and Formatting Text

## Lesson 9: Organizing your Illustrations with Layers

## Lesson 10: Working with Symbols

## Lesson 11: Using Effects and Transparency

## Lesson 12: Exporting and Saving Files

## Lesson 13: Advanced Blending Techniques

## Lesson 14: Adobe Illustrator CC New Features

# Starting up

## About Illustrator Digital Classroom

The *Adobe® Illustrator® CC Digital Classroom* lets you create artwork for a variety of uses. Illustrator's drawing tools let you take advantage of many ways to control color, text, and artwork in your designs. Illlustrator provides you with ways to express your creative ideas and experiment with the presentation.

The *Adobe Illustrator CC Digital Classroom* helps you get up-and-running right away. You can work through all the lessons in this book, or complete only specific lessons. Each lesson includes detailed, step-by-step instructions, along with lesson files, useful background information, and video tutorials on the included DVD–it is like having your own expert instructor guiding you through each lesson while you work at your own pace. This book includes 14 self-paced lessons that let you discover essential skills, explore new features, and understand capabilities that will save you time. You'll be productive right away with real-world exercises and simple explanations. The *Adobe Illustrator CC Digital Classroom* lessons are developed by the same team of Illustrator experts who have created many official training titles for Adobe Systems.

## Prerequisites

Before you start the *Adobe Illustrator CC Digital Classroom* lessons, you should have a working knowledge of your computer and its operating system. You should know how to use the directory system of your computer so that you can navigate through folders. You also need to understand how to locate, save, and open files, and you should also know how to use your mouse to access menus and commands.

Before starting the lessons files in the *Adobe Illustrator CC Digital Classroom*, make sure that you have installed Adobe Illustrator CC. The software is sold as part of the Creative Cloud, and is not included with this book. Find more information about the Creative Cloud at *www.adobe.com/CreativeCloud*. You can use the free 30-day trial version of Adobe Illustrator CC available at the *adobe.com* website, subject to the terms of its license agreement.

### System requirements

Before starting the lessons in the *Adobe Illustrator CC Digital Classroom*, make sure that your computer is equipped for running Adobe Illustrator CC. The minimum system requirements for your computer to effectively use the software are listed below and you can find the most current system requirements at *http://www.adobe.com/products/Illustrator/tech-specs.html*.

### Windows

- Intel® Pentium® 4 or AMD Athlon® 64 processor
- Microsoft® Windows® 7 with Service Pack 1 or Windows 8
- 1 GB of RAM (3 GB recommended) for 32 bit; 2 GB of RAM (8 GB recommended) for 64 bit
- 2 GB of available hard-disk space for installation; additional free space required during installation (cannot install on removable flash storage devices)
- 1024 × 768 display (1280 × 800 recommended)
- Internet connection and registration are necessary for required software activation, membership validation, and access to online services.

### Mac OS

- Multicore Intel processor with 64-bit support
- Mac OS X v10.6.8, v10.7, or v10.8
- 2 GB of RAM (8 GB recommended)
- 2 GB of available hard-disk space for installation; additional free space required during installation (cannot install on a volume that uses a case-sensitive file system or on removable flash storage devices)
- 1024 × 768 display (1280 × 800 recommended)
- Internet connection and registration are necessary for required software activation, membership validation, and access to online services.

## Starting Adobe Illustrator CC

As with most software, Adobe Illustrator CC is launched by locating the application in your Programs folder (Windows) or Applications folder (Mac OS). If you are not familiar with starting the program, follow these steps to start the Adobe Illustrator CC application:

### Windows

1   Choose Start > All Programs > Adobe Illustrator CC.

2   If a Welcome Screen appears, you can close it.

### Mac OS

1   Open the Applications folder, and then open the Adobe Illustrator CC folder.

2   Double-click the Adobe Illustrator CC application icon.

3   If a Welcome Screen appears, you can close it.

*Menus and commands are identified throughout the book by using the greater-than symbol (>). For example, the command to print a document appears as File > Print.*

## Access lesson files and videos any time

Register your book at *www.digitalclassroombooks.com/CC/Illustrator* to gain access to your lesson files on any computer you own, or to watch the videos on any Internet-connected computer, tablet, or smart phone. You'll be able to continue your learning anywhere you have an Internet connection. This provides you access to lesson files and videos even if you misplace your DVD.

## Checking for updated lesson files

Make sure you have the most up-to-date lesson files and learn about any updates to your *Adobe Illustrator CC Digital Classroom* book by registering your book at *www.digitalclassroombooks.com/CC/Illustrator.*

## Resetting Adobe Illustrator CC preferences

When you start Adobe Illustrator, it remembers certain settings along with the configuration of the workspace from the last time you used the application. It is useful for you to start each of the Adobe Illustrator lessons in this book using the default settings so that you do not see unexpected results. You can use the following steps to reset the Adobe Illustrator CC preferences.

In order to reset your preferences you will need to quit Illustrator and locate the preferences. In Windows and the Mac OS these are in two separate locations. If you are working on a Windows system you might need to change the folder's view settings in order to find the preferences. Keep in mind that when you reset your preferences you lose saved colors, styles and other preferences that might be important to you. If you wish to save your preferences, rename them instead of deleting them; Illustrator will create all new preferences if it cannot locate the appropriately named folder.

### Steps to resetting Windows preferences

1  Quit Adobe Illustrator CC.

2  In Windows, verify that you can find the hidden AppData folder by opening your Control Panel and typing **Folder Options** into the search text field in the upper-right of the Control panel dialog box.

3  When Folder Options appears, click Show hidden files and folders.

**4**   In the View tab of Folder Options click the radio box to select Show hidden files, folders and drives. Click OK.

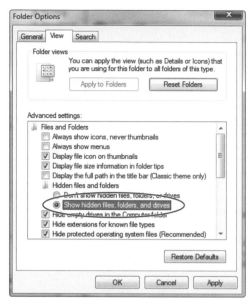

*In Windows, you might have to change your folders to show Hidden folders.*

**5**   Select C:\Users\user name\AppData\Roaming\Adobe\Adobe Illustrator\.

**6**   Select the folder named Adobe Illustrator CC Settings. If you want to save custom settings to restore at a later time, rename this file **Adobe Illustrator CC Settings folder_old**.

**7**   If you want to delete the preferences and start with new clean preferences, delete the entire Adobe Illustrator CC Settings folder.

**8**   Relaunch Adobe Illustrator CC. Your preferences are back to the original settings.

## Steps to resetting Mac OS preferences

**1**   Quit Adobe Illustrator CC.

**2**   Choose User > Library > Preference and select the Adobe Illustrator CC Settings folder.

**3**   Select the folder named Adobe Illustrator CC Settings. If you want to save custom settings to restore at a later time, rename this file **Adobe Illustrator CC Settings folder_old**.

**4**   If you want to delete the preferences and start with new clean preferences, delete the entire Adobe Illustrator CC Settings folder.

**5**   Relaunch Adobe Illustrator CC. Your preferences are back to the original settings.

To restore custom settings, Quit Adobe Illustrator, and then delete the new AIPrefs file and restore the original name of the previous AIPrefs file.

# Loading lesson files

The *Adobe Illustrator CC Digital Classroom* DVD includes files that accompany the exercises for each of the lessons. You can copy the entire lessons folder from the supplied DVD to your hard drive, or copy only the lesson folders for the individual lessons you want to complete.

For each lesson in the book, the files are referenced by file name. The exact location of each file on your computer is not used, as you might have placed the files in a unique location on your hard drive. We suggest placing the lesson files in the My Documents folder (Windows), at the top level of your hard drive (Mac OS), or on your desktop for easy access.

## Copying the lesson files to your hard drive

1    Insert the *Adobe Illustrator CC Digital Classroom* DVD supplied with this book.

2    On your computer desktop, navigate to the DVD and locate the folder named ailessons.

3    You can install all the files, or just specific lesson files. Do one of the following:

   • Install all lesson files by dragging the ailessons folder to your hard drive.

   • Install only some of the files by creating a new folder on your hard drive named ailessons. Open the ailessons folder on the supplied DVD, select the lesson you want to complete, and drag the folder(s) to the ailessons folder you created on your hard drive.

## Unlocking Mac OS files

Macintosh users might need to unlock the files after copying them from the accompanying disc. This only applies to Mac OS computers and is because the Mac OS might view files that are copied from a DVD or CD as being locked for writing.

If you are a Mac OS user and have difficulty saving over the existing files in this book, you can use these instructions so that you can update the lesson files as you work on them and also add new files to the lessons folder.

Note that you only need to follow these instructions if you are unable to save over the existing lesson files, or if you are unable to save files into the lesson folder.

1    After copying the files to your computer, click once to select the ailessons folder, then choose File > Get Info from within the Finder (not Illustrator).

2    In the ailessons info window, click the triangle to the left of Sharing and Permissions to reveal the details of this section.

3    In the Sharing and Permissions section, click the lock icon, if necessary, in the lower-right corner so that you can make changes to the permissions.

4    Click to select a specific user or select everyone, then change the Privileges section to Read & Write.

5    Click the lock icon to prevent further changes, and then close the window.

# Working with the video tutorials

Your *Illustrator CC Digital Classroom* DVD comes with video tutorials developed by the authors to help you understand the concepts explored in each lesson. Each tutorial is approximately five minutes long and demonstrates and explains the concepts and features covered in the lesson.

The videos are designed to supplement your understanding of the material in the chapter. We have selected exercises and examples that we feel will be most useful to you. You might want to view the entire video for each lesson before you begin that lesson. Additionally, at certain points in a lesson, you will encounter the DVD icon. The icon, with appropriate lesson number, indicates that an overview of the exercise being described can be found in the accompanying video.

*DVD video icon.*

## Setting up for viewing the video tutorials

The DVD included with this book includes video tutorials for each lesson. Although you can view the lessons on your computer directly from the DVD, we recommend copying the folder labeled videos from the *Adobe Illustrator CC Digital Classroom* DVD to your hard drive.

### Copying the video tutorials to your hard drive

1   Insert the *Adobe Illustrator CC Digital Classroom* DVD supplied with this book.

2   On your computer desktop, navigate to the DVD and locate the folder named videos.

3   Drag the videos folder to a location on your hard drive.

### Viewing the video tutorials with the Adobe Flash Player

The videos on the *Adobe Illustrator CC Digital Classroom* DVD are saved in the Flash projector format. A Flash projector file wraps the Digital Classroom video player and the Adobe Flash Player in an executable file (.exe for Windows or .app for Mac OS). Note that the extension (on both platforms) might not always be visible. Projector files allow the Flash content to be deployed on your system without the need for a browser or prior stand–alone player installation.

### Playing the video tutorials

**1** On your computer, navigate to the videos folder you copied to your hard drive from the DVD. Playing the videos directly from the DVD could result in poor quality playback.

**2** Open the videos folder and double-click the Flash file named PLAY_AICCvideos to view the video tutorials.

**3** After the Flash player launches, click the Play button to view the videos.

The Flash Player has a simple user interface that allows you to control the viewing experience, including stopping, pausing, playing, and restarting the video. You can also rewind or fast-forward, and adjust the playback volume.

Lesson 06: Creating a Good Image

*A. Go to beginning. B. Play/Pause. C. Fast-forward/rewind. D. Stop. E. Volume Off/On. F. Volume control.*

*Playback volume is also affected by the settings in your operating system. Be certain to adjust the sound volume for your computer, in addition to the sound controls in the Player window.*

# Additional resources

The Digital Classroom series goes beyond the training books. You can continue your learning online, with training videos, at seminars and conferences, and in-person training events.

### On-demand video training from the authors

Comprehensive video training from the authors are available at *DigitalClassroom.com*. Find complete video training along with thousands of video tutorials covering Illustrator and related Creative Cloud apps along with digital versions of the Digital Classroom book series. Learn more at *DigitalClassroom.com*.

### Training from the Authors

The authors are available for professional development training workshops for schools and companies. They also teach classes at American Graphics Institute, including training classes and online workshops. Visit *agitraining.com* for more information about Digital Classroom author-led training classes or workshops.

### Additional Adobe Creative Cloud Books

Expand your knowledge of creative software applications with the Digital Classroom book series. Books are available for most creative software applications as well as web design and development tools and technologies. Learn more at *DigitalClassroomBooks.com*

### Seminars and conferences

The authors of the Digital Classroom seminar series frequently conduct in-person seminars and speak at conferences, including the annual CRE8 Conference. Learn more at *agitraining.com* and *CRE8summit.com*.

### Resources for educators

Visit *digitalclassroombooks.com* to access resources for educators, including instructors' guides for incorporating Digital Classroom into your curriculum.

## What you'll learn in this lesson:

- Setting up an Artboard
- Creating and combining shapes
- Applying color with the new Kuler panel and effects
- Adding and adjusting text with the new Touch Type Tool
- Importing an image
- Cloning objects

# Adobe Illustrator CC Jumpstart

*In this lesson, you have the opportunity to dive right into Adobe Illustrator CC and create an exciting illustration. This lesson helps you quickly discover some of the essential features available in CC. If you are a completely new user, you might want to start with Lesson 2, "Getting to Know the Workspace," and then return to this lesson.*

## Starting up

Register your book at *www.digitalclassroombooks.com/CC/Illustrator* to gain access to updated lesson files on any computer or watch the videos online.

Before starting, make sure that your tools and panels are consistent by resetting your workspace. See "Resetting Adobe Illustrator CC Preferences" in the Starting up section of this book.

You will work with several files from the ai01lessons folder in this lesson. Make sure that you have loaded the ailessons folder onto your hard drive from the included DVD. See "Loading lesson files" in the Starting up section of this book.

**See Lesson 1 in action!**

*Use the accompanying video to gain a better understanding of how to use some of the features shown in this lesson. You can find the video tutorial for this lesson on the included DVD.*

## The project

In this lesson, you will create a comp (rough design) of an ad using some features that have been around for years, as well as newer features recently added to Adobe Illustrator CC.

**1**   Launch Adobe Illustrator CC.

**2**   Choose File > Browse in Bridge or click the Go to Bridge button (Br) in the Application bar at the top of the workspace.

By clicking the Go to Bridge button, you launch a separate application called Adobe Bridge. Bridge is an indispensable application that acts as the central command center for all your CC applications, and helps you to organize your Adobe Illustrator projects. You can use Bridge to help you easily locate files, since it provides a preview of every file within any folder.

**3**　Once Bridge opens, navigate to the ai01lessons folder within the ailessons folder that you copied to your computer, and double-click **ai0101_done.ai** to open it. If an embedded Profile Mismatch dialog box appears, leave it at the defaults and click OK. The artwork for a rough design of an ad appears. You can keep this completed file open for reference, or choose File > Close to close it. If you are asked to save the file, choose No (Windows) or Don't Save (Mac OS).

*The completed rough design of an ad.*

*The Illustrator CC workspace is nearly identical to CS6, so that fewer steps are needed to accomplish daily tasks. You will explore this new interface in Lesson 2, "Getting to Know the Workspace."*

**4**　For this lesson, you want to have multiple panels showing at the same time. To make sure that you can follow the lesson more easily, choose Window > Workspace > Essentials, or choose Essentials from the drop-down menu on the right side of the application bar.

## Setting up the Artboard

You will now set up the artboard to create your comp for an ad.

**1** Choose File > New. The New Document dialog box appears. Type **ai0101_work** into the Name text field.

**2** Choose Print from the New Document Profile drop-down menu. By choosing the Print preset your default colors, patterns, and gradients are built from CMYK (Cyan, Magenta, Yellow, and Black) colors.

**3** Make certain that Letter is selected from the Size drop-down menu, and select Inches instead of Points in the Units drop-down menu. Set the document to Landscape by clicking the Orientation button on the right (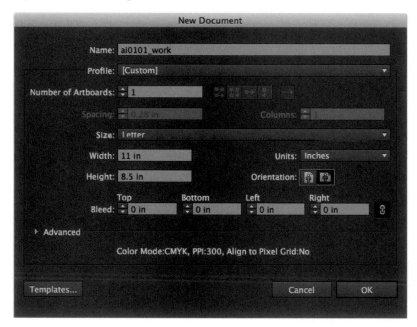). Click OK; the new document is created. The document window contains a blank artboard, which represents the region that contains printable artwork.

*Define the settings in the New Document dialog box.*

# Creating the background shape

You will now create the fundamental shape that will be used as the background of the ad. You will use two separate shapes and then combine them using the Shape Builder tool (⊕).

**1** Click and hold the Rectangle tool in the Tools panel to select the Rounded Rectangle tool (▢) and click once on the artboard; the Rounded Rectangle dialog box appears.

*In order to enter exact values, you are clicking and releasing with your mouse on the artboard. If you accidently drag your mouse, the Rounded Rectangle dialog box will not appear. If the Rounded Rectangle dialog box does not appear, press Ctrl+Z (Windows) or Command+Z (Mac OS) to undo your last step and try clicking again.*

**2** Enter **9** into the Width text field, **7** into the Height text field, and **2.5** into the Corner Radius text field. Click OK.

**3** Use the Selection tool (▸) to reposition the new shape in the center of the artboard. No exact position is necessary.

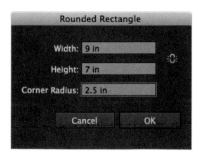

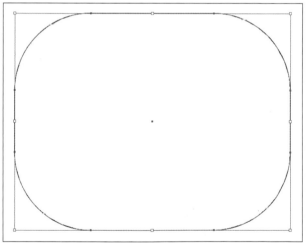

*Enter the values for the Rounded Rectangle.*     *The result.*

## Combining shapes

You will now use the Shape Builder tool to combine two shapes to create your own unique shape.

1  Smart Guides offer assistance when aligning one shape with another and also tracking the size and position of your objects as you are creating them. Verify that Smart Guides are turned on by looking under the View menu. If the Smart Guides command does not have a checkmark on the left, select it now.

2  Click and hold the Rounded Rectangle tool (▣) and select the Rectangle tool (▣). Click and drag from the center of the rounded rectangle shape and release when the rectangle is flush with the bottom and right sides of the rounded rectangle. You are essentially creating the sharp corner that will be in the lower-right of this shape. The shape will also take on the current white fill color.

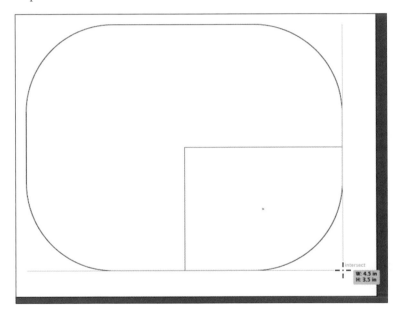

*Click and drag to create a rectangle.*

3  Using the Selection tool, Shift+click the rounded rectangle shape. Both the rectangle and the rounded rectangle are selected.

4  Select the Shape Builder tool (◉) from the Tools panel.

**5**    With the Shape Builder tool, click and drag from the larger rounded rectangle all the way down into the lower-right corner of the rectangle shape and release. (Make sure your cursor reaches the extreme lower-right corner of the rectangle.) The shapes are now combined into one shape.

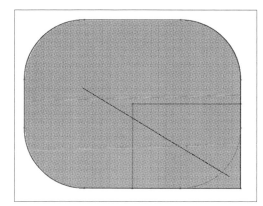 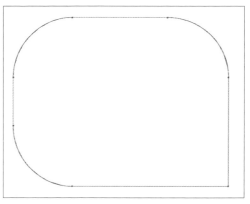

*Click and drag through the shapes.*          *The result.*

## Using the new Kuler panel

Adobe Kuler® is a Creative Cloud-based application for making color themes using an iPhone or your browser. You can capture colors from photos you take with your iPhone, such as flowers in a garden or whatever you want. You can also browse thousands of themes from the Kuler community and then sync your themes into Adobe Illustrator CC to use them in your designs.

**1**    Using the Selection tool, click the new background shape to select it.

**2**    Click the Kuler icon (█) in the dock to open the Kuler panel. Once you have signed-in using your Adobe ID and created colors on the Kuler website (by clicking the Launch Kuler website button at the bottom of the panel) you can click the Refresh button at the bottom of the panel to update your list of themes. You can also use the free Kuler for iPhone app to create and sync colors.

3  You can now apply any Kuler colors you want to the selected background shape.

*Use the new Kuler panel to assign colors you create on the Kuler website or your iPhone.*

 *You can also download the free Adobe Ideas app for your iPhone or iPad to create sketches that you can import into Adobe Illustrator CC. Search the Apple iTunes store for more information.*

## Applying a fill and stroke

1  At the bottom of the Tools panel, click the Fill color icon (⬚). Any color you click in the Kuler panel will now be applied to the fill, or interior color, of the selected background shape.

2  Click a Kuler panel swatch to select a color for the fill of the background shape. An exact color choice is not necessary for this exercise.

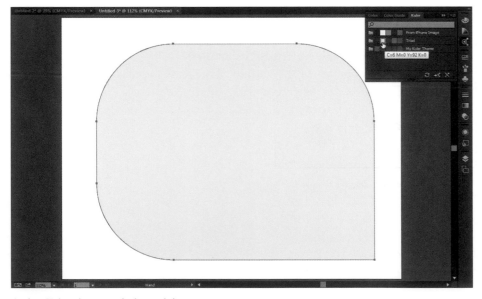

*Apply a Kuler color to your background shape.*

**3**    Now click the Stroke icon at the bottom of the Tools panel. You will add a gradient stroke to your background shape, which was a new capability in Illustrator CS6.

**4**    In the Control panel at the top of your workspace, choose 14 pt from the Stroke drop-down menu to increase the weight of the background shape's stroke. This will make the gradient stroke easier to see.

**5**    In the Tools panel, click the Gradient button beneath the Fill and Stroke icons to apply the default gradient to the background shape's stroke.

## Creating the smaller combined shape

You will now create the smaller shape used on the left side of the page. You will create a new rounded rectangle shape so that you can visually set how rounded you would like the corners to be.

**1**    Click and hold the Rectangle tool to select the hidden Rounded Rectangle tool.

**2**    Click and drag (but don't release) to start creating the new rounded rectangle shape. While dragging, press the down arrow key repeatedly to reduce the size of the rounded corner. You might have to press the down arrow many times to see the difference. Keep in mind that this shortcut will not work if you release the mouse; it only works while you are initially clicking and dragging out the shape. Experiment by pressing the up arrow key (repeatedly) to increase the corner radius. Adjust the corner radius to a point where you are visually happy with it but do NOT release the mouse yet.

**3**    An exact height and width are not important for this shape. In this example, the mouse was released when the measurement reached approximately 2.5 inches in width and 1.75 inches in height.

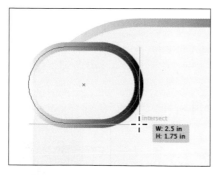

*Press the down arrow while dragging the rounded rectangle shape to reduce the corner values.*

*It is best to avoid stretching the width or height of a rounded rectangle, since you can distort the corners. If you need a wider or taller rounded rectangle, it is best to recreate it.*

4   Select the Rectangle tool (▣), and (repeating what you did with the large background shape) click and drag from the center point down to the lower-right of the small rounded rectangle.

5   Select the Selection tool (▶) and Shift+click to select the smaller rounded corner shape. Both the rectangle and the rounded rectangle are selected.

6   Select the Shape Builder tool (⬮), and then click and drag from the rounded rectangle all the way down into the lower-right corner of the rectangle shape and release. The shapes are now combined into one shape.

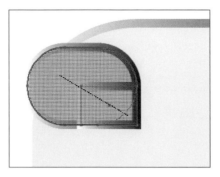

*Combine the newly created shapes.*

7   Choose File > Save to save this file. In the Save As dialog box, leave the File name the same and make sure Adobe Illustrator (*.AI) is selected for the type. Using the Save in text field, navigate to the ai01lessons folder, and then click Save. In the Illustrator Options window, leave the settings at their default and click OK. Keep the file open for the next part of this lesson.

## Applying color and effects

You will now apply a different color and use the Zig Zag effect on just the stroke of this shape. Using the Appearance panel you can apply a different effect to either the stroke or fill, offering more options for you to create unique artwork.

1   Select the new combined shape and then click Fill in the Control panel and select the CMYK Green color in the first row of the swatches.

2   Click the Appearance icon (▣) in the panel docking area, or choose Window > Appearance to show the Appearance panel.

**3**   Using the Appearance panel, click the Stroke color menu and select Black, and then click the Stroke Weight drop-down menu to the right and change the value to **1**.

*Make sure that you have a 1-point black stroke.*

**4**   Click Stroke in the Appearance panel, and then choose (from the main menu) Effect > Distort and Transform > Zig Zag. The Zig Zag dialog box appears.

Using the Zig Zag effect you can apply this effect with sharp corners or points, or smooth waves. In this example, you will create a smooth wavy effect.

**5**   In the Zig Zag dialog box, check Preview.

- In the Size text field, enter **.07**.
- Type **4** in the Ridges per segment text field.
- Select Smooth in the Points section of the dialog box.
- Click OK.

The stroke is now wavy, but the fill in the shape remains unchanged.

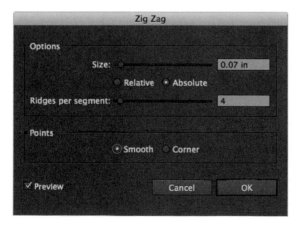 

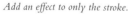
*Add an effect to only the stroke.*          *The result.*

## Cloning the small shape

You will now clone (or copy) the shape two times and then apply different colors to each shape.

**1** Make sure that the smaller shape you just created is selected.

**2** Choose the Selection tool and then position your cursor over the smaller shape that you created.

**3** Press and hold the Alt (Windows) or Option (Mac OS) key, and when the double cursor (⯍) appears, click and drag down to create a copy of the original shape directly underneath itself. Don't worry about alignment or position. That will be addressed in a later step.

**4** Repeat the same process to clone a third shape underneath the second.

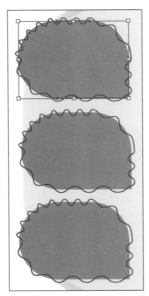

*Press and hold the Alt/Option key    The result.*
*and drag.*

**5**    Select the middle shape and then click the Fill box in Appearance panel. Click the arrow that appears on the right of the Fill box and select the purple (C=**50**, M=**100**, Y=**0**, K=**0**) color at the beginning of the third row of swatches.

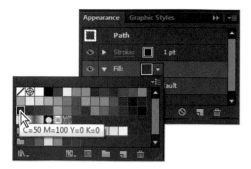

*Use the Appearance panel to change the fill color.*

**6**    Select the bottom shape, click the arrow that appears on the right of the Fill box in the Appearance panel, and select the orange (C=**0**, M=**50**, Y=**100**, K=**0**) color at the end of the first row of swatches.

*The artwork at this stage.*

## Aligning and distributing the shapes

You will now align and distribute the shapes.

1  Use your Selection tool (▶) to Shift+click and select all three shapes.

2  If the Align buttons do not automatically appear in your Control panel, click Align in the Control panel, or select Window > Align to show the Align panel.

3  Select Horizontal Align Left from the Align Objects row.

4  Click the Vertical Distribute Center button in the Distribute Objects row.

*Align and distribute the shapes.*

The shapes are now aligned and distributed.

5  With all three shapes selected, click Transform in the Control panel. The Transform panel appears.

Next you will position your shapes.

6  With all three shapes selected, click the upper-left corner of the reference point (in the upper-left corner of the Transform panel) and change the X value to **.5**, and the Y value to **1.25**.

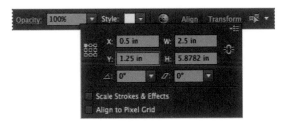

*Set the position for the three shapes.*

**7**    Select the large shape (background), click Transform in the Control panel, type **1.25** in the X text field and **.75** into the Y text field. Ignore it if the value changes slightly after you have entered it.

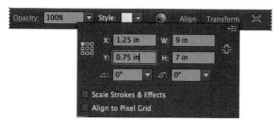

*Set the position for the background shape.*

**8**    Choose File > Save to save this file. Keep it open for the next part of this lesson.

## Adding text

Next, you will add text to your comp, as well as to the boxes that you have already created.

**1**    Select the Type tool (T) and click the artboard, making sure not to accidently click in an existing shape. By clicking (and not dragging) you do not limit the width of your text area.

**2**    Select Character in the Control panel at the top of the work area. The Character panel appears.

**3**    Change the size of your text to **48** and press Enter (Windows) or Return (Mac OS).

**4**    Type **Rufus' What's Happening**.

*Change the font size.*          *Type text.*

5   With the Type tool still active, press Ctrl+A (Windows) or Command+A (Mac OS) to select your text.

*You can select the Font family name that appears in the Set the font family text field of the Control panel and then press the down arrow. By pressing the down arrow, you cycle through your font list in your system. You also see the font applied to your selected text. Press the Up arrow to go up the list. This feature, previously only available on the Windows platform, is now available in the Mac OS.*

6   Choose Type > Font to choose a font you would like to use. In this example, the font name Cooper was selected, but you can use any font you wish. If you do not see the font being applied to your text, make sure your text is still selected.

7   Choose File > Save to save this file. Keep it open for the next part of this lesson.

## Applying the Warp effect

In this next exercise, you will apply the Flag warp effect to your text.

1   Choose the Selection tool (▸), and click the text area you just created to make sure it is active.

2   Choose Effect > Warp > Flag. The Warp Options dialog box for the Flag warp appear.

   • Check Preview.

   • Type **50** into the Bend text field.

   • Type **40** into the Horizontal Distortion text field.

   • Click OK. The Flag warp is applied.

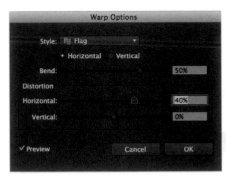

*Apply the Flag warp.*

**3**    With the warped type area still selected, click Fill in the Control panel and select
CMYK Red from the Swatches panel that appears.

*Change the color of the text to Red.*

Depending upon the font that you have selected, you might have to increase or
decrease the size of your text. If you want to resize your text, follow this next step.

**4**    Make sure that the text area is selected (with the Selection tool) and press
Ctrl+Shift+< (Lesser than) or > (Greater than) (Windows), or Command+Shift+<
or > (Mac OS) to visually decrease or increase your font size.

If you would rather, you can grab any corner of the visible bounding box and click
and drag (press and hold the Shift key to maintain proportions) to resize the text area.

*Resize the text if necessary.*

## Adding text to the small shape areas

In this next exercise, you will create text for the smaller shapes.

**1**    Select the Type tool (T), and then click Character in the Control panel, and then
change the Font size to **24**. Click a blank area on the Control panel to put the
Character panel away.

**2**    Click the Align Center icon in the Control panel to center the text that you are about
to enter.

*Center the text.*

**3**    With the Type tool, click a blank area on the artboard, and type **Kids**.

**4**    Switch to the Selection tool (▸) and position the text over the top shape.

**5** Click Fill in the Control panel and select White.

*Change the font color to white.*     *The result.*

**6** With the Selection tool still active, press and hold the Alt (Windows) or Option (Mac OS) key and click and drag the text (in one motion), so that it is in approximately the same location in the second shape. If you must nudge the text, press Ctrl+Z (Windows) or Command+Z (Mac OS) to undo and try again to clone the text to the right position in one movement.

**7** Press Ctrl+D (Windows) or Command+D (Mac OS) to repeat the transformation and place another copy of the text in the third shape.

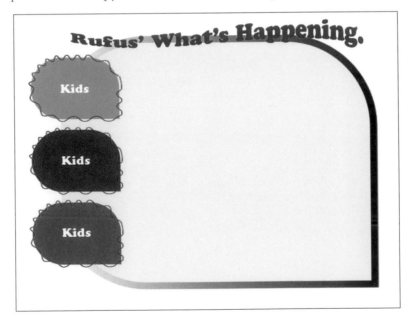

*The comp at this stage.*

**8** Switch to the Text tool (T) and select the text in the middle text box. With the text selected, type **Teens**. The Kids text is replaced with the word Teens.

**9**   Change the text in the third text box to **Families**.

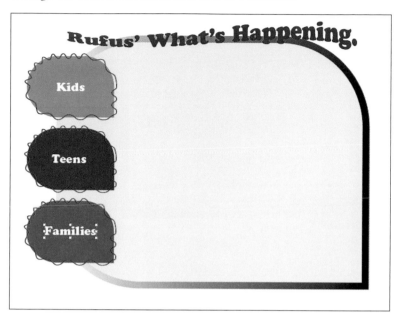

*The comp after the text has been replaced.*

**10**   Choose File > Save to save this file. Keep it open for the next part of this lesson.

## Distorting a shape

In this section, you will create the green shape that appears behind the image of the dog in the comp.

**1**   Select the rectangle tool and click once on the artboard. When the Rectangle dialog box appears, type **3.5** for the Width and **4** for the Height, and then click OK.

**2**   Click Fill in the Control panel and select the CMYK Green color in the first row of swatches. The green color is applied.

**3** Using the Selection tool, reposition the new rectangle in the lower-right of the background.

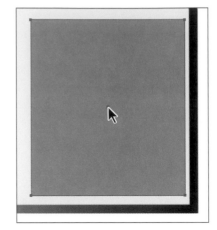

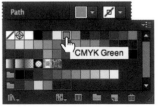

*Create a green rectangle.*     *Position on the artwork.*

**4** Click and hold the Scale tool (⊞) to select the hidden Shear tool (☑).

**5** With the Shear tool active, click the middle of the bottom edge and drag slightly to the left. This skews the shape. No exact increment is necessary.

*Select the Shear tool.*     *Click and drag to the left.*

You will now apply a Zig Zag effect to this shape.

**6** Click the rectangle with the Selection tool, then click the Stroke color in the Control panel and select None. Make sure that you are not selecting Stroke in the Appearance panel.

**7** From the main menu, choose Effect > Distort & Transform > Zig Zag. The Zig Zag dialog box appears.

**8**    In the Zig Zag dialog box, enter the following:

- Turn on Preview
- Size: **.15**
- Ridges per Segment: **4**
- In the Points section choose Smooth
- Click OK.

**9**    Make sure Fill is selected in the Tools panel, then click Opacity in the Control panel, and change the opacity to **50%**.

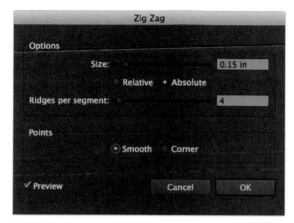

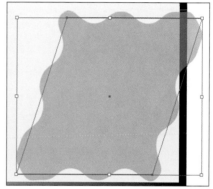

*Apply the Zig Zag effect and change the opacity.*          *The result.*

**10**    Choose File > Save to save this file. Keep it open for the next part of this lesson.

## Importing an image

In this section, you will import the dog image, as well as some of the other images you will use in the comp.

**1**    Making sure that nothing is selected in your file, choose File > Place, and the Place dialog box appears. Navigate to the ai01lessons folder and select the image named **rufusdog.psd**, ensure that the Link option is checked and click Place. The image is added to the center of the artboard.

**2**    Using your Selection tool (⬆), click and drag to position the dog over the sheared green rectangle in the lower-right of your page.

**3** Then, click and drag a corner of the bounding box outward (while pressing and holding the Shift key) to enlarge the image of the dog.

*Resize and reposition the image of Rufus.*

## Adding lines of text

In this section you will create the wavy lines that are meant to represent body copy on the comp. When creating a rough draft of a document, it is often a good idea to use graphics to represent the look and feel of text without adding actual content.

**1** If the Layers panel is not visible, choose Window > Layers.

**2** From the Layers panel menu, select New Layer. The Layer Options panel appears.

**3** Type **Textblocks** in the Name text field and click OK. By creating a separate layer for the text art you have the opportunity to turn off the visibility, or delete the layer if you want to add actual content.

*Create a new layer for the textblocks.*

**4**   Click the Stroke color box in the Control panel and choose Black. Choose 1 pt for the Stroke weight from the Stroke pull-down menu.

**5**   Select the Line Segment Tool (/) and position your cursor next to the Kids graphic, then click and drag until you see the smart measurement guide indicate that the line is approximately 2.5 inches long. You can also type **2.5** into the Width text field of the Transform panel. If it makes it easier, you can press and hold the Shift key to keep your line segment straight as you drag it.

*Create a new line segment.*

**6**   With the line segment still selected, choose Effect > Distort & Transform > Zig Zag. The Zig Zag dialog box appears. This time you will use the Zig Zag effect to represent body text with squiggly lines.

**7** In the Zig Zag dialog box, click the Preview check box and enter the following:

- Size: **.05**
- Select Absolute.
- Ridges per segment: **45**
- Points: Smooth
- Click OK.

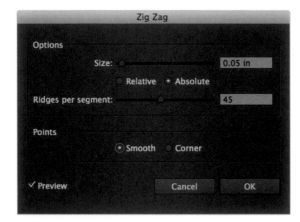

*Zig Zag the line segment.*

*The result.*

You will now clone this line segment.

**8** Choose the Selection tool and then press and hold the Alt (Windows) or Option (Mac OS) key and click and drag down. Press and hold the Shift key as you are dragging to keep the line segment aligned with the original. You are cloning the line segment, so make sure that you have enough space between the lines to look like rows of text.

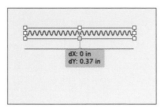

*Clone the line segment.*

**9** Press Ctrl+D (Windows) or Command+D (Mac OS) to repeat your last movement, or transformation. Another line segment appears beneath the second. Continue pressing Ctrl/Command+D until you have a total of eight line segments. If you spaced them out too much or not enough, drag to reposition the last segment, then select all of the line segments and click Vertical Distribute Center in the Align panel.

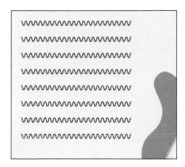

*Duplicate the line segment for a total of 8 lines.*

**10** Select the top line segment, and choose 3 pt from the Stroke Width drop-down menu in the Control panel.

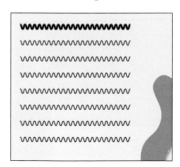

*Change the top segment to 3 pt.*

**11** Select the last three line segments and press and hold the Alt/Option key and drag down, so that the cloned lines start at about the top of the Families artwork.

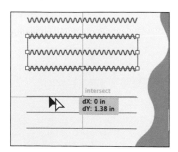

*Clone the last three lines down further on the page.*

**12** Select the top line in the newly created group of line segments and change its width to 3 pt.

**13** Choose File > Place. Select the **pictures.psd** file in the ai01lessons folder, then click Place. An image of the Kids, Teens and Families appear on the artboard. Using the Selection tool, reposition the image above Rufus.

*The comp at this stage. Your version might have slight variations in positioning and text.*

**14** Choose File > Save.

## Using the new Touch Type tool

In this section, you will have an opportunity to explore the new Touch Type Tool.

**1**   Press and hold the Type tool (T) and select the new Touch Type tool ( ).

**2**   Click the letter *K* in Kids; handles appear around the character. Click and drag down to change the baseline shift of just the letter *K*.

Using the Touch Type tool, you can customize each individual character's properties. Adjusting the letter and word spacing (known as kerning and tracking) has never been easier.

**3**   Click other letters and click and drag up, down, left or right to change their alignment, size and rotation, using the corner handles, plus the one above the character to rotate.

You can even work with text on a path. For example, after you are done experimenting with the Touch Type Tool, try changing the period at the end of the Rufus headline to a question mark using the regular Type Tool.

The only rules for this exercise are to have fun and be creative.

*Explore the possibilities with the new Touch Type Tool to create a unique text effect.*

**4**   Press Ctrl+S (Windows) or Command+S (Mac OS) to save your file when finished.

## Self study

Now that you've had an introduction to some of the essential tools and techniques in Illustrator, try the following:

1   Create several Kuler themes using the Kuler website and/or your Kuler iPhone app photos. Also explore the possibilities with the free Adobe Ideas app for iPhone and iPad.

2   Finally, change the colors in your design using your Kuler theme and import an Adobe Ideas file from Creative Cloud into Illustrator CC. You can post a portfolio of your best designs on the Behance social network, which is integrated into the Creative Cloud app.

## Review

### Questions

1   What does choosing Essentials from the Application bar do to your workspace?

2   How can you combine shapes with the Shape Builder tool?

3   What keyboard modifier can you use to clone a shape in Illustrator?

4   Why would you create a separate layer for artwork that you're adding to your illustration?

5   How can you repeat a transformation (such as a move)?

### Answers

1   Choosing the Essentials workspace resets the panels on your screen to their original, factory default settings.

2   Dragging over multiple selected shapes with the Shape Builder tool combines them into one united shape.

3   Pressing and holding Alt (Windows) or Option (Mac OS) while dragging an object clones, or duplicates, that object.

4   Creating a separate layer for new artwork allows you to turn off the visibility of that content, or delete it with one click by deleting the layer.

5   Pressing Ctrl+D (Windows) or Command+D (Mac OS) repeats your last movement or other transformation. You can also choose Object > Transform > Transform Again to achieve the same result.

## What you'll learn in this lesson:

- Opening an existing Illustrator file

- Navigating the document window

- Finding and using common panels

- Selecting and using tools

- Saving workspaces and keyboard shortcuts

# Getting to Know the Workspace

*The Adobe Illustrator workspace includes tools, panels, and windows that you use to create and manipulate your artwork. In this lesson, you find out where all these necessary components are located and how they can be organized. You also discover how to customize the workspace for your specific needs.*

## Starting up

Before starting, make sure that your tools and panels are consistent by resetting your workspace. See "Resetting Adobe Illustrator CC Preferences" in the Starting up section of this book.

You will work with several files from the ai02lessons folder in this lesson. Make sure that you have loaded the ailessons folder onto your hard drive from the included DVD. See "Loading lesson files" in the Starting up section of this book.

**See Lesson 2 in action!**

*Use the accompanying video to gain a better understanding of how to use some of the features shown in this lesson. You can find the video tutorial for this lesson on the included DVD.*

## Opening Illustrator

When you launch Illustrator for the first time you will see the Tools panel on the left, Menu bar at the top, and panels on the right.

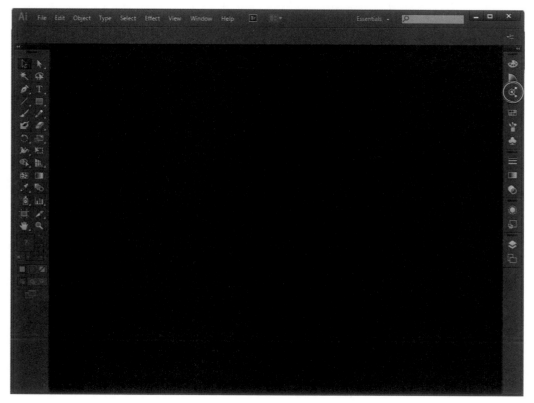

*The Illustrator CC workspace as it appears when first launched.*

## Exploring the Illustrator CC interface

You can adjust the interface incrementally from bright to dark, giving you the ability to choose a design that is more pleasing to the eye than previous versions. Additionally, the canvas color can be keyed to match the brightness of the interface, toning down the white expanse on either side of the artboard.

**1**    Choose Edit > Preferences > User Interface (Windows) or Illustrator > Preferences > User Interface (Mac OS) to display the new interface options.

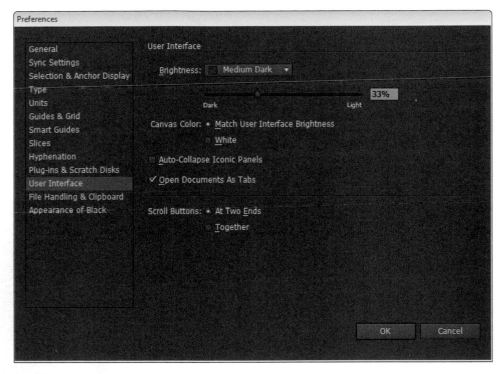

*Change the contrast settings of the Illustrator CC workspace.*

**2**    From the Brightness drop-down menu, choose Medium Light to return the interface to the brighter contrast of previous settings.

**3**    Drag the slider below from Light to Medium Dark to return the interface to the low-contrast view that is the default in Illustrator CC.

**4**    Under Canvas Color, verify that Match User Interface Brightness option button is selected. This will ensure that the canvas remains consistent with the contrast of the rest of the workspace.

**5**    Leave the other settings at their defaults, and click OK.

# Choosing a workspace

Workspaces define which panels are visible on your screen. Illustrator starts you off with a number of workspaces: Automation, Essentials, Layout, Painting, Printing and Proofing, Tracing, Typography and Web. You will learn a little more about these later in the lesson.

1   Choose the Essentials workspace from the Workspace Switcher drop-down menu, in the top right corner of the screen, to display the Illustrator Application bar, Tools panel, Control panel, and five panel groups that are collapsed into tabs and docked on the right side of the workspace.

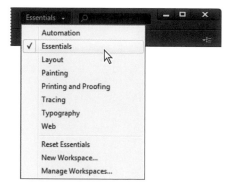

*Choosing the Essentials workspace displays the most commonly used panels.*

You could also have selected the Typography workspace, which gives you instant access to the docked, expanded panels you'll use most frequently for type formatting, or the Painting or Printing and Proofing workspaces, which are reserved for those common Illustrator functions.

**2**  Click one of the icons in the panel docking area on the right side of the workspace. This expands the panel. Click the same panel icon again to collapse the panel.

*Click the panel icon to expand the panel.*

The panels currently listed in the dock are displayed by default, but you can add any panel to the workspace by selecting it specifically from the Window menu. You can also save and manage your own custom workspaces from the Window > Workspace menu. These functions are described in more detail later in this lesson.

## Opening a file

To begin this lesson, you'll open an existing file using Adobe Bridge.

**1**  Choose File > Browse in Bridge to open Adobe Bridge. In Bridge, if the Folders panel is not in the foreground, select the Folders tab (by default in the upper-left of the Adobe Bridge workspace) to bring it forward, then choose Desktop from the list of folders.

**2**  In the large Content panel to the right of the Folders panel, double-click the ailessons folder that you copied onto your computer, and then open the ai02lessons folder.

**3** Locate and double-click the file named **ai0201.ai** to open it within Illustrator.

*A Convert to Artboards dialog box might appear when you open certain files. Click OK to continue opening the file.*

*Illustrator files can be opened using Adobe Bridge.*

**4** In Illustrator, choose File > Save As. In the Save As dialog box, navigate to the ai02lessons folder. In the Name text field, type **ai0201_work.ai** and click Save.

*If a dialog box appears warning you about converting spot colors in transparency to process colors outside of Illustrator, take note, then click Continue.*

**5** In the Illustrator Options dialog box, make sure the Version is set to Illustrator CC, and the other settings are at their defaults, and click OK.

# The document window

The document window displays the entire contents of your file. In this example, it shows a design for the liner notes (front and back) for a CD. In addition to the artwork, the document window also displays the following:

- **Artboards**: The artboard represents the printable page containing your artwork. It's bounded by solid lines and can be enlarged or reduced to accommodate larger or smaller artwork. The default artboard size is U.S. Letter (8.5 inches wide by 11 inches tall), but it can be set as large as 227 inches by 227 inches, or almost 19 feet by 19 feet. You can have up to 100 artboards in a single Illustrator document. You will use multiple artboards later in this lesson.

- **Scratch Area**: The scratch area is a space for experimenting with and storing elements of your design before moving them onto the artboard. It consists of the blank area outside of the artboard, and extends to 227 inches in each direction. Although visible on screen, elements placed on the scratch area will not print, and should be removed before printing to reduce file complexity.

- **Imageable and Non-imageable Areas**: The imageable and non-imageable (or printable and non-printable) areas of a page can also be displayed on the Illustrator artboard, and are delineated by a series of dotted lines. To see the printable area you can choose View > Show Print Tiling.

 *If you turned on the print tiling view, turn it back off by selecting View > Hide Print Tiling. Since you are using multiple artboards, the print tiling is not accurate at this time.*

# Using Artboards

Adobe Illustrator offers the ability to build illustrations using multiple artboards. This gives you the ability to crop several pieces of artwork to different sizes, print components of your illustration separately, as well as provide you with an easy method to keep related artwork together. You can have up to 100 artboards per document (depending on the size of those artboards). You can specify the number of artboards for a document when you create it, and add and remove artboards at any time. You can create artboards in different sizes, resize them by using the Artboard tool, and position them anywhere on the screen—even overlapping one another. In this lesson file, two artboards are used: one for the front side of the artwork, and one for the back.

## Navigating multiple Artboards

You can easily navigate artboards by clicking and holding the Artboard Navigation drop-down menu in the lower-left of the work area.

1    Click and hold the Artboard Navigation drop-down menu in the lower-left and choose 2. This navigates you to the second artboard.

*Click and hold Artboard Navigation
to switch from one artboard to another.*

2    Press Ctrl+0 (zero) (Windows) or Command+0 (zero)(Mac OS) to fit the artboard into the window.

3    Click the Previous button to navigate to Artboard 1.

*Navigate to the other artboards by using
the arrows.*

## Using the Artboards panel

You can manage your artboards more easily by using the Artboards panel. Using the Artboards panel, you can select, add, reorder, and duplicate artboards.

1    Choose Window > Artboards to show the Artboards panel.

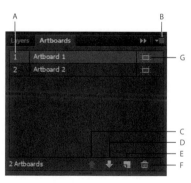

*A. Name and number of artboard. B. Panel Menu.
C. Move Up. D. Move Down. E. New Artboard.
F. Delete Artboard. G. Page Icon.*

2    Double-click the number to the left of Artboard 2 in the Artboards panel to view the second artboard.

**3**  Click the page icon to the right of Artboard 2, in the Artboards panel, to open the Artboard options. Type **Artwork-Back** into the Name text field. Notice that you can change the size of an artboard using the Artboard Options dialog box. In this example, you will only change the name. Click OK.

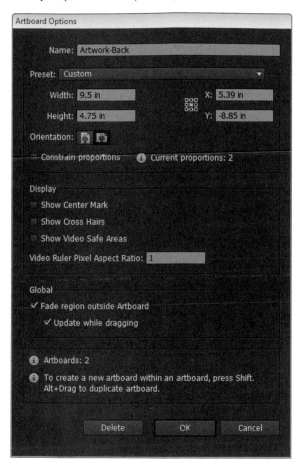

*The Artboard Options dialog box.*

## Creating new Artboards

Now that you know how to navigate from one artboard to another, you can give creating a new one a try. In this example, you will duplicate one of the existing artboards.

You can create a new artboard using several methods:

- Click the New Artboard button (⬄) in the Artboards panel. This creates a new artboard for you to work with that is the same size as the artboard you selected. This is good if you are working on a project that has multiple pages, or a front and back as in our example.

- Create a custom artboard by selecting the Artboard tool (□) in the Tools panel, and then clicking and dragging a new artboard anywhere in your document window.

- Duplicate an existing artboard by selecting it in the Artboards panel and then selecting Duplicate Artboards from the panel menu.

To duplicate an artboard, follow these steps.

1   Select Artboard 1 in the Artboards panel, then click the panel menu (⋅≡ ) to select Duplicate Artboards. The artboard is replicated, and *Artboard 1 copy* appears in the Artboards panel.

*Duplicating an existing artboard.*

2   With Artboard 1 copy still selected, click the Delete Artboard button at the bottom of the Artboards panel. The new artboard is deleted, but the artwork is still positioned in the scratch area of the document. When using the Artboard panel, the artwork can be repositioned using an artboard, but does not delete with it.

3   Choose File > Revert to return to the last saved version of this file. When asked if you want to Revert to the saved version of the document, click Revert.

## Switching screen modes

For easier viewing of the artwork, the display properties of the document window and accompanying menu bar can be changed by switching screen modes. By switching screen modes, you can open up your workspace.

**1** With the **ai0201_work.ai** file open, click the Change Screen Mode button (⟳) at the bottom of the Tools panel to expand the Screen Mode drop-down menu, and cycle through the options.

*Switching screen modes allows easier viewing of artwork.*

**2** If necessary, choose Normal Screen Mode to show the artwork in a standard document window that contains a menu bar, scroll bars, and a title bar.

**3** Choose Full Screen Mode with Menu Bar to show the artwork in a full-screen document window with only a menu bar (and no scroll bars or title bars).

**4** Choose Full Screen Mode to show the artwork in a full-screen document window without menu bars, or title bars.

Even without the Tools panel in view, you can still access the tools using keyboard shortcuts. In this next section, you have the opportunity to use some of these shortcuts; you can find more in the Tools panel section in this lesson.

**5** Press **Z**. The cursor turns into the Zoom cursor (🔍). Click to zoom into the image.

**6** Now press **V**. By pressing V, you have switched to the Selection tool. Each tool has a keyboard shortcut to access it. You will discover more shortcuts later, in this lesson, in the section covering the Tools panel.

**7** Press the Escape key to return to Normal Screen mode to continue this lesson.

## Changing your view

Because you'll be creating artwork visually in Illustrator, the way in which that artwork is displayed on-screen (the size, color, and location of objects) is a primary concern. Illustrator provides the flexibility with which you can change the view of your artwork to best suit your needs.

### Preview versus Outlines

By default, Illustrator displays artwork colors, gradients, meshes, and complex paths. The more complex the elements are, the more time it takes Illustrator to render the artwork. This can cause a delay when you are editing an illustration.

You might also discover that attributes of the objects that you are creating, such as strokes and colors, can make it difficult to make precise adjustments to detailed artwork. To help you, Illustrator provides you with several view modes, the most commonly used modes being the Preview (default) and Outline modes.

**1**    To toggle between view modes, choose View > Outline, or use the keyboard shortcut Ctrl+Y (Windows) or Command+Y (Mac OS). In Outline mode, Illustrator displays artwork so that only its outlines (or paths) are visible.

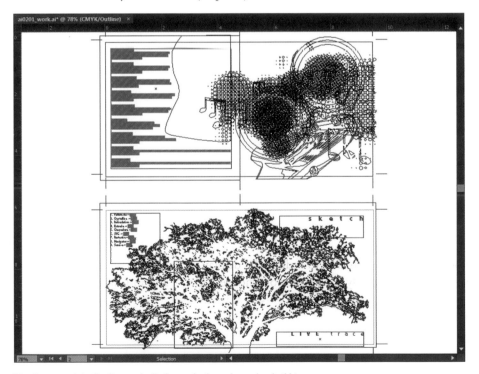

*Viewing artwork in Outline mode displays only the paths used to build it.*

**2**    Choose View > Preview. In Preview mode, the paint attributes of the artwork are displayed.

## Zooming and scrolling

It is amazing how details seem different when you zoom in and out of artwork. Usually, you discover that the artwork isn't as precise as you think it should be. Fortunately, you have the opportunity to zoom in to 6400 percent in Adobe Illustrator CC. Keep in mind that changing the view of a file changes the on-screen display only, not the actual size of your artwork. There are many ways to change the view of your artwork in Illustrator:

### Zooming with the View commands

The easiest, but most time-consuming, method for zooming in and out is using the View menu. You will be using keyboard shortcuts throughout the lessons in this book, but it is helpful to know where you can find the zoom menu items in case you have a lapse in keyboard shortcut memory.

**1**   Choose View > Zoom In to enlarge the display of the CD artwork. The view depth increases incrementally each time you choose View > Zoom In from this menu, and allows you to closely examine portions of the design that were not otherwise visible.

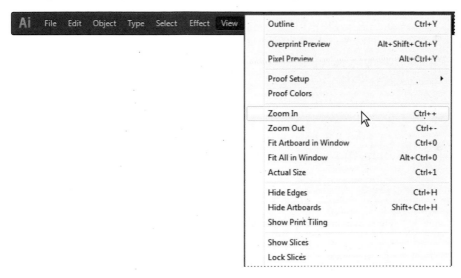

*Commands under the View menu allow you to change the magnification of your artwork.*

**2**   Choose View > Zoom Out to reduce the display of the CD artwork. The view depth decreases incrementally each time you choose View > Zoom Out from this menu, and allows you to view the artwork from a distance to see how the elements work together.

*By default, Illustrator zooms in or out on the center of your document window when the View commands are used. You can then scroll to different areas of your artwork using the scroll bars.*

Keep in mind that the Illustrator Artboard can be up 227″ × 227″. If your artboard is much smaller, perhaps letter-sized, that remaining area becomes your scratch area. The scratch area frequently becomes "nowhere land" for new users as they accidently navigate into blank space. Once in this blank area, it can be difficult to find your artwork again.

**3**  Choose View > Fit All in Window to instantly center the document window (both artboards) into your viewing area. The keyboard shortcut is Alt+Ctrl+0 (zero) (Windows) or Option+Command+0 (zero) (Mac OS).

**4**  If the Artboards panel is not visible, choose Window > Artboards now. Double-click the number to the left of Artboard 1 to make sure it is the selected artboard. Choose View > Fit Artboard in Window to center the artboard only in the workspace.

### Zooming using the View Depth text field and drop-down menu

Whenever you zoom in or out on your artwork, the view depth percentage is displayed in a field in the lower-left corner of the document window. This field, along with an attached drop-down menu, allows you to make further changes to the view depth of your artwork.

**1**  In the lower-left corner of the document window, type **120%** into the View Depth text field. Typing into this field allows you to choose whatever enlargement or reduction percentage you'd like to view your artwork at. Press Enter (Windows) or Return (Mac OS) on your keyboard to enlarge the view of your artwork to 120 percent.

*Type 120% in the View Depth text field to zoom in on the document.*

**2**  Click the arrow to the right of the View Depth text field. A drop-down menu appears that allows you to choose a preset zoom percentage, from 3.13 percent to 6400 percent, by selecting it.

**3**   Choose 66.67 percent from the drop-down menu to continue this lesson.

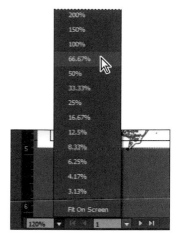

*Choose magnifications from 3.13 percent to 6400 percent.*

## Zooming with the Zoom tool

**1**   Select the Zoom tool (🔍) from the Tools panel on the left of the workspace.

**2**   Using the Zoom tool, click the photo of the guitarist in the lower-left corner of the document window to enlarge the view. Each click enlarges the photo at a higher (preset) magnification.

**3**   Press and hold the Alt (Windows) or Option (Mac OS) key on your keyboard, and note that the zoom cursor now contains a minus sign (🔍).

**4**   Click the photo of the guitarist to reduce the view of the photo. Release the Alt (Windows) or Option (Mac OS) key to return the Zoom tool to its default Zoom In function.

You might have discovered that by clicking to Zoom (with the Zoom tool) that you have very little control over the resulting zoomed in view. You can better control your zooming by clicking and dragging with the Zoom tool selected.

5   With the Zoom tool, drag a marquee (box) around the photo of the guitarist to zoom in on that particular area of the artwork, without the redundancy of clicking multiple times. Note that you cannot draw a marquee to reduce the display size.

*Drag a marquee around selected portions of your artwork with the Zoom tool.*

There might be times when you wish to access the Zoom controls without leaving the active tool. You can use keyboard shortcuts to temporarily activate the Zoom tool, then quickly return back to your work in progress.

6   Press **V** to switch to the Selection tool.

7   Press and hold the Ctrl+Spacebar keys (Windows) or Command+Spacebar (Mac OS) to temporarily switch to the Zoom tool. Note that on the Mac OS, you can start Spotlight, which will not affect the Zoom tool in Illustrator.

8   While keeping the Ctrl/Command+Spacebar keys pressed, click and drag in any area in the image to zoom into a specific area.

9   Release the Ctrl+Spacebar, or Command+Spacebar, and the tool is returned to the Selection tool.

10   Easily zoom back out by pressing Ctrl+0 (zero) (Windows) or Command+0 (zero) (Mac OS).

## Scrolling with the Hand tool

Much like moving a piece of paper around on your desk, you can use the Hand tool to push your artboard around. This is much more time efficient than using the scroll bars, and you can even access the Hand tool without leaving any other tools that you have active.

**1**    Select the Hand tool (✋) from the Tools panel.

**2**    Click and drag in the document window. The artwork moves in the direction you drag.

*The Hand tool moves the artwork as if it were a piece of paper on your desk.*

**3**    Now press **V** to return to the Selection tool, click any item to select it, then press and hold the spacebar. Notice that the cursor now changes into the Hand tool.

**4**    Click and drag to reposition your artboard, then release the spacebar. You are returned to the Selection tool. This feature is extremely handy, especially when you are working with operations that require you to be zoomed into your artwork.

The Hand tool can also be used as a Zoom tool, to fit all artwork in the document window.

**5**    Double-click the Hand tool in the Tools panel to return the file to Fit Artboard in Window view.

## Changing views with the Navigator panel

If you prefer a more visual method for zooming in and out of an image, you can use the navigator panel.

**1**   Choose Window > Navigator to open the Navigator panel.

**2**   In the Navigator panel, click the Zoom In button ( ▲ ) at the bottom-right of the panel, or drag the slider to the right to enlarge the view percentage of your artwork. As you do so, watch the View Depth percentage change in the lower-left corner of this panel, and stop enlarging when you reach 150 percent. If it is easier, you can type **150** into the view percentage text box. The current view of your artwork increases to 150 percent.

*The Navigator panel.*

**3**   Note that a red box is visible in the panel, showing the content currently being displayed inside your document window. This red box shrinks as you increase the magnification of your artwork, and can also be used to scroll around your illustration. Position your cursor over the red box in the Navigator panel, and when the cursor changes to a hand, drag the red box to scroll to the lower-left corner of the artboard. This allows you to view the intricate branches of the tree illustration in closer detail.

*Using the Navigator panel simplifies the process of zooming and scrolling in your artwork.*

**4**   In the Navigator panel, drag the slider to the left to reduce the view percentage of your artwork. Note that the red box increases in size to show the increased content inside your document window.

**5**   Position your cursor over the red box in the Navigator panel, and when the cursor changes to a hand, drag the red box to scroll to the upper-right corner of the artboard. This enables you to view the guitar illustration from farther away and see how it interacts with the other parts of the design.

6   Control the zoom even more by pressing and holding the Ctrl key (Windows) or Command key (Mac OS) and then dragging over an area that you want to zoom into in the Navigator panel. By essentially drawing a zoom area with the cursor, you control the final zoom result in the artboard.

7   Type **100** into the View Depth text field in the Navigator panel and press Enter (Windows) or Return (Mac OS) to return to actual size.

## The Tools panel

In Illustrator, you use the tools in the Tools panel to create, select, and edit portions of your Illustrator artwork.

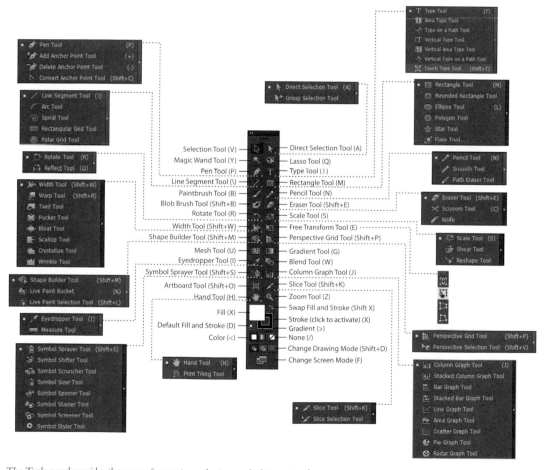

*The Tools panel provides the means for creating, selecting, and editing artwork.*

*Nearly all the tools in the Tools panel have keyboard shortcuts that can be used to access them. Place your cursor over a tool in the panel to display its tooltip, which includes the tool's name and its shortcut (in parentheses).*

## Using tools and panels

To keep all the options organized, Adobe Illustrator uses panels. Some panels are displayed in the default Illustrator workspace, and all other panels can be displayed by choosing them from the Window menu. Most panels have panel menus containing options specific to that panel's functions.

By default, when you open Illustrator, you'll see the Essentials workspace. The Essentials workspace includes the Tools panel on the left side of your screen, the Control panel at the top of your screen (under the application bar), and five panel groups collapsed into the panel dock on the right side of your screen.

**1** The Selection tool (⬉) is used to identify objects in your artwork for editing. Choose the Selection tool from the Tools panel.

**2** Select the closeup photo of the guitarist in the lower part of your document window.

**3** Certain tools offer additional options for selecting, drawing, painting, and repositioning objects. To access the Selection tool's options, double-click the Selection tool in the Tools panel. In the Move dialog box that appears, activate the preview option to explore the possibilities. For example, you can use your up or down cursor keys in the fields, to reposition the photo. Click the Cancel button when you are finished experimenting.

**4** To switch to another tool, you can either click the new tool to select it, or access it using a keyboard command. Press **T** on your keyboard or select the Type tool (T) in the Tools panel to access the Type tool.

**5** Using the Type tool, select the s in the word *sketch* in the top-right corner of the artwork's bottom panel, and type an uppercase **S** to replace it.

*Replace the character using the Type tool.*

*Due to the spacing between the letters, you might have some difficulty selecting just the letter S. If this is the case, click to the left of the letter K, press and hold the Shift key, and then press the left arrow once.*

**6** Press the Esc key. This closes the text frame and returns you to the Selection tool.

## Hidden tools

Some tools in the Tools panel have white triangles in the lower-right corner of their icons, which indicate that there are hidden (related) tools beneath them.

1   Choose Select > Deselect to deselect items on the artboard that might be selected, then click and hold the Type tool (T) in the Tools panel.

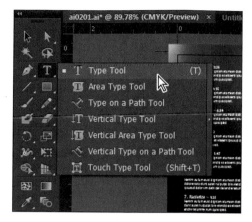

*Some tools have hidden tools nested beneath them.*

2   Notice the keyboard shortcuts in parenthesis for the Type Tool (T) and the new Touch Type Tool (Shift-T) that appear while pressing and holding the mouse button to reveal hidden tools.

*Tooltips display tools' names.*

*These and other keyboard shortcuts can be changed and saved as part of a personal workspace. Techniques for creating shortcuts and saving workspaces are discussed later in this lesson.*

### Tearing off tools

Related tools (both default and hidden) can be separated from the Tools panel and displayed as a separate, repositionable panel.

1    Click and hold the Type tool in the Tools panel. With the mouse button held down, move the cursor to the tab marked with an arrow at the far right of the hidden tools menu.

*Tearoff tabs allow you to separate groups of tools.*

2    When the tooltip Tearoff appears, release your mouse button to tear off the tools into a separate panel.

*The separated tools.*

*In Illustrator CC, you can tear off and dock previously hidden tools, such as the Shape and Pen tools. You can also dock tools horizontally or vertically for a more efficient workspace.*

## Adjusting the Tools panel

The Tools panel can be reconfigured to different views, and repositioned to different locations on your screen.

1   To change the visual configuration of the Tools panel, click the double-arrow in the upper-left corner of the Tools panel to change it from its default two-column configuration to a one-column configuration.

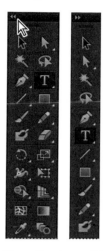

*Change the column width of the Tools panel from two columns to one column by clicking the double arrows at the top of the panel.*

2   Select the double arrow again to return the Tools panel to two-column view.

3   To move the Tools panel, click the dark gray bar at the top of the Tools panel and drag it to a new location on your screen.

4   Release the mouse button when the Tools panel is at the desired location.

5 Dock your Tools panel at any time by dragging it back to the left side of the workspace and pausing. When a blue bar appears, release the mouse. The Tools panel is docked again.

*Dock the Tools panel by dragging it back to the left side of the workspace.*

## The Control panel

The Control panel provides easy access to options used to modify your artwork. It is context-sensitive, meaning that the options displayed will change depending on the type of object you select, and the tool you used to select it. For example, text-formatting settings are displayed in the Control panel when a text object is selected in your artwork.

*When text is selected in your artwork, text-formatting settings are displayed in the Control panel.*

When an option name is orange and underlined in the Control panel, you can click it to display a related dialog box or panel. Click anywhere outside the panel or dialog box to close it.

You can customize the content of the Control panel at any time by making choices from its panel menu.

1    Click the Control panel menu button (-≡) in the upper-right corner of the Control panel to show the settings that can be displayed in the Control panel. Those that are currently being displayed have check marks next to them.

*The Control panel options can be found by clicking the panel menu button.*

2    Select Fill and Stroke from the menu, and notice that the Fill and Stroke settings disappear from the Control panel to the left.

3    Access the panel menu again, and select Fill and Stroke again to turn these settings on in the panel.

## Moving the Control panel

As with other panels, the Control panel can be repositioned on your screen to further customize your workspace.

1    Drag the dashed bar on the left edge of the Control panel away from its default position.

2    Drop the Control panel at another location in your workspace.

3    From the Control panel menu (-≡), choose Dock to Top or Dock to Bottom to change the docking location of the panel.

*You can quickly find what you need in Illustrator CC's more efficient Control panel, now with consistency across options, anchor point controls, clipping masks, envelope distortions, and more.*

## Panel groups and the dock

The ability to arrange panels in groups, and then dock them to the Illustrator workspace, allows for both better organization and increased functionality.

### Panel groups

Panels with related functions can be nested and displayed together in panel groups. An example is the Navigator panel (described earlier in this chapter), which is part of a panel group that also includes the Info panel.

1   From the Window menu, choose Window > Align. The Align panel appears as part of a panel group that includes the Transform and Pathfinder panels.

2   Choose Window > Attributes to also display the Attributes panel in the workspace.

3   Select the Attributes tab at the top of the Attributes panel and drag it to the Align panel.

*Drag the Attributes tab to the Align panel.*

4   Release the mouse button to add the Attributes panel to the panel group.

*Release the mouse button to add the Attributes panel to the group.*

5   To remove the Align panel from the panel group, select the Align tab at the top of the panel and drag it away from the panel group you just created.

6   Release the mouse button to separate the Align panel from the panel group.

## Using the dock

If you choose, you can store panels and panel groups in the panel dock, located on the right side of your screen. In the Essentials workspace, there are five panel groups displayed by default, including panels such as Color, Swatches, Stroke, Appearance, and Layers.

1   To dock a panel, select the Align panel, which you made independent in the last exercise, and drag it to the dock at the top, bottom, left, right, or in between existing panels.

2   When you see a light-blue line marking the panel's desired position in the dock, release the mouse button and the panel becomes docked.

*Drag a panel by its tab,*
*and position it over the*
*dock to store it there.*

## Docking a panel group

To dock a panel group, you'll need to drag the group by its title bar (not individual panel tabs) into the dock.

1   Select the bar at the top of the Attributes panel and drag it into the dock.

2   Release the mouse button when a light-blue line marks the panel's desired position, and it becomes docked.

## Removing a panel or panel group from the dock

To remove a panel or panel group, drag it out of the dock by its tab or title bar. You can drag it into another dock or make it free-floating.

1   To remove a panel from the dock, select the desired button and drag it away from the dock. To remove a panel group, select the dashed bar at the top of the group in the dock and drag it away from the dock.

**2**  Release the mouse to move it into another dock or make it a floating panel group.

*If you remove all panels and panel groups from the dock, the dock will disappear. It will reappear when new panels or groups are dragged into it.*

### Adjusting the dock

Like the Tools panel (which, incidentally, can also be docked), the panel dock can be reconfigured to further customize your workspace.

**1**  To change the configuration of the dock, press the double arrow in the upper-right corner of the dock to expand all the panels therein to their full width.

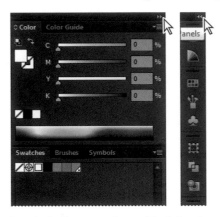

*Press the double arrow at the top of the dock to change from Icon to Expanded mode.*

**2**  Press the double arrow again to collapse the panels to icons.

**3**  Expand the width of panels in the panel dock by clicking and dragging the left side of the dock to the left.

**4**  Reduce the width of panels in the panel dock by clicking and dragging the left side of the dock to the right.

**5**  Alternately, double-click the dark gray bar at the top of the dock to toggle between Icon and Expanded modes.

# Custom workspaces

Once you've configured, moved, and manipulated Illustrator's panels to your liking, you can save custom workspaces and switch among them.

## Saving workspaces

When you save the current size and position of panels as a custom workspace, you can restore that workspace even if you've moved or closed panels in the meantime.

**1**   Dragging them by their name tabs, pull the Color and Swatches panels out from the dock and drop them on your artboard. Nest the Swatches panel inside the Color panel by dragging it on top of the Color panel. Drag the new panel group by its title bar and position it next to the Tools panel on the left side of your screen.

**2**   Collapse all other panels in the dock by clicking the double-arrow in the upper-right corner of the dock.

**3**   To save this customized workspace, choose Window > Workspace > New Workspace.

**4**   In the New Workspace dialog box, type **Color Workspace** in the text field to label your new workspace, and click OK.

**5**   Choose Window > Workspace again, and notice that your named workspace is now at the top of the list.

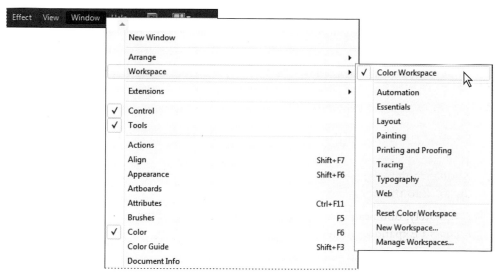

*Choose Window > Workspace to save a customized workspace.*

**6**   To restore a default workspace, choose Window > Workspace to display both the preset workspaces and the custom workspace you just saved. Choose Essentials, then choose Window > Workspace > Reset Essentials to return to that workspace. All panels return to their original appearance.

Now you can see how Illustrator allows you to return to the custom workspace you've saved.

7   To restore your custom workspace, choose Window > Workspace, noting that your Color Workspace appears at the top of the list. Choose the Color Workspace from the list to return to that workspace. All panels return to the customized appearance you chose to save.

## Using the Manage Workspaces dialog box

Custom workspaces can also be saved (and deleted) using the Manage Workspaces dialog box.

1   To add a new custom workspace using the Manage Workspaces feature, choose Window > Workspace > Manage Workspaces. The Manage Workspaces dialog box appears.

2   Click the New Workspace button (⊒) at the bottom of this dialog box to save the current panel configuration as a custom workspace.

3   Name the new workspace **Color Workspace 2** in the text field at the bottom and click OK. You are creating this replica merely to practice deleting an undesired workspace.

4   Your new workspace is added to both the list in the Manage Workspaces dialog box, and the Window > Workspace menu.

*Choose Window > Manage Workspaces*
*to add and delete custom workspaces.*

### Deleting a custom workspace

Using the Manage Workspaces dialog box to delete a custom workspace is just as easy as it was to add one.

1  To delete a custom workspace using the Manage Workspaces feature, choose Window > Workspace > Manage Workspaces. The Manage Workspaces dialog box appears.

2  Select the Color Workspace 2 you just added from the list at the top.

3  Click the Delete button (🗑) at the bottom of the dialog box.

4  The Color Workspace 2 is deleted from both the list in the Manage Workspaces dialog box and the Window > Workspace menu. Click OK.

5  Choose Window > Workspace > Essentials to revert back to the original workspace.

*The default workspaces are not listed in the Manage Workspaces dialog box and cannot be deleted.*

## Customizing keyboard shortcuts

A keyboard shortcut is a combination of keys that, when pressed simultaneously, perform some task that ordinarily could take longer to do if you use a mouse or other input device. In Illustrator, keyboard shortcuts are provided for many tools and commands to save you the trouble of searching for these options in its menus and panels. You can view a list of all the shortcuts, and create or edit your own, using the Keyboard Shortcuts dialog box.

### Default shortcuts

Illustrator's set of default shortcuts can be viewed and printed from an easy-to-create plain-text file.

1  To view a list of default keyboard shortcuts, choose Edit > Keyboard Shortcuts.

**2**   In the Keyboard Shortcuts dialog box, choose Illustrator Defaults from the Set drop-down menu.

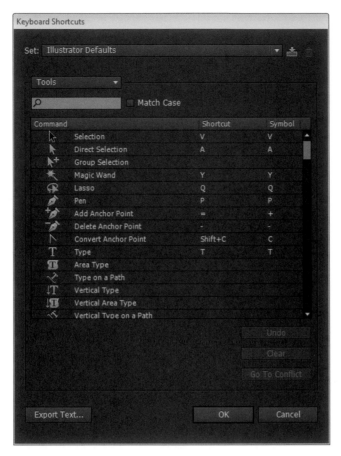

*The Keyboard Shortcuts dialog box allows you to view a list of all shortcuts, and create or edit your own.*

**3**   To create a text file containing the default shortcuts, click the Export Text button.

**4**   When prompted, save your Illustrator Defaults text file to the desktop, leaving the name as Illustrator Defaults.

**5**   Use Notepad (Windows), TextEdit (Mac OS), or another text editing application to open, view and print your default shortcuts file.

## Custom shortcuts

For missing or hard-to-remember keyboard shortcuts, Illustrator allows you to add to or edit its list of defaults. It is highly recommended that you make a copy of the default keyboard shortcuts first before altering the original shortcut list. To do so, click the Save button and rename the new listing, then choose that new listing from the Set drop-down menu.

**1**   To add a custom shortcut, choose Edit > Keyboard Shortcuts.

**2**  In the Keyboard Shortcuts dialog box, choose the Menu Commands shortcut type from the drop-down menu above the shortcut list.

**3**  In the shortcut list below, click the arrow next to the File menu designation to expand that portion of the list.

**4**  Scroll down the menu list to the Place command, which, by default, doesn't have a keyboard shortcut.

**5**  Click the Shortcut column next to the Place command, and press Ctrl+E (Windows) or Command+E (Mac OS) to enter that shortcut.

**6**  Click the Symbol column next to the Place command, and type **E**, if there's not already one there. This is the symbol that will appear in the menu next to the Place command.

If you enter a shortcut that's already assigned to another command or tool, you'll get a warning about this at the bottom of the Keyboard Shortcuts dialog box.

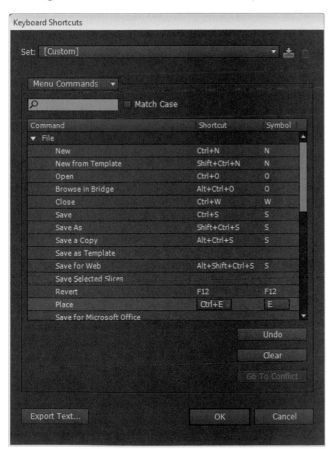

*Change the keyboard shortcut for the Place command.*

If this happens, do one of the following:

- Click the Undo button below to withdraw the entry.
- Click the Go To Conflict button to enter a different shortcut for the other command.
- Ignore the warning, and Illustrator will delete the shortcut for the other command in favor of your new one.

**7** To edit an existing shortcut, click the shortcut you want to change in the Shortcut column of the list, and type a new shortcut.

**8** If that shortcut has already been assigned, follow the directions above to Undo or Go To the other command.

## Saving shortcut sets

Saving sets of custom shortcuts in Illustrator will allow you to return to them and use them whenever you choose.

**1** To save a new set of custom shortcuts, make changes to an existing shortcut set in the Keyboard Shortcuts dialog box, as noted in the previous section, "Custom shortcuts."

**2** Click OK to save those changes to the currently selected shortcut set.

*You cannot save changes to the Illustrator Defaults set.*

**3** When the Save Keyset File dialog box appears, type **MySet** in the Name text field, and then click OK. The new keyset will appear in the Set drop-down menu under its new name.

*Save the new set.*

## Deleting shortcut sets

You can delete unused or unwanted shortcut sets in the Keyboard Shortcuts dialog box.

1   To re-visit your shortcut set, choose Edit > Keyboard Shortcuts.

2   Select the unwanted new set from the Set drop-down menu at the top of the dialog box.

3   Click the Delete button (🗑), then click Yes to confirm in the alert box that appears to remove that set from the list. Note that you cannot delete the Illustrator Default set.

*Illustrator warns you when you try to delete an existing set of keyboard shortcuts.*

4   Click OK to exit the dialog box. Choose File > Save, then choose File > Close.

Now that you're familiar with the features and customization options of Illustrator workspaces, you're ready to begin creating and editing artwork in the next chapter.

## Self study

Using your new knowledge of Illustrator workspaces, try some of the following tasks to build on your experience. Use the **ai0201.ai** file from your ai02lessons folder as an example file.

1   Choose the Selection tool (▸) from the Tools panel, and select different objects within the example artwork. Watch as the options available in the Control panel change based on what's selected, and try to make yourself familiar with how and why these options change.

2   Explore the default workspaces. Rearrange the panels in each workspace to meet your needs. Create and save your own custom workspace, and then return to the Essentials workspace, noting the differences between the workspaces.

3   Create your own set of keyboard shortcuts, changing those that you think are less intuitive than others, and adding shortcuts where there aren't any by default. Think about how these shortcuts can speed up your workflow and customize the way Illustrator creates and edits artwork.

# Review

## Questions

**1** Describe the advantages of using the Navigator panel to change the view of your artwork.

**2** How do you select hidden tools in Illustrator?

**3** Describe three ways to change the configuration of the panel dock.

**4** How can saving workspaces help you work more efficiently?

**5** What can you do if a keyboard shortcut you've added is the same as one already in existence?

## Answers

**1** The Navigator panel allows you to reduce or enlarge the view of your artwork in the document window by dragging its Zoom slider. It also allows you to scroll to different locations within your artwork by dragging the box in its proxy window. These options, along with the ability to marquee-zoom in on areas of your illustration, are all available in the same panel and do not require you to switch tools or choose different commands to access them. This makes it a more efficient choice for changing the view of your artwork while you're working.

**2** Tools that have other, related tools hidden beneath them are indicated by a small white triangle in the lower-right corner of the tool icon. To access these hidden tools, position your cursor over any tool that has a white triangle displayed, then click and hold the mouse button to expose the hidden tools nested within it. Once the hidden related tools appear, you can click to switch to the desired tool.

**3** The panel dock can be reconfigured by clicking the double-arrow in its upper-right corner. This toggles the dock between expanded and collapsed view. In addition, you can click and drag the left edge to expand or reduce the width of the panels contained in it. You can also double-click the dark gray bar at the top of the dock to toggle between icon and expanded mode.

**4** Saving a workspace allows you to lock in the position and visibility of panels on your screen. It also allows you to return to that workspace whenever you choose, even after you've opened and closed panels or switched to other workspaces. This ability to customize your workspace ensures that you only have to work with the panels that you need the most at any given time, and streamlines your workflow in the process.

**5** If you've added a keyboard shortcut in Illustrator, either to an existing set or to a new custom set, and you get a warning about another command that already uses the same shortcut, you have three choices: you can ignore the warning and forfeit the shortcut for the other command in favor of a new choice; you can click the Undo button in the Keyboard Shortcuts dialog box to reverse the change; or you can click the Go To Conflict button to change the other command's shortcut so they no longer conflict.

## What you'll learn in this lesson:

- Creating shapes
- Selecting objects using the selection tools
- Transforming shapes
- Using layers to organize artwork

# Illustrator CC Essentials

*Illustrator is used to create many types of artwork from simple icons to complicated illustrations and technical documentation. In this lesson, you'll use the shape tools, work with basic selection techniques, and complete artwork. Along the way, you will learn some helpful tips for creating artwork on your own.*

## Starting up

Before starting, make sure that your tools and panels are consistent by resetting your workspace. See "Resetting Adobe Illustrator CC Preferences" in the Starting up section of this book.

You will work with several files from the ai03lessons folder in this lesson. Make sure that you have loaded the ailessons folder onto your hard drive from the supplied DVD. See "Loading lesson files" in the Starting up section of this book.

### See Lesson 3 in action!

*Use the accompanying video to gain a better understanding of how to use some of the features shown in this lesson. You can find the video tutorial for this lesson on the included DVD.*

## Using the shape tools

Making shapes is an important part of using Adobe Illustrator. In Lesson 5, "Working with the Drawing Tools," you learn how to make your own custom shapes and lines using the Pen tool, but many times you will work with shapes that are ready-to-go, right off the Tools panel.

Though it might seem simple if you have used Illustrator before, transferring a shape from the Tools panel to the artboard can be a little confusing for new users. To start this lesson, you'll create a new blank document; think of it as a piece of scratch paper that you can use for practice. You will put a number of shapes on this new document throughout the exercise; feel free to delete or reposition them as you move on to make room for new ones. You won't use this document in any other lessons.

1    In Illustrator, choose File > New, or use the keyboard shortcut Ctrl+N (Windows) or Command+N (Mac OS). The New Document dialog box appears.

2    If they are not already selected, choose Print from the New Document Profile drop-down menu and Inches from the Units drop-down menu. When you change the units to inches, the New Document Profile setting changes to [Custom]. Keep in mind that the Document Profile can be changed after the file has been created, as can the units of measurements.

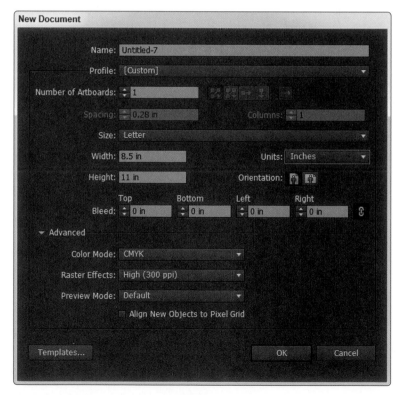

*Specify the settings of your new Illustrator document.*

**3**   Click OK. A new blank document appears.

**4**   Select the Rectangle tool (□) from the Tools panel. Click and drag anywhere on the artboard. By clicking and dragging, you determine the placement and size of the rectangle. Typically, you would pull from the upper-left corner diagonally to the lower-right corner.

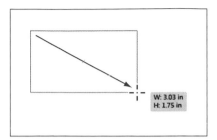

W: 3.03 in
H: 1.75 in

*Click and drag from the upper-left corner to the lower-right corner.*

**5**   It is wise to save your files often after you start working. Choose File > Save As to save this file. The Save As dialog box appears.

**6**   Type **ai0301_work** into the File name (Windows) or Save As (Mac OS) text field, leave the Save as type as Adobe Illustrator (AI), and then navigate to the ai03lessons folder. Click Save.

**7**   When the Illustrator Options dialog box appears, leave the version set to Illustrator CC and click OK. The file is saved.

*If you are not able to save in the ai03lessons folder, the folder might be locked. See the Starting up section at the beginning of this book for instructions on how to unlock your lessons folder.*

## Repositioning and visually resizing the rectangle

Now that you have your first shape on the page, perhaps you want to relocate it or alter its shape or size.

1   Choose the Selection tool (➤) from the Tools panel. A bounding box with eight handles appears around the rectangle you just drew. If you do not see the eight handles, make sure you have the rectangle selected by clicking it once. If the bounding box is still not visible, choose View > Show Bounding Box. The bounding box is a feature that can be toggled on or off, and that allows you to transform a shape without leaving the Selection tool.

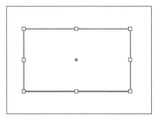

*The bounding box provides handles to help transform shapes.*

2   Using the Selection tool, click inside the rectangle and drag it to another location on the page (do not click the handles, since that resizes the shape).

*If you click inside a shape and it becomes unselected, it probably has no fill. Fill and stroke are discussed in Lesson 4, "Adding Color." By pressing the letter **D**, you revert back to the default white fill and black stroke, then you can easily select the shape.*

3   Hover over the bottom-middle handle until the cursor becomes a vertical arrow and the word path appears. Click and drag. When you click a middle handle and drag, you adjust the size of the selected handle's side only.

4   Click a corner handle and drag. When you click a corner handle, you adjust both sides that are connected to the corner point.

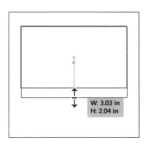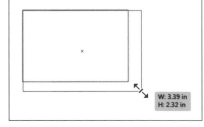

*Click and drag a middle point.*          *Click and drag a corner point.*

5   Choose File > Save to save your work.

## Finding or changing the shape's dimensions using the Transform panel

What if you need to know a shape's dimensions, or need it to be an exact size? This is when you should refer to the Transform panel.

**1** Make sure the rectangle is still selected and open the Transform panel by choosing Window > Transform. The Transform panel appears. The values displayed are for the selected item, which in this case is the rectangle.

The Transform panel displays information about the rectangle's location and size. Here is something to keep in mind: the values (except for the X and Y values, which refer to the selected reference point) displayed in the Transform panel refer to the rectangle's bounding box. By default, the reference point is the center of the shape.

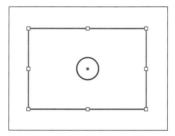

The center reference point locator.     The reference point in the shape.

**2** Click the upper-left corner of the reference point locator to see that the X and Y values change, reflecting the shape's position based upon the upper-left corner as the reference point. Because you created your rectangle without given parameters, its values are different from those displayed in the figure below.

The X and Y coordinates change depending
on the reference point selected.

**3** Choose View > Rulers > Show Rulers to display the rulers, or use the keyboard shortcut Ctrl+R (Windows) or Command+R (Mac OS).

4    In the Transform panel, type **2** into the X text field and press the Tab key to move the cursor to the Y text field. Type **2** into the Y text field. Make sure the Constrain Width and Height proportions button (⊛) is not selected, then type **1** into the W (Width) text field and **1** into the H (Height) text field. The rectangle is now positioned and sized according to these values.

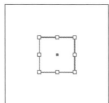

*Manually enter values.*         *The result.*

5    Choose File > Save to save your work.

## Rotating and shearing using the Transform panel

You can also use the Transform panel to enter exact rotation and shear values for the shapes on the artboard.

1    With the shape still selected, type **25** into the Rotate text field at the bottom of the Transform panel and press Enter (Windows) or Return (Mac OS). The square rotates 25 degrees counterclockwise and the dimensions in the Transform panel are updated.

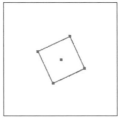

*Type **25** into the Rotate text field.*         *The result.*

**2**    Click and hold the arrow to the right of the Shear text field and choose -30° from the drop-down menu. Illustrator shears the shape by 30 degrees.

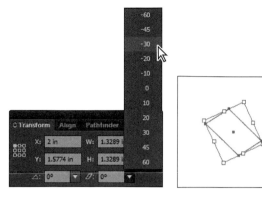

*Choose a value from the Shear drop-down menu.*    *The result.*

**3**    Choose File > Save.

## Constraining a shape

You have created a shape visually and then used the Transform feature to make the rectangle a square. You can also use keyboard commands to create the shape that you want right from the Tools panel.

**1**    Select the Rectangle tool (□) from the Tools panel.

**2**    Press and hold the Shift key and click and drag on an empty area on the artboard. Note that the Shape tool is constrained to create a square. In order for the finished product to remain a square (and not become a rectangle), you must release the mouse before you release the Shift key. Now try this with the Ellipse tool.

**3**    The Ellipse tool (○) is hidden beneath the Rectangle tool. Click and hold the Rectangle tool in the Tools panel to reveal and select the Ellipse tool.

*Select the hidden Ellipse tool.*

**4** Press and hold the Shift key, click an empty area of the artboard, and drag to create a circle. Remember to release the mouse before you release the Shift key to keep the shape a circle.

**5** Choose File > Save. Keep this file open for the next part of the lesson.

## Entering exact dimensions

You can also modify a shape's properties and dimensions through the shape tool's dialog box. You'll do that now using the Ellipse tool.

Before you start, you should know where to set the units of measurement. Even after indicating that you want the rulers to use inches, you might still have values recognized in points.

**1** Choose Edit > Preferences > Units (Windows) or Illustrator > Preferences > Units (Mac OS). The Preferences dialog box appears.

**2** Select Inches from the General drop-down menu, if it is not already selected. Leave all other measurements the same and click OK.

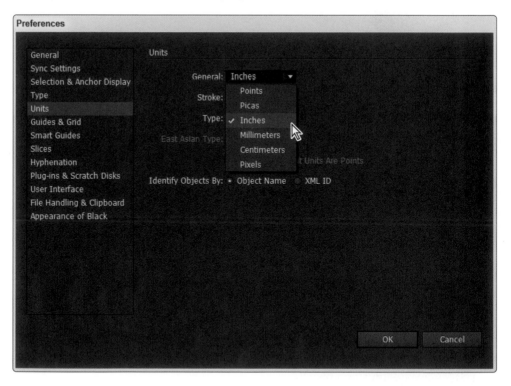

*Change the general units of measurements to inches.*

**3**    Using the Ellipse tool (○), click once on the artboard. The Ellipse dialog box appears.

*If the Ellipse dialog box does not appear, you might have inadvertently clicked and dragged. Even a slight drag instructs Illustrator to create a tiny shape rather than open the dialog box. If this happens, press Ctrl+Z (Windows) or Command+Z (Mac OS) and click the artboard again.*

**4**    Type **4** into the Width text field, and then press the Tab key to highlight the Height text field. Type **4** into the Height text field and click OK.

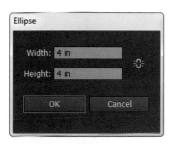
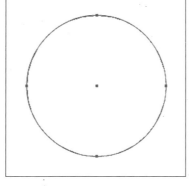

*Change the Width and Height to matching values.*    *The result.*

You can use this same method to change shape options.

**5**    Hidden beneath the Ellipse tool in the Tools panel are a number of other shape tools. Click and hold the Ellipse tool to see the other options. Select the Star tool (☆) and click once on a blank area of the artboard. The Star dialog box appears.

**6**    Set the star's Radius 1 to **1.5** inches and its Radius 2 to **2** inches; then type **15** in the Points text field. Click OK.

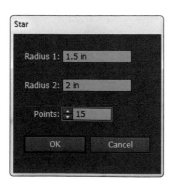
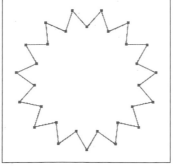

*Enter star values.*    *The result.*

**7** Choose File > Save, then File > Close. You won't be working with this file anymore.

You will now create a basic illustration using some of these basic shapes as well as additional fundamental features.

## Selecting artwork

In this part of the lesson, you will receive a quick primer on the selection tools and techniques in Adobe Illustrator. As the old saying goes, you have to select it to affect it. You need to know how to select objects in order to reposition, color, transform, and apply effects to them.

### Helpful keyboard shortcuts for selections

| FUNCTION | WINDOWS | MAC OS |
|---|---|---|
| Switch to last-used selection tool | Ctrl | Command |
| Switch between Direct Selection tool and Group Selection tool | Alt | Option |
| Add to a selection | Shift+click | Shift+click |
| Subtract from a selection | Shift+click | Shift+click |
| Change pointer to cross hair for selected tools | Caps Lock | Caps Lock |

### The selection tools

While there are several selection tools in Adobe Illustrator, the three main tools are the Selection tool, the Direct Selection tool, and the Group Selection tool. You will have an opportunity to experiment with selections in this part of the lesson.

**1** Choose File > Open and navigate to the ai03lessons folder. Select the file named **ai0302.ai** and click Open. A file opens with a completed fish illustration on the top and the individual components of that fish at the bottom. The top fish artwork is locked and not accessible; use this for reference as you follow the exercise.

**2** Choose File > Save As. The Save As dialog box appears.

**3** Type **ai0302_work** into the File name text field and click Save. When the Illustrator Options dialog box appears, click OK.

**4**  Choose the Selection tool (▸) from the Tools panel and pass the cursor over the shape pieces at the bottom of the artwork. As you pass over the objects, notice that the cursor changes to reflect where there are selectable objects. Do not click to select any of these objects just yet.

*Selectable object.*

*Anchor point.*

*No selectable object.*

**5**  Click the large red fin; the entire fin is selected. If you do not see the bounding box appear around the fin, choose View > Show Bounding Box.

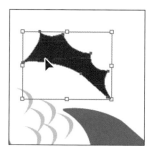
*The entire shape is selected and has a bounding box surrounding it.*

**6**  Click and drag to reposition the fin anywhere on the page. When you use the Selection tool, you select an entire object or group.

**7**  Choose the Direct Selection tool (▸) from the Tools panel. Using this tool allows you to select individual points or path segments of an object.

8 Without clicking the selected large fin, reposition the cursor over one of the tips of the fin to see how the cursor changes to indicate that there is a selectable anchor beneath the cursor. A light-gray box giving the X- and Y-coordinates of the anchor point also appears. Click when you see the arrow with the small white square.

*Cursor changes to show the selectable item.*
*Individual anchor point selected.*

9 Notice that only the anchor point that you clicked on is solid; all the other anchor points are hollow and not active.

10 Click the solid anchor point and drag upward to reposition the anchor point and change the shape of the fin. By using the Direct Selection tool, you can alter the shape of an object.

*Click and drag with the Direct Selection tool to alter a shape.*

11 Press Ctrl+Z (Windows) or Command+Z (Mac OS) to undo the last step, or choose Edit > Undo Move.

12 Choose File > Save. Keep this file open for the next part of this lesson.

## Grouping the scales

You will now turn the individual scales in the artwork into a group that you can move and modify as a collective unit.

**1**   Activate the Selection tool (➤). Click one of the pale orange scales, then add to the selection by pressing and holding the Shift key and clicking one of the other five scales.

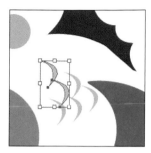

*Shift+click to add to the selection.*

**2**   With the two scales selected, choose Object > Group or use the keyboard shortcut Ctrl+G (Windows) or Command+G (Mac OS). The two scales are grouped together. When you select one with the Selection tool, the other is also selected.

**3**   Shift+click a third scale to add to the selection, then Shift+click the remaining scales. All the scales are now selected.

**4**   Press Ctrl+G (Windows) or Command+G (Mac OS) to group all six scales together.

**5**   Choose Select > Deselect, or press Shift+Ctrl+A (Windows) or Shift+Command+A (Mac OS), to deselect the scales.

**6**   Using the Selection tool, click one of the first scales you selected. The scales act as a collective group now, and all the scales are selected.

**7**   Press Shift+Ctrl+A (Windows) or Shift+Command+A (Mac OS) to deselect everything again.

You will now use the Group Selection tool to select individual items in a group.

**8**   Click and hold the Direct Selection tool (▷) in the Tools panel and choose the hidden Group Selection tool (▷).

**9**   Click once on the top-most scale of the group; only the one scale is selected.

**10**  Now click the same scale again and the second scale that you grouped back in step 2 also becomes selected.

**11**  Click the same scale a third time and the entire last group of items becomes selected. By using the Group Selection tool, you can select individual items and even groups within groups.

**12** With all the scales selected, click and drag the scales on top of the fish's orange body.

*Click and drag to reposition the scales.*

**13** Now switch back to the Selection tool to reposition the rest of the separate components together to complete the fish. The positioning guides help you to best position and arrange the different pieces into one fish.

*The completed fish.*

**14** Choose File > Save, then File > Close to close the document. You won't be working with this file anymore.

## Isolation mode

Isolation mode is an Illustrator mode in which you can select and edit individual components or sub-layers of a grouped object. There are four ways to enter into isolation mode:

- Double-click a group using the Selection tool (⬧).

- Click the Isolate Selected Object button (⊞) in the Control panel.

- Right-click (Windows) or Ctrl+click (Mac OS) a group and choose Isolate Selected Group.

- Select a group and choose Enter Isolation Mode from the Layers panel menu (⋅☰).

# Using shape and transform tools to create artwork

You will add to the basics that you have discovered to complete some different fish artwork.

**1**    Choose File > Open and navigate to the ai03lessons folder. Double-click **ai0303_done.ai** to open the file in Adobe Illustrator. Artwork of two swimming fish appear.

**2**    This is the file you will create. You can choose File > Close, or keep it open for reference throughout this exercise.

*You can leave this file open for reference or choose File > Close.*

**3**    Choose File > Open, navigate to the ai03lessons folder, and double-click the **ai0303.ai** file. A document with four guides in the center of the page opens.

**4**    If your units are not in inches choose Edit > Preferences > Units (Windows) or Illustrator > Preferences > Units (Mac OS) and change the measurement units in the General drop-down menu to Inches. Click OK.

**5**    Choose File > Save As. The Save As dialog box appears.

**6**    Type **ai0303_work** into the File name text field and navigate to the ai03lessons folder you saved on your hard drive; then click Save.

**7**    When the Illustrator Options dialog box appears, click OK.

## Using the transform tools

There are several basic transform tools. Though each performs a different task, they are essentially used in the same manner.

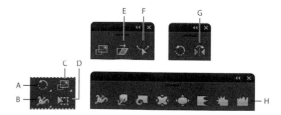

*A. Rotate. B. Width tool. C. Scale. D. Free Transform. E. Shear.*
*F. Reshape. G. Reflect tool. H. Additional Warp tools.*

You used the Transform panel to rotate and shear earlier in this lesson. You will now use the transform tools to make changes by entering exact values.

1    Click and hold the Star tool (☆) in the Tools panel to reveal the hidden tools. Select the Rounded Rectangle tool (▢).

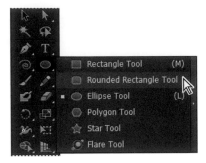

*Select the Rounded Rectangle tool.*

2    Click and drag to create a rectangle with rounded corners of any size.

3    Activate the Selection tool (▶), and using the bounding box's anchors, click and drag until the rounded rectangle fits the dimensions of the guides located in the center of the document.

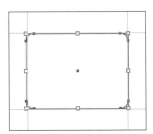

*Manually drag anchors to fit the
rectangle inside the guides.*

## Adding a fill color

You will now fill the rounded rectangle with a color.

**1** Make sure the rounded rectangle is still selected. If it is not selected, click it using the Selection tool (➤).

**2** Locate the Control panel at the top of your workspace and click the Fill box on the left side of the panel. Color swatches appear, from which you can choose a color. Pass your cursor over the swatches, and each color's name appears in a tooltip. Select the color named *CMYK Blue*. If the tooltip does not appear, select the color you see highlighted in the figure below. The shape's fill becomes blue.

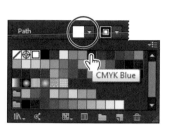

*Select CMYK Blue for the fill.*    *The result.*

**3** Lock the selected rectangle by pressing Ctrl+2 (Windows) or Command+2 (Mac OS), or by choosing Object > Lock > Selection. This makes it impossible to select the rectangle unless you unlock it. This feature is extremely helpful when you start creating more complicated artwork.

## Modifying a shape

You will now use the shape tools to create and add light rays to the illustration.

**1** From the list of hidden shape tools beneath the Rounded Rectangle tool in the Tools panel, select the Polygon tool (○) and click once on the artboard. The Polygon dialog box appears.

**2** Leave the radius as it is; type **3** into the Sides text field and click OK. A triangle is drawn.

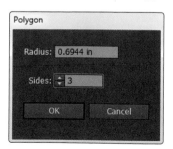

*Change the amount of sides.*    *The result.*

**3** Choose the Selection tool (➤), and click and drag the top-center anchor of the bounding box upward, to stretch the triangle.

**4** Elongate the triangle more by clicking the lower-right corner of the bounding box, pulling down, and dragging the anchor to the left.

  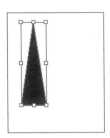

Click and drag upward.     Drag inward and down.     The result.

By clicking and dragging the anchor, you visually resize the shape.

## Entering a shape size in the Transform panel

For the purpose of this illustration, you will use the Transform panel to make sure that the triangle is sized correctly.

**1** If it is not visible, choose Window > Transform, or click the word Transform in the Control panel. The Transform panel appears.

**2** With the triangle still selected, type **.5** in the W (Width) text field, and type **2** into the H (Height) text field. Press Enter (Windows) or Return (Mac OS).

 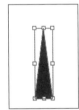

Enter values in the Transform panel.     The result.

**3** Press **D**; the triangle's color reverts to the default white fill and black stroke colors.

**4** Click once on the Stroke box in the Control panel at the top of the Illustrator work area and select None from the Stroke swatches drop-down menu. The triangle is not visible at this time (as it is white on a white background), but you can still see its anchor points.

 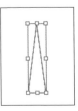

Change the stroke color to None.     The result.

## Viewing in Outline view

By default, previews of Adobe Illustrator artwork are in color. There will be times, however, when you create shapes that are white, or possibly have no fill or stroke color. Finding these items on your white artboard after you deselect them can be difficult. This is where Outline view can help.

1    With the Selection tool (▶), click somewhere on the artboard to deselect the triangle. Unless your triangle crosses over the rectangle you created earlier, you can no longer see the shape.

2    Choose View > Outline, or press Ctrl+Y (Windows) or Command+Y (Mac OS). Outline view displays artwork so that only its outlines (or paths) are visible. Viewing artwork without fill and stroke attributes speeds up the time it takes Illustrator to redraw the screen when working with complex artwork; it is also helpful when you need to locate hidden shapes.

3    With the Selection tool, click one of the triangle's sides and reposition it so its tip touches the center (indicated by an X) of the rectangle.

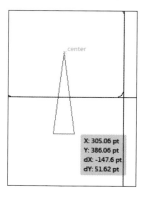

*The triangle and rectangle arranged in the Outline view.*

4    Choose View > Preview, or press Ctrl+Y (Windows) or Command+Y (Mac OS) once more. The color attributes are visible again.

## Rotating the shape

You will now create a series of triangle shapes and rotate them 360 degrees, creating what will look like rays of light.

1    Make sure the triangle is selected.

2    Select the Rotate tool (◌) from the Tools panel. The Rotate tool allows you to visually rotate objects, as well as enter specific rotation angles. In this example, you will enter values so that the triangles are evenly spaced.

**3**    Alt+click (Windows) or Option+click (Mac OS) the tip of the triangle aligned with the rectangle's center. When you have the Rotate tool selected, and you Alt+click (Windows) or Option+click (Mac OS) on the artboard, you define the reference point from which the selected shape is rotated. Doing this also displays the Rotate dialog box, in which you can enter an exact value for the angle.

**4**    Type **18** into the Angle text field and click Copy. This rotates a copy of your triangle 18 degrees and keeps the original triangle intact. The value of 18 degrees evenly divides into 360 degrees, which will make the distribution of these rays even when you circle back to the starting point.

*Enter rotate values and click Copy.*                                      *A rotated copy is created.*

**5**    Press Ctrl+D (Windows) or Command+D (Mac OS) to repeat the transformation. The triangle shape copies, and rotates again.

**6**    Continue to press Ctrl+D (Windows) or Command+D (Mac OS) until you reach the original triangle.

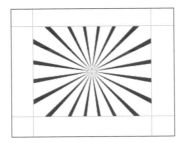

*The triangle after being rotated.*

**7**    If you are still in Outline view, press Ctrl+Y (Windows) or Command+Y (Mac OS) to return to the Preview view.

## Changing the color of the triangles

You will now select the triangles and change their opacity.

**1**    Switch to the Selection tool (↖) and select any one of the white triangles.

**2**    Choose Select > Same > Fill Color and all the white triangles become selected. The Select > Same feature can be helpful when selecting objects that share a common feature, including fill color, stroke color, stroke point size, and more.

**3**    Choose Object > Group. Grouping these shapes together makes it easier to select them later.

**4**    Type **50** into the Opacity text field in the Control panel and press Enter (Windows) or Return (Mac OS) to change the opacity of the white triangles to 50 percent.

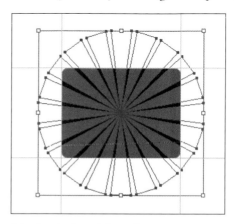

*Select the triangles and change the opacity to 50 percent.*

**5**    Choose File > Save to save your work.

# Using layers when building an illustration

Layers have many uses in Adobe Illustrator. In this lesson, you will find out how to use layers to lock and temporarily hide artwork that you don't want to inadvertently select while you work on other things.

**1**   Open the Layers panel by clicking the Layers button () in the dock on the right side of the workspace. Notice that when you start to work in Illustrator, you begin with a layer named Layer 1. All the artwork that you have created throughout this lesson is added as a sub-layer to this layer. You will now lock a layer and create a new layer onto which you can put additional artwork.

**2**   Click the Toggles lock (a small empty box) to the left of Layer 1 in the Layers panel. A Padlock icon (🔒) appears, indicating that this layer is locked. You cannot select or change any items on this layer.

*The Toggles lock area of the Layers panel.*

*Earlier in this lesson, you selected and locked the rectangle using the Object > Lock menu item. That method works well for individual items, especially if you don't typically work with layers. Locking a layer is different, since it locks all items on the layer at once.*

**3**   To unlock the layer, click the Padlock icon. The layer unlocks.

**4**   Relock Layer 1 by clicking the Toggles lock square again.

## Creating a new blank layer

You will now create a new blank layer onto which you can paste artwork.

**1** Alt+click (Windows) or Option+click (Mac OS) the Create New Layer button (◻) at the bottom of the Layers panel. The Layer Options dialog box appears. By pressing and holding the Alt/Option key, you can name the layer before its creation.

**2** Type **Fish** into the File name text field and click OK. A new empty layer appears on top of the original (Layer 1) displayed in the Layers panel. You are now ready to copy and paste artwork from another Illustrator file into this one.

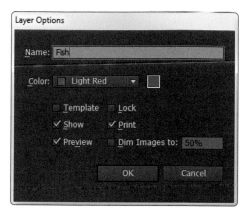

*Name the new layer.*

*The layer in the Layers panel.*

## Cutting and pasting objects

You will now open another document and cut and paste artwork from one Illustrator file to another.

**1** Choose File > Open. In the Open dialog box, navigate to the ai03lessons folder and double-click the file named **ai0304.ai**. Artwork of two fish appears.

*The fish artwork.*

**2**    Use the Selection tool (➤) to click once on the larger of the two fish, then Shift+click the second fish to add it to the selection.

**3**    Choose Edit > Cut, or press Ctrl+X (Windows) or Command+X (Mac OS), to cut the fish.

**4**    Return to the work file by choosing Window > **ai0303_work.ai**. Choose Edit > Paste, or press Ctrl+V (Windows) or Command+V (Mac OS), to paste the fish onto the artboard. The fish are pasted onto the Fish layer, which is the active layer.

**5**    Press Shift+Ctrl+A (Windows) or Shift+Command+A (Mac OS), or click a blank area of the artboard, to deselect the fish.

**6**    Activate the Selection tool; click the smaller of the two fish and drag it to a spot on top of the larger fish. Notice that the smaller fish disappears behind the larger fish. The order in which artwork appears is based on the order in which artwork is created. Newer artwork is placed higher in the object stacking order, which can be changed using the Arrange feature.

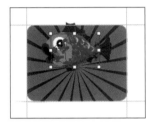

*The smaller fish falls behind the*
*larger fish in the stacking order.*

**7**    With the smaller fish still selected, choose Object > Arrange > Bring to Front.

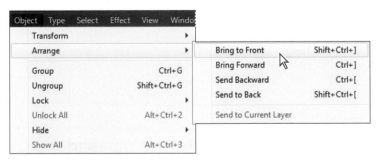

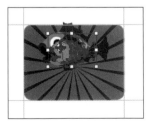

*Choose to bring the small fish to*
*the front, and then view the result.*

**8**    Select the smaller fish and reposition it so that it slightly overlaps the bottom of the larger fish.

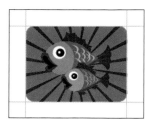

*Reposition the smaller fish to overlap the larger fish slightly.*

**9**    Choose File > Save. Keep this file open for the next part of this lesson, but close **ai0304.ai**. When asked if you'd like to save the changes made to the document, choose No (Windows) or Don't Save (Mac OS).

## Creating bubbles

You will now create a bubble, and then clone it several times to finish the illustration.

**1**    Click and hold the last-used shape tool (the Polygon tool) in the Tools panel and select the hidden Ellipse tool (○).

**2**    Click once on the artboard to display the Ellipse dialog box.

**3**    Type **.5** into the Width and Height text fields. Click OK. A small circle is created.

**4**    Click the Fill color swatch in the Control panel and choose the color *CMYK Cyan* from the drop-down swatches menu.

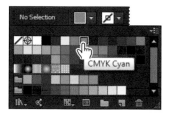    

*Change the fill color to CMYK Cyan.*    *The result.*

**5**    If the Stroke is not set to none (☒), choose the Stroke box in the Control panel and choose None from the drop-down swatches menu.

Now you will create a smaller circle to use as a reflection in the circle you already created.

**6**    With the Ellipse tool still active, click once on the artboard.

**7**  In the resulting Ellipse dialog box, type **.1** into the Width and Height text fields and click OK.

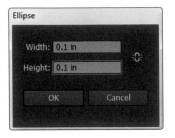

*Create a smaller circle.*

*The result.*

**8**  Use the Fill box in the Control panel to select White for the small circle's fill.

**9**  Activate the Selection tool (▸), then click and drag the smaller circle on top of the larger cyan (blue) circle. Position it anywhere you want on the circle, as long as it looks like a light reflection on the bubble.

*Position the smaller
white circle on top
of the cyan circle.*

**10**  Shift+click the larger and smaller circles to select them both. Choose Object > Group, or press Ctrl+G (Windows) or Command+G (Mac OS), to group the circles.

**11**  Choose File > Save to save your work.

### Cloning the bubble group

You will now clone, or duplicate, the bubble several times.

**1**  Make sure the bubble group is selected.

**2**  Hover your cursor over the bubble and press and hold the Alt (Windows) or Option (Mac OS) key. Note that the icon becomes a double cursor (▸▸).

**3**    While pressing and holding on the Alt/Option key, click and drag to the right. Notice that as you drag, the original group of circles remains intact and you create a second group. Release the mouse when you are off to the right and the cloned bubble no longer touches the original.

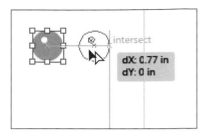

*Press and hold the Alt (Windows) or*
*Option (Mac OS) key, then click and drag.*

**4**    Press Ctrl+D (Windows) or Command+D (Mac OS) to repeat the duplication. Illustrator remembers the distance and angle of the last movement. You can also perform this function by selecting Object > Transform > Transform Again.

**5**    Press Ctrl+D (Windows) or Command+D (Mac OS) once more to create a total of four circle groups.

*If you press and hold the Shift key while cloning, you can constrain the cloned objects to move on a straight path, or a 45 or 90-degree angle.*

*Clone the circle group three times.*

**6**    Choose File > Save to save your work. Keep the file open for the next part of the lesson.

## Repeating a resize transform

You will now use the Transform Again keyboard shortcut to transform the bubbles so they are varying sizes.

**1**    Select the second bubble. You will leave the original bubble at its current size.

**2**    Press and hold the Shift key (to constrain the proportions as you resize), and click and drag a corner anchor point to resize the bubble only slightly. An exact amount is not important for this. Once you resize, do not perform any other actions, such as repositioning. The resizing has to be the last action that you performed for the Transform Again feature to work properly.

**3**   Select the third bubble group and press Ctrl+D (Windows) or Command+D (Mac OS). This applies the same transformation to the third bubble. With the same bubble still selected, press Ctrl+D (Windows) or Command+D (Mac OS) again and the resize transformation is applied, making it even smaller.

**4**   Select the last (fourth) bubble and press Ctrl+D (Windows) or Command+D (Mac OS) three times, making this the smallest bubble.

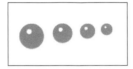

*The bubbles after they have been transformed into differently sized bubbles.*

 *Remember that the Transform Again feature (Ctrl+D [Windows] or Command+D [Mac OS]) repeats the most recent transformation, including positioning, that you performed. If you resize and then move an object, the repositioning, not the resizing, is repeated. If this occurs, press Ctrl+Z (Windows) or Command+Z (Mac OS) until you return to the point where all the bubbles are the same size. Then restart at step 1.*

**5**   Using the Selection tool (&#9733;), click and drag each bubble down and position them around the fish, on top of the rectangle. No exact position is necessary.

*Click and drag the bubbles to reposition them in the artwork.*

**6**   Choose File > Save to save your work. Keep the file open for the next part of the lesson.

## Moving objects from one layer to another

You will now move the bubbles onto Layer 1, under the rays of light.

**1**   Select one of the bubble groups, then Shift+click the remaining three so that all four
bubble groups are selected.

**2**   If the Layers panel is not visible, open it by clicking the Layers button () in the dock
or by choosing Windows > Layers.

A colored square appears to the right of the Fish layer in the Layers panel. This colored
square is called the selection indicator. If Illustrator's settings are at their defaults, the
indicator is red, matching the layer selection color.

*When something on a layer is selected, the
selection indicator appears.*

**3**   Click the Padlock icon (🔒) to the left of Layer 1 to unlock the layer.

**4**   Click and drag the selection indicator from the Fish layer down to Layer 1. The
bubbles are now on Layer 1 instead of on the Fish layer.

*Click and drag the selection indicator to
the layer beneath.*

**5**   Click any one of the triangles that you used to create the rays of light. Because they
were grouped earlier, selecting one selects the entire group.

**6**   Choose Object > Arrange > Bring to Front; the triangles are now on top of the
bubbles, but not on top of the fish. This is because the Fish layer is higher in the
stacking order than any objects on Layer 1.

**7**   Choose File > Save, then File > Close.

## Self study

Practice will help you to create the shapes that you want. To practice on your own, open the file named **ai0305.ai** and create the shapes that are locked on the base layer.

## Review

### Questions

1   Which selection tool allows you to select an individual anchor point or path segment?

2   What key modifier do you press and hold to constrain a shape to equal width and height values?

3   What are two methods of inputting exact height and width values for shapes?

### Answers

1   The Direct Selection tool allows you to select an individual anchor point or path segment.

2   Constrain a shape's proportions by pressing the Shift key while dragging the shape.

3   You can enter values for shapes by doing either of the following:

**a.** Select a Shape tool and click once on the artboard. This opens the shape options dialog box, in which you can enter width and height values.

**b.** After a shape has been created, choose Window > Transform and enter values into the Width and Height text fields.

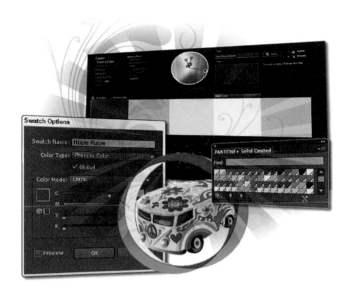

## What you'll learn in this lesson:

- Using the Appearance panel
- Applying and adjusting fills and strokes
- Using the Live Paint Bucket tool
- Creating and applying a gradient
- Creating and updating a pattern swatch

# Adding Color

*Adobe Illustrator CC provides a number of methods to help add color to your artwork. In this lesson, you'll discover how to enhance your artwork with color.*

## Starting up

Before starting, make sure that your tools and panels are consistent by resetting your workspace. See "Resetting Adobe Illustrator CC Preferences" in the Starting up section of this book.

You will work with several files from the ai04lessons folder in this lesson. Make sure that you have loaded the ailessons folder onto your hard drive from the included DVD. See "Loading lesson files" in the Starting up section of this book.

### See Lesson 4 in action!

*Use the accompanying video to gain a better understanding of how to use some of the features shown in this lesson. You can find the video tutorial for this lesson on the included DVD.*

# Basics of the Appearance panel

The Appearance panel in Illustrator allows you to adjust an object's fill and stroke, in addition to keeping track of any effects that have been applied to the object. The Appearance panel is also an indispensable tool for determining the structure of an object. Fills and strokes are shown in the order that they are applied to an object, the same way that other effects are ordered chronologically. As your Illustrator artwork increases in complexity, the Appearance panel becomes more important, since it makes the process of editing your illustration much easier. In this section, you have the opportunity to explore the Appearance panel by creating a simple illustration from scratch.

**1**   Launch Adobe Illustrator CC and choose File > New. The New Document dialog box appears.

**2**   In the Name text field, enter **Appearance**. Choose Print from the New Document Profile drop-down menu. Leave all other items the same and click OK. The new artboard appears.

To help you understand how powerful the Appearance panel is, you will create a simple shape and apply attributes to it.

**3**   Click and hold the Rectangle tool (□) and select the hidden Star tool (☆).

**4**   To make sure that you have the default color settings of a white fill and black stroke, press the letter **D**. This returns your colors to the default black stroke and white fill.

**5**   Click and drag out on the artboard anywhere to create a new star shape. Any size is fine for this exercise.

**6**   If the Appearance panel is not visible, choose Window > Appearance now.

The Appearance panel offers you the ability to track or make changes to the properties that have been applied to a selected object.

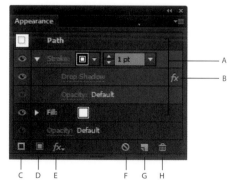

*A. Path with stroke, fill, and drop shadow.*
*B. Indicates path has effect applied.*
*C. Add New Stroke.*
*D. Add New Fill.*
*E. Add New Effect.*
*F. Clear Appearance.*
*G. Duplicate Selected Item.*
*H. Delete Selected Item.*

Click the tab of the Appearance panel and drag it out of the docking area. This ensures that the Appearance panel does not go away when you select other panels.

*Click and drag the Appearance panel out of the panel group.*

The Appearance panel indicates that this shape has a Stroke of 1 pt and it is black, and a Fill of white. The Opacity is also noted as being the default (100%).

## Changing colors

When you have a shape active in Adobe Illustrator, you can change the colors using multiple methods, including using the Appearance panel.

1   Click the color box to the right of Stroke in the Appearance panel, then click the arrow; this makes the Swatches panel accessible from within the Appearance panel.

2   With the Swatches panel open, choose *CMYK Red*. The stroke is changed to red.

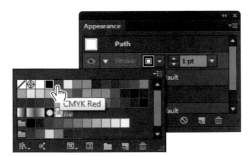

*Change colors right in the Appearance panel.*

3   Now click the fill color box to the right of Fill, and click the arrow. Choose *CMYK Yellow* from the Swatches panel.

## Adding effects

In this next section, you will discover how you can apply effects and then update them using the Appearance panel.

Keep in mind that, by using the Appearance panel, you can independently apply effects, such as drop shadows, outer glows, scribble effects and more, to strokes and fills. For example, you can apply the drop shadow effect to the stroke, but not to the fill.

1   Select the Stroke in the Appearance panel, then click the Add New Effect (*fx*) button at the bottom. From the list that appears, choose Stylize > Drop Shadow; the Drop Shadow dialog box appears. Leave the default settings and click OK. A drop shadow appears on the stroke, and Drop Shadow is listed as a property applied to the Stroke in the Appearance panel. Note that you can click to expand the arrow to the left of Stroke or Fill to see individual properties associated with them.

*The Property is listed in the Appearance panel.*      *The star with a drop shadow effect.*

2   Double-click the Drop Shadow property listed under Stroke, the Drop Shadow dialog box appears. Use this method to make changes to any effects that are applied to your object, otherwise you might end up applying an additional effect.

3   In the Drop Shadow dialog box change the following settings:

   **Opacity**: Change to 100% by either entering **100** into the Opacity text field, or clicking the arrow buttons to the left of the field.

   **X Offset**: Use the down-arrow to change the offset to a value of **3**.

   **Y Offset**: Use the down-arrow to change the offset to a value of **3**.

   **Blur**: Change to 1 pt by either entering **1** into the Blur text field, or clicking the arrow buttons to the left of the field.

4   Change the color of the drop shadow by clicking the color box; this displays the Color Picker. The Color Picker provides a color spectrum from which you can visually select colors, or enter color values into the text fields to manually define colors.

**5**   Click and drag the slider down toward red on the color spectrum, then click a red color in the Color Field. Click OK.

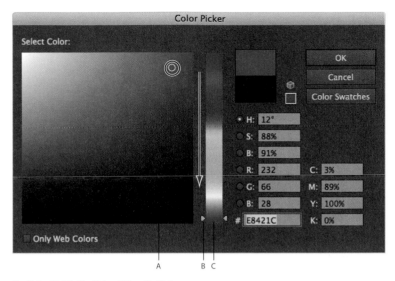

*A. Color Field.* **B.** *Color slider.* **C.** *Color spectrum.*

**6**   Click OK in the Drop Shadow dialog box. The drop shadow has been changed.

    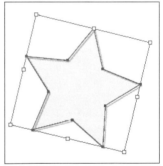

*Make changes to the drop shadow.*            *The result.*

**7**   You will not be saving this file, choose File > Close, and choose No (Windows), or Don't Save (Mac OS) when the Adobe Illustrator warning dialog box appears.

Throughout this lesson, you will be using alternate methods from which you can select color. But, keep in mind the power and ease of use the Appearance panel provides.

## Creating a colorful illustration

In this next exercise, you create a colorful illustration. While creating this illustration, you have the opportunity to use features that will speed up your production time, and also offer you creative solutions for color.

1   To begin, you will open the finished file. Choose File > Browse in Bridge and click the Favorites tab (in the upper-left corner). Click Desktop and open the ai04lessons folder.

2   Locate the file named **ai0402_done.ai** inside the ai04lessons folder, and double-click it to open it in Illustrator CC. An illustration of a retro bus appears.

You are looking at the final illustration that you will create. In this lesson, you will have the opportunity to experiment with fills, strokes, patterns, Live Paint and gradients.

3   You can either choose File > Close, to close this file, or keep it open as a reference.

## Using Live Paint

Illustrator provides two methods of painting: you can select a fill, stroke, or both to an object, or you can convert the object(s) to a Live Paint group and assign fills and strokes to the separate edges and faces of paths within. Live Paint is a brilliant solution to painting illustrations with multiple faces that are not necessarily independent shapes that can be easily filled.

1   Choose File > New to create a new file. In the Name text field, type **ai0402_work**.

2   Choose Print as the New Document Profile.

3   Select Inches from the Units drop-down menu. Leave all other settings at their default and click OK.

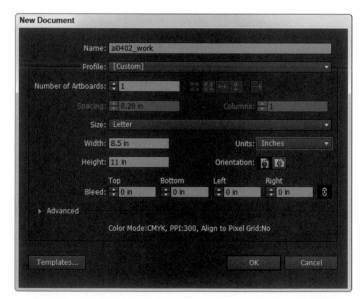

*Create a new print document.*

**4**   Choose File > Save to save this file. Make sure that you are saving into the ai04lessons folder. Leave **ai0402_work** in the File name text field and make sure that Illustrator is selected in the Save as type drop-down menu and then click Save. When the Illustrator Options dialog box appears, click OK.

**5**   Press **D** to make sure that you are at the default color settings of a black stroke and a white fill.

**6**   Click and hold the Star tool (☆) to select the Ellipse tool (○). Instead of clicking and dragging to create a shape, you will enter exact values into the shapes dialog box. Click once out on the artboard. The Ellipse dialog box appears. Enter **5** into the Width and Height text fields. Click OK. The circle appears on the artboard.

**7**   Choose the Selection tool, and then press and hold the Alt (Windows) or Option (Mac OS) key and position your cursor over the ellipse. When you see a double cursor, click and drag to clone (copy) the ellipse toward the lower-right by about .25 inch. Exact position is not important.

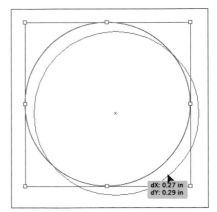     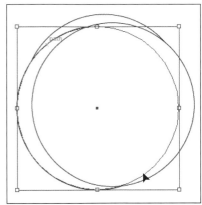

*Press and hold the Alt/Option key to clone the ellipse   Clone again to the lower-left.*
*to the lower-right.*

**8**   Click the original ellipse that you created and press and hold the Alt/Option key and drag to the lower-left to clone another ellipse.

For the next step, you will make the fill transparent.

9   Using the Selection tool, click and drag so that you create a marquee area that touches all three ellipses. This selects all the ellipses that the marquee crosses over.

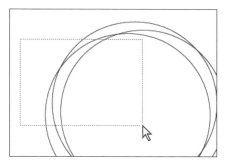

*Click and drag with the Selection tool to create a*
*selection of all three ellipses.*

10   Click Fill in the Control panel at the top of the workspace and choose None (⬜). This allows you to see all the intersecting faces that have been created. These individual faces are not individual objects that can easily be filled in with the traditional fill and stroke options available in Illustrator. To fill the faces, you will create a new Live Paint object.

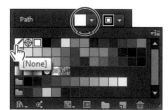

*Change the fill to None.*

## Converting the artwork to a Live Paint group

**1** Make sure that all three ellipses are still selected and then click and hold the Shape Builder tool (⬡) in the Tools panel to select the hidden Live Paint Bucket tool.

**2** Position the cursor over the selected ellipses, and when you see the message, click to make a Live Paint group, click. The ellipses are converted to a group of faces that can now be easily filled with color.

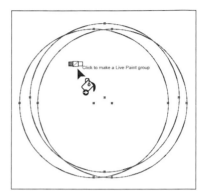

*Use the Live Paint Bucket tool to convert your ellipses to a Live Paint group.*

## Applying Live Paint to the group

In this next step, you will select colors and apply them to the individual faces in the newly created Live Paint group.

**1** If the Swatches panel is not visible, choose Window > Swatches. Click the tab of the panel and drag it out into the workspace to undock it from the panel docking area.

**2** Select the color named *CMYK Red*, and then (with the Live Paint Bucket tool still selected) hover over anyone of the faces in the Live Paint group. Notice that the individual face becomes highlighted. When you have picked a face that you want to fill with red (any one will do) click. The face fills with the red color.

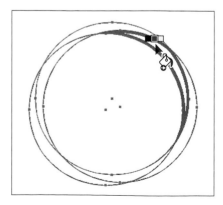
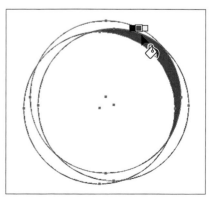

*Hover over a face in the Live Paint group and then click.*     *The result.*

You might have noticed the color selection appearing above the cursor. You can use this color selection to navigate through the rest of your colors in the swatches panel.

3    Hover over another face in your Live paint group, but this time press the right-arrow key to navigate to the color to the right of *CMYK Red* in the Swatches panel (*CMYK Yellow*), then click to fill the face.

4    For the rest of this lesson, use the colors in the Swatches panel to fill random faces in the Live Paint group. No specific color assignment is necessary.

*Fill the faces of the Live Paint group with color.*

5    Select File > Save, or press Ctrl+S (Windows) or Command+S (Mac OS) to save this file. Keep it open for the next part of this lesson.

6    Choose Window > Workspace > Reset Essentials to reset the panels.

## Adding a symbol to your artwork

Symbols offer you the ability to create artwork that can be used dynamically throughout your illustration. For example, you can create a snowflake and use it over 100 times in the illustration. Every time you use the snowflake, it is referred to as an instance. If you edit the symbol, all instances are updated.

Symbols can also be used to store frequently used artwork, such as logos, or clip art. In this lesson you use an existing symbol to add the retro bus to the illustration.

1    Choose Window > Symbols, the Symbols panel appears. There are only a few symbols included in the Symbols panel by default, but many more that you can access in the library.

2    Click the panel menu in the upper-right of the Symbols panel and select Open Symbol Library > Retro. A separate panel appears with retro symbols included in it.

*Select Open Symbol Library from the panel menu.*

*The Retro symbols.*

3    Click the Mini Bus symbol and drag it to the artboard.

*Easily navigate through all the Symbol libraries by clicking the arrow buttons at the bottom of an open Symbol Library panel.*

4    Using the Selection tool ( ), reposition the mini bus so that it is in the center of the ellipses.

5    With the bus still selected, double-click the Scale tool ( ) in the Tools panel. The Scale dialog box appears.

**6**    Type **175** in the Uniform Scale text field, and click OK. The bus is scaled to 175% of
the original size.

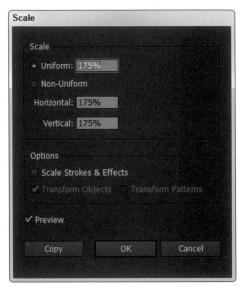

*Use the Scale tool to enter an exact scale amount.*

*If you want to visually resize the bus, you can position your cursor over any corner point in the
bounding box. Click, then press and hold the Shift key and drag inward or outward to scale
down or up proportionally.*

**7**    Press Ctrl+S (Windows) or Command+S (Mac OS) to save this file, keep it open for
the next part of this lesson.

## Expanding the symbol

As mentioned earlier, using symbols as clip art is an easy way to access lots of artwork, but perhaps you want to edit the symbol without affecting the original stored version. In this next lesson, you expand the mini bus so that you can recolor some of the artwork.

**1**    With the bus still selected, choose Object > Expand. The Expand dialog box appears.

*Expanding a symbol.*

**2**    Leave the options in the Expand dialog box the same and click OK. Most of the vector paths are now accessible and ready for you to edit. This has also removed any link to the original symbol.

## Saving swatches

The Swatches panel allows you to store colors for multiple uses in your document. You can create colors using several different methods in Illustrator, and by adding them to the Swatches panel, you can store them for frequent and consistent use. Storing a swatch of a color that you plan to reuse guarantees that the color is exactly the same each time it is used. Let's create a new swatch for your document.

**1**    Click the artboard (the white area surrounding the page) to deselect any objects in your document. You can also use the keyboard shortcut, Shift+Ctrl+A (Windows) or Shift+Command+A (Mac OS).

**2**    Double-click the Fill color at the bottom of the Tools panel.

**3** When the Color Picker appears, type the values of C:**0** M:**70** Y:**100** K:**0**. Click OK.

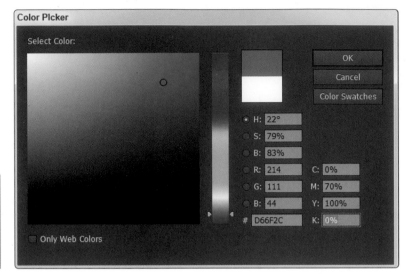

*Click Fill.*     *Enter values into the Color Picker. .*

**4** If the Swatches panel is not open, choose Window > Swatches now, then click the New Swatch icon (⬐) at the bottom of the panel.

**5** In the Swatch Name text field, type **Hippie Orange**, then check the box to the left of Global and click OK. The color has been added to the Swatches panel, and has a white triangle in the lower-right side of the swatch indicating that this color has been defined as Global.

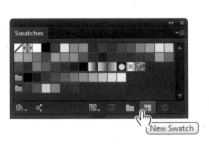

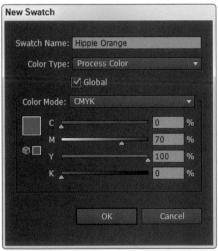

*Click the New Swatch icon.*     *Name the Swatch and select Global.*

## What is a Global Color?

Taking advantage of global colors allows you to apply a color to multiple fills and strokes, and make updates to the colors dynamically. This is extremely useful when you want to tweak your color, or perhaps replace it with an entirely different set of color values.

In this part of the lesson, you will apply the new Hippie Orange to several shapes in the bus, and then update them.

1   Click and hold the Direct Selection tool (⬚) and select the Group Selection tool.

2   Select any shape on the bus and then click the newly added Hippie Orange swatch.

3   Assign the Hippie Orange color to at least three other shapes. Select any shapes in the mini bus art except for the purple windshield, which you will use in the next exercise.

*Select at least four shapes to apply the new global color to.*

4   Choose Select > Deselect, or use the keyboard shortcut Shift+Ctrl+A (Windows) or Shift+Command+A (Mac OS) to deselect everything.

5   Double-click the Hippie Orange swatch in the Swatches panel; the Swatch Options dialog box appears.

6   Type **50** into the M (Magenta) text field, and click OK. All the instances of Hippie Orange have been changed.

## Selecting the Same color

Editing colors when they have been defined as global is fairly simple, but what if you already used a non-global swatch in multiple instances in your illustration? For these situations you can take advantage of selecting the Same fill, stroke or both.

1   Using the Group Selection tool (⬚) select the large purple windshield.

2   Choose Select > Same > Fill Color. Any additional objects using that same fill are selected.

To make editing colors easier in the future, you should save this color and convert it to global.

**3** With the objects still selected, click the New Swatch button at the bottom of the Swatches panel. The New Swatch dialog box appears.

**4** Type **Hippie Purple** into the Swatch Name text field and check Global, then click OK.

*Collect like colors and convert them to global.*

## Reusing swatches

When you create swatches in an Illustrator document, those swatches are available only in that document. However, users commonly repurpose swatches in other Illustrator documents. Instead of recreating frequently used swatches in every document, you can choose Save Swatch Library as AI from the Swatches panel menu. This creates a new file containing the swatches in your current document. To reuse the swatches in another document, choose Open Swatch Library > Other Library from the Swatches panel menu. Now all those swatches are available to apply to objects in your new document.

There is also an option called Save Swatch Library as ASE (Adobe Swatch Exchange) in the Swatches panel menu. This performs a very similar task to Save Swatch Library as AI, except that the ASE format is interchangeable with other CC applications. These swatch libraries can be opened within Adobe Photoshop and Adobe InDesign, making it very easy to share colors between multiple applications. Unfortunately, any swatch patterns that have been added to the swatch library will not be accessible inside programs other than Illustrator.

## Saving a set of colors as a group

When working in Illustrator, you'll often end up with quite a few swatches in your Swatches panel. As you experiment with colors and make adjustments, the number of swatches can increase to a point that makes it difficult to find a particular color. Fortunately, Illustrator simplifies the process of locating specific swatches by allowing you to create color groups to organize swatches into logical categories. Let's organize the swatches in the Swatches panel into color groups.

**1** In the Swatches panel, press and hold the Ctrl key (Windows) or the Command key (Mac OS) and select the Hippie Orange, Hippie Purple, CMYK Green, and CMYK Cyan color swatches.

**2** Click the New Color Group button (▢) at the bottom of the panel. The New Color Group dialog box appears.

**3** In the New Color Group dialog box, type **Retro Colors** in the Name text field. Choose the *Selected Swatches* option button, and then click OK. The colors are collected in a group at the bottom of the Swatches panel, making it easy to locate them.

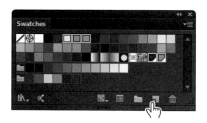

*Select five colors, then click the New Color Group button.*

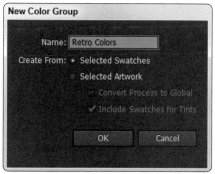

*Save them to a color group.*

## Creating a color group from selected colors

You can also extract colors from existing artwork to create a color group.

**1** Choose the Selection tool (▸) and then click the ellipses you created earlier.

**2** Click the New Color Group button at the bottom of the Swatches panel; the New Color Group dialog box appears.

**3** Type **Base Colors** into the Name text field, then click the Selected Artwork option button and make sure that the Convert Process to Global and Include Swatches for Tints check boxes are selected. Click OK; the color group is added to your Swatches panel.

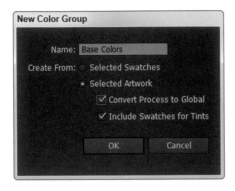

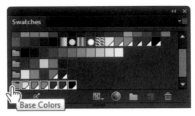

*Create a color group from colors already used.*     *The Color group is added to the Swatches panel.*

**4** Choose File > Save to save your work. Keep the file open.

*You can add a color to an existing color group by selecting the color in the Swatches panel, then dragging it to the folder to the left of the color group.*

## Using the Color panel

Another method for creating or editing colors is the Color panel. The Color panel displays color sliders depending upon the color model you choose to work in.

**1** Open the Color panel by clicking the Color button (🎨) in the dock on the right side of the workspace, or choose Window > Color.

*As a default, the Color panel comes up displaying the default color model. If you want to switch from CMYK, RGB, HSB (Hue, Saturation, and Brightness), or Grayscale modes, press and hold the Shift key and click the color ramp at the bottom of the Colors panel. This cycles you through the available color models.*

**2**    Make sure that you have the CMYK values displaying, if not, choose CMYK from the Color panel menu. From the panel menu in the upper-right, choose Show Options to expand the panel.

**3**    Using the Group Selection tool, click an instance where you used the Hippie Orange color to notice that only one color slider (named Hippie Orange) is displayed. This is another benefit of using a global color.

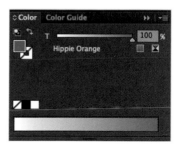

*You can easily apply tints of a global color.*

**4**    Click the slider and change the value to 50%. By defining this color as global, you now have the ability to use it multiple times at various shades.

**5**    Click a color (any) that was not defined as global to notice that all four CMYK color sliders appear in the Color panel.

**6**    Using the color slider choose any color and drag its slider to the left or right to change the color value.

**7**    Now, press and hold the Shift key and drag the same slider. Notice that multiple sliders now move simultaneously. By pressing and holding the Shift key, you can create tints of a CMYK color that was not defined as global.

**8**    Choose File > Save. Then choose File > Close to save the illustration.

## Adding Pantone (Spot) Colors

In the next example, you will open a completed color logo and convert it to be used as a logo on a business card. When creating artwork that will be printed in multiple locations on various media, it is important to use spot colors.

---

### Spot colors

When designing a product that will be reproduced on a printing press, some decisions need to be made regarding what colors will be used in the document. So far in this lesson, you have created all your swatches based on the CMYK color space. CMYK colors—Cyan, Magenta, Yellow, and Black—are referred to in the printing industry as process colors. Using these four inks, printed in succession, it is possible to create a wide range of colors on a printed piece. Photographs, for example, are printed using process colors. However, process colors do have limitations. Certain colors are not achievable using CMYK due to the somewhat limited gamut of the CMYK color space. To more accurately achieve a specific color on a printed piece, spot colors come in handy.

Spot colors are colored inks that are specifically mixed to produce a desired color. The most common spot colors in the printing industry are made by a company called Pantone, Inc. Pantone and spot color are used almost synonymously in the printing industry, since Pantone colors are the primary inks used to specify spot colors for a printing job.

Spot colors can be used in many ways, but the primary reasons for using a spot color are:

- If color matching is critical. If a company logo is required to appear in the exact same color each time it is printed, a spot color might be used to reproduce the color consistently. In this example, adding a spot color to an existing process color job increases the costs of the project.

- Instead of printing a product, such as a business card, using four process colors, you might choose to print the card in two spot colors or one spot color and black to reduce the cost of the printed product.

- To produce very rich, vibrant colors. These might be colors that process printing cannot recreate. This type of print job is often very expensive to produce.

---

1   Choose File > Browse in Bridge or click the Go to Bridge button (Br) in the application bar.

2   Navigate to the ai04lessons folder within Bridge and open the file **ai0403.ai** by double-clicking it.

3   After the file opens in Illustrator, choose File > Save As. In the Save As dialog box, navigate to the ai04lessons folder and type **ai0403_work** in the File name text field. Choose Adobe Illustrator (ai) from the Save as type drop-down menu and choose Save. Click OK when the Illustrator Options dialog box appears.

4   Choose Select > All and then press **D**. By pressing D, you change all selected objects to the default stroke and fill of black-and-white.

# Adding Pantone colors

The PANTONE COLOR MATCHING SYSTEM®, also referred to as PMS colors, is a largely standardized color reproduction system. By standardizing the colors, different manufacturers in different locations can all refer to the Pantone system to make sure colors match without direct contact with one another. Adobe Illustrator groups Pantone colors into a color library called Color Books.

Pantone colors are numbered, making it easy to identify a frequently used color, whether for corporate identity or for ease of use, when searching for a specific color. In this lesson, you add several Pantone colors to the document.

1   If the Swatches panel is not visible, choose Window > Swatches.

2   Click the Swatches panel menu and choose Open Swatch Library > Color Books > Pantone+ Solid Coated. The Pantone+ Solid Coated panel appears.

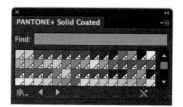

*Opening a Pantone color book.*

*Choose Solid coated for illustrations that will be printed as solid ink colors (not combinations of CMYK color) on coated paper. Choose Pantone+ Solid Uncoated for uncoated paper.*

3   In the Pantone+ Solid Coated panel, locate the Find field, which is a text field that you can input a Pantone number into.

Next, you will identify color values and their associated numbers easier by changing the view of the Pantone Solid Coated panel.

4   Click the Pantone Solid Coated panel menu and choose Small List View. The Pantone colors are now listed with descriptive text.

*The Pantone colors in a list with the Find Field visible.*

5  Type **3005** into the Find Field. Pantone 3005 is highlighted in the list.

6  Select the Group Selection tool (image), then click a shape on the artboard, then click the highlighted Pantone 3005 color in the list. The shape is filled with the Pantone color, and the Pantone swatch is automatically added to the Swatches panel.

7  If the Swatches panel is not visible, choose Window > Swatches. Note that the Pantone 3005 swatch has been added, and it not only has the white triangle identifying it as a global color, but also has a dot, indicating that this color is a spot color. It is made up of one ink color, not a combination of multiple inks.

8  Choose Select > Deselect all, or use the keyboard shortcut Shift+Ctrl+A (Windows) or Shift+Command+A (Mac OS) to make sure nothing is selected.

9  Type **173** into the Find field to select an orange color.

*Depending on the numerical value you select, you might have to press the spacebar at the end of the value to see only the three digit PMS color.*

10  Click Pantone 173 C in the panel to add the color to your swatches panel without using it. This technique allows you to set up your entire color palette before you start to work.

11  Select any object in the illustration and then click Fill in the Control panel. Select the Pantone 173 color from the swatch panel that appears.

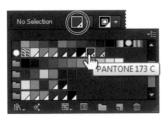

*Assign colors using the Control panel.*

12  Choose Window > Color to open the Color panel. Using the tint slider, apply various shades of the Pantone color throughout your Illustration. Repeat this procedure with the Pantone 300 color.

13  Choose File > Save, then File > Close. Keep in mind that if you used spot colors, they are automatically imported and added to the Swatches panel in InDesign when you use the File > Place command.

## Taking advantage of the new and improved Kuler panel

If you like using color in your illustrations, you'll love being able to save combinations of colors as themes. You can do this by accessing the Kuler website directly from Adobe Illustrator.

In this part of the lesson, you create a new document to take advantage of some existing color themes from the Kuler website.

**1**　Choose File > New and select Devices for the Profile. Note that you can select the device you are building graphics for in the Size drop-down menu. You can leave it set to iPad and click OK.

**2**　If you do not see the Kuler panel, choose Window > Kuler now. Note that it will most likely be empty, unless you have previously used the Kuler website with an Adobe log in.

**3**　Click the Launch Kuler website button ( 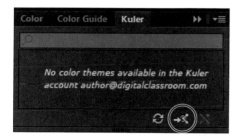 ); *kuler.adobe.com* launches.

*Select the Launch Kuler website button.*

**4**　Sign in using your Adobe ID in the upper-right corner. Once you are signed in you can save, edit and create color themes.

**5**    Select Most Popular in the column on the left and the most popular themes populate the column to the right.

*Select the Most Popular themes.*

*Keep in mind that you can use the Search text field to search existing color themes as well. Themes can be found by creator, keyword, and title.*

**6**    Select any one of the Most Popular themes and note that you now have the option Add to Favorites, Download the theme as an Adobe Swatch Exchange file, or Make changes to this theme and view color values.

*A. Add to Favorites. B. Download the theme as an Adobe Swatch Exchange file. C. Make changes to this theme and view color values.*

**7**  For this lesson, choose Make changes to this theme and view color values. A window appears where you can select each color and edit its values. For this lesson, you will make a simple change to one of your color values. You can experiment more with the Kuler website on your own after you have a better idea of how to use it.

**8**  Select the any color, and then use the color sliders beneath it to change the value.

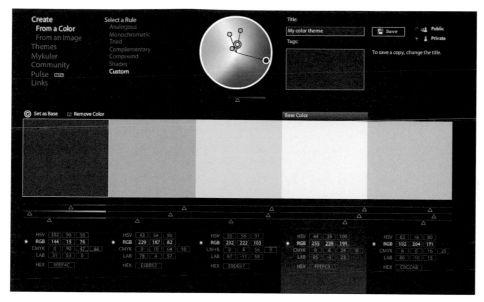

*Change the color values of any one of the color swatches.*

**9**  Add a name to the Title text field. In this example My color theme was used as the name, but you can name your color theme anything you would like. Click Save. This color theme has been saved under your account. You will now return to Adobe Illustrator to access it.

**10**  Return to Adobe Illustrator and locate the Kuler panel.

**11**  Click the Refresh (■) button; your color theme appears.

*Click Refresh to see your own color themes in Illustrator.*

**12**  Select my color theme in the Kuler panel and then select the Panel menu in the upper-right corner and choose Add to Swatches. You can now use your color theme in your own graphics. This was just an introduction to using Kuler. There are many other capabilities that you will want to explore on your own.

# Self study

In this lesson, you were introduced to several great new features of Adobe Illustrator CC, as well as some features that aren't so new, but deserve further investigation nonetheless.

The Appearance panel is a highly underused feature of Adobe Illustrator; practice on your own by exploring the capabilities harnessed in it. Start by drawing a line with the Line Segment tool then expanding the weight of the stroke. Add another stroke to it from within the Appearance panel, setting it to a different weight and color; you'll see that you can apply more than one stroke to a single object.

Explore Live Paint and Live Color in more detail. See Lesson 5, "Working with the Drawing Tools," for information about converting a picture into a vector-based piece of art using the Live Trace feature and then coloring it using Live Paint. Furthermore, you can experiment with Color Groups and the Recolor Artwork dialog box to change how your artwork is colorized in Illustrator.

Launch the Kuler website from the Kuler panel and experiment with creating your own color themes or editing existing themes.

# Review

## Questions

1   What does the appearance of a dot in the lower-right corner of a swatch indicate?

2   In Adobe Illustrator CC, where would you look to identify the fill and stroke properties of a selected object?

3   True or false: You can share swatches that you created in Adobe Illustrator CC with other Adobe CC programs.

4   What is a global color?

5   What is the benefit of using Live Paint?

## Answers

1   If a swatch has a dot in the lower-right corner, it is defined as a spot color.

2   You can locate the attributes of a selected object in the Appearance panel.

3   True. You can choose the Save Swatch Library as ASE command from the panel menu of the Swatches panel. This saves all your swatches as a separate Swatch Library file (.ase) that can be imported into other CC applications.

4   A global color is one that is dynamically linked to all instances in the illustration. Use a global color if you want color updates to be less time-consuming.

5   The Live Paint feature allows you to individually paint faces of an illustration without defining new shapes.

## What you'll learn in this lesson:

- Using the Pen tool
- Editing existing paths
- Working with tracing presets
- Creating vector artwork from placed images

# Working with the Drawing Tools

*Adobe Illustrator includes a number of impressive drawing tools that allow you to create a wide variety of artwork with speed and precision.*

## Starting up

Before starting, make sure that your tools and panels are consistent by resetting your workspace. See "Resetting Adobe Illustrator CC Preferences" in the Starting up section of this book.

You will work with several files from the ai05lessons folder in this lesson. Make sure that you have loaded the ailessons folder onto your hard drive from the included DVD. See "Loading lesson files" in the Starting up section of this book.

 **See Lesson 5 in action!**

*Use the accompanying video to gain a better understanding of how to use some of the features shown in this lesson. You can find the video tutorial for this lesson on the included DVD.*

# Working with the Pen tool

The Pen tool is one of the most powerful tools in Illustrator and it allows you to create any line or shape that you need. The Pen tool creates anchor points that can be rounded, smooth, sharp, or angular. Using the Pen tool, you can create any line or shape that you can conceive. Using the Pen tool and mastering line construction is all about understanding the nature of anchor points and how to create and work with them.

*There are two kinds of anchor points that you can create in Illustrator: corner points and smooth points. Corner points are usually seen on linear, hard-edged shapes such as polygons and squares, while smooth points are used to construct sinuous, curved lines. There are two mouse actions that are repeated over and over again when creating anchor points: click and release, which creates corner points; and click and drag, which creates smooth points.*

The Pen tool has a versatile feature that allows you to create new anchor points, add anchor points to existing paths, and remove anchor points from existing paths. The tool's appearance changes based on what your cursor is hovering over on the artboard. Pay attention to what the tool cursor looks like, since it will assist you in using all the Pen tool's functions.

| PEN TOOL VARIATION | DESCRIPTION |
| --- | --- |
| | Only appears as you are in the process of creating a line; it signals that the next anchor point created will continue that line. |
| | Indicates that the Pen tool will create a new line. |
| | Indicates that the Pen tool can be used to convert the anchor point it is currently hovering over. This icon only appears when the Pen tool is hovering over the last anchor point that was created in a selected path. |
| | Indicates that the Pen tool will pick up a path and continue from the end point you are hovering over. This icon only appears next to the Pen tool when it is hovering over the endpoint of a path that you are not currently creating. |
| | Indicates that the Pen tool will connect the path that is currently being created to the end point of a different path. |
| | Indicates that the Pen tool will close the path that you are currently creating. |
| | Indicates that the Pen tool will remove the anchor point that it is currently hovering over. This icon only appears when the Pen tool is hovering over an anchor point on a selected path. |
| | Indicates that the Pen tool will add an anchor point to the line segment that it is currently hovering over. This icon only appears when the Pen tool is hovering over a line segment on a selected path. |

## Drawing straight lines

The first Pen tool skill you need to master is creating a straight line. To do this, you make corner anchor points with the Pen tool. Straight lines are automatically generated as a result.

**1**  In Illustrator, choose File > Open. When the Open dialog box appears, navigate to the ai05lessons folder and select the **ai0501.ai** file. Click OK. This is a practice file containing several different line templates that you will work through in the following exercises.

**2**  Choose File > Save As. In the Save As dialog box, navigate to the ai05lessons folder and type **ai0501_work.ai** into the File name text field; then click Save. In the Illustrator Options dialog box, click OK to accept the default settings.

**3**  In the Control panel at the top of the workspace, select None (☑) from the Fill color drop-down menu. If necessary, select the color black from the Stroke color drop-down menu and select 2 pt from the Stroke Weight drop-down menu.

**4**  Select the Pen tool (✎) from the Tools panel and locate the template labeled Exercise 1 on the artboard. Click and release your left mouse button while hovering over label 1. This starts the line by creating the first anchor point.

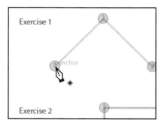

*Use the Pen tool to create the first anchor point.*

**5**  Move your cursor to the part of the line labeled 2, and click and release your mouse. The second point of the line is created. The Pen tool automatically draws a straight line between the two points.

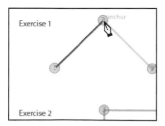

*Click to create the second anchor point.*

**6**  Continue to click and release to complete the line through labels 3, 4, 5, 6, and 7. Notice how the Pen tool automatically continues the line to include each new anchor point.

**7**  After you have set a final anchor point at label 7, press and hold Ctrl (Windows) or Command (Mac OS) and click any empty area of the page. This deselects and ends the line. If you don't deselect and end the line, the Pen tool continues to link the path to the next anchor that you create.

**8**  Position the cursor over label 1 of Exercise 2. Click and release the left mouse button to create the first anchor point of the new line.

**9**  Position the cursor over label 2. Press and hold the Shift key, then click and release to create the second point of the line; the Pen tool automatically connects the two points with a straight line. Because you were pressing and holding the Shift key when the second point was created, Illustrator automatically draws a perfectly horizontal line.

**10**  Position the cursor over label 3. Again press and hold the Shift key and click and release the left mouse button to set a third anchor point. This time, the line created is a perfect vertical line.

**11**  Continue pressing and holding the Shift key while clicking at labels 4, 5, and 6. Doing this draws the line between points 4 and 5 at a perfect 135-degree angle, since the Shift key constrains the angle to 45-degree increments.

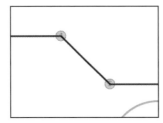

*Pressing Shift while clicking allows you to create
90 and 45-degree angles with the Pen tool.*

**12**  With a final anchor point at label 6, press and hold the Ctrl key (Windows) or Command key (Mac OS) and click the artboard to deselect and end the line.

**13**  Choose File > Save to save your work.

## Drawing curved lines

Straight lines can only take you so far; more organic and complex compositions require you to use curved lines to render objects. You will now complete Exercise 3.

**1** Position your cursor over label 1 at the beginning of the curved line. Click, and without releasing the mouse, drag your cursor up slightly above the hump of the line to create your first anchor point. As you drag your cursor up, it looks like you are dragging a line away from the point. You are, in fact, creating a direction handle for the anchor point.

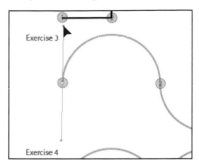

*Dragging while clicking with the Pen tool allows you to create direction handles.*

## What are direction handles?

When you select or create a smooth point, you can see the direction handles of that point. Direction handles control the angle and length of curves. Direction handles comprise two parts: direction lines and the direction points at the ends of the lines. An anchor point can have zero, one, or two direction handles, depending on the kind of point it is. Direction handles serve as a kind of road map for the line, controlling how the lines approach and leave each anchor point. If the exiting handle is downward-facing, the line leaves the anchor point and goes down. Similarly, the line faces upward if the direction handle is pointing upward.

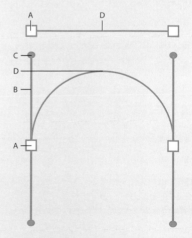

*A. Anchor point. B. Direction Line.*
*C. Direction Handle. D. Line Segment.*

**2** Place your cursor over label 2, located at the end of the first curve in Exercise 3. Click and drag straight down to create the second anchor point. Continue to drag the mouse until you form the curve in the template. As you drag your cursor down, you will notice that a curve is being formed between the two anchor points in real time. As long as you do not release the mouse button, you can reshape this line by dragging the mouse in different directions.

If you need to modify any of the previous points, choose Edit > Undo or use the keyboard shortcut, Ctrl+Z (Windows) or Command+Z (Mac OS). Do not worry if the curves do not follow the template perfectly, they can be adjusted later.

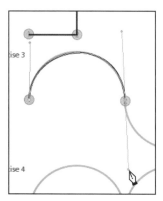

*Dragging while creating the second anchor
point allows you to curve the path.*

**3** Place your cursor over label 3, located at the end of the second curve. Click and drag up to create the third anchor point of the line. Continue to drag the mouse until you form the curve displayed in the template. Again, as long as you do not release the mouse, you can reshape this path by changing the mouse direction.

**4** Place your cursor over label 4, located at the end of the second curve. As in step 3, click and drag down to create the fourth and final anchor point of the line. Continue to drag the mouse until you form the curve displayed in the template.

**5** As in the previous exercise, after you have created your final anchor point at label 4, press and hold Ctrl (Windows) or Command (Mac OS) and click the artboard to deactivate the path.

**6** If necessary, use the Direct Select tool (⬧) to reposition the handles and points so the curves follow the path more closely, then choose File > Save to save your work.

## Drawing hinged curves

In the previous exercise, you created S-curves, lines curved in the opposite direction from the previous one. In this exercise, you will create hinged curves, lines that curve in the same direction; in this case, they will all curve up like a scallop. You will now complete Exercise 4.

**1**   Select the Pen tool (✎) from the Tools panel and position your cursor over label 1 at the beginning of the curved line in Exercise 4. As you did in the previous exercise, click and drag your cursor up slightly above the arch to create your first anchor point.

**2**   Place your cursor over label 2, located at the end of the first curve. Click and drag straight down to create the second anchor point. Continue to drag the mouse until you form the curve in the template.

**3**   Press and hold the Alt (Windows) or Option (Mac OS) key on the keyboard. This temporarily changes the Pen tool into the Convert Anchor Point tool (⊳), which is also a separate tool in the Pen tool grouping. Among other things (covered later in this lesson), this tool is used to edit direction handles. Position the Convert Anchor Point tool over the direction handle for the exiting direction line, and click and drag this point so that it points upward. The two direction lines now form a V.

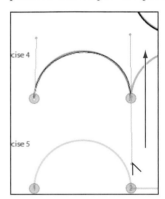 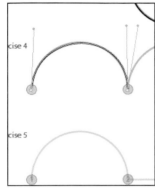

*Move the direction handle to change the direction of the next path.*

 *Direction handles control the curvature of the lines in a path. Because the exiting direction handle created in step 3 is pointing down, the line will want to go down. To draw the hinged curve, you must change the angle of this direction handle so that it points upward.*

**4**   Place your cursor over label 3, located at the end of the second curve. Click and drag straight down to create the third anchor point. Continue to drag the mouse until you form the curve in the template.

**5**   Again, press and hold Alt (Windows) or Option (Mac OS) to temporarily switch the Pen tool to the Convert Anchor Point tool. Once again, position the Convert Anchor Point tool over the direction handle for the exiting direction line, and click and drag this point so that it points upward and the direction lines form a V.

**6**   Repeat step 4 for the final curve at label 4. After you have created this final anchor point, press and hold the Ctrl (Windows) or Command (Mac OS) key and click the artboard to deactivate the path.

**7**   Choose File > Save to save your work.

## Drawing curved lines to straight lines

The following two exercises cover how to draw straight and curved lines together as part of the same path. You will now complete Exercise 5.

**1**   Position your cursor over label 1 at the beginning of the curved line in Exercise 5. Hold the Shift key, and click and drag your cursor up slightly above the arch to create your first anchor point. As you drag your cursor upward, your movement is constrained to a perfectly vertical line. Release the mouse before releasing the Shift key.

**2**   Place your cursor over label 2, located at the end of the first curve. Again, while pressing and holding the Shift key, click and drag straight down to create the second anchor point. Continue to drag the mouse until you form the curve in the template.

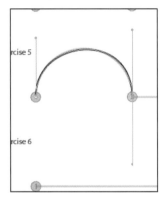

rcise 5

rcise 6

*Create another curved path.*

*Direction handles control the curvature of the lines in a path. Because the exiting direction handle created in step 2 is pointing down, the line will want to go down. If you drag the direction point so that the line points up as in the previous exercise, it will want to curve up. To form a straight line, however, remove this direction handle entirely, thus converting the anchor point into a corner point.*

**3**    Position your cursor over the anchor point you created in step 2. The Pen tool cursor changes, giving you the ability to convert the anchor point you just created.

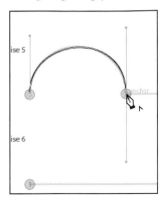

*The Pen tool cursor changes, allowing you to modify the anchor point.*

**4**    While hovering over the anchor point, click the mouse. This collapses the anchor's outgoing direction handle, allowing you to create a straight line.

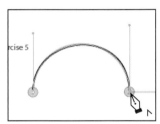

*Collapse the direction handle.*

**5**    Place the cursor over label 3. Hold the Shift key on the keyboard, and click at label 3 to create a straight line to finish the path.

**6**    After you have created your final anchor point at label 3, press and hold Ctrl (Windows) or Command (Mac OS) and click the artboard to deselect and end the line.

**7**    Choose File > Save to save your work.

## Drawing straight lines to curved lines

Now, you will work from the opposite direction and connect straight lines to curved lines. Practice with Exercise 6.

**1** Locate the template labeled Exercise 6. Hold the Pen tool over the start of the line (labeled 1). The cursor changes (♦ₓ), indicating that you will start a new line. Click and release your left mouse button while hovering over label 1. This starts the line by creating the first anchor point.

**2** Place the cursor over label 2. Press and hold the Shift key and click at label 2 to create a perfectly straight line between points 1 and 2 on the path.

**3** Position your cursor over the anchor point you created in step 2. The Pen tool cursor changes (♦.), indicating that you can change the direction of the direction handle.

**4** While hovering over the anchor point, click and drag upward in the direction of the curve you want to draw. This creates a new direction handle.

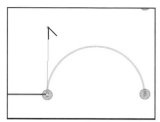

*Change the direction of the direction handle.*

**5** Position the Pen tool over label 3. Click and drag down to create the curve displayed in the template.

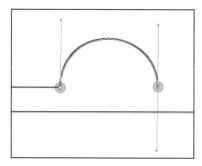

*Finish the path by creating a curve.*

**6** After you have created your final anchor point at label 3, press and hold the Ctrl (Windows) or Command (Mac OS) key and click the artboard to deselect and end the line.

**7** Choose File > Save, then choose File > Close.

# Tracing images

Illustrator is often used to convert artwork that has been scanned or rendered in a pixel-based painting program, like Adobe Photoshop, into crisp vector line art. There are two ways to trace images in Illustrator CC. You can manually trace them using template layers and drawing tools or you can use the Image Trace feature, discussed in further detail later in this section, that automatically converts a bitmap image into a vector graphic.

In the first part of the exercise, you will place a scanned image as a template and retrace it using the skills you just learned with the Pen tool. In the second part of the exercise, you will learn how to use the Image Trace feature, equipped with built-in presets and custom settings, to convert a bitmap image into a vector graphic.

## Placing an image as a template

1   Create a new Illustrator document by choosing File > New. In the New Document dialog box, type **ai0502_work** into the File name text field. Choose Print from the Profile drop-down menu. Choose Letter from the Size drop-down menu, if it is not already selected. Click OK.

2   Select File > Save. Make sure that you are in the ai05lessons folder, and keep the type Adobe Illustrator. When the Illustrator Options dialog box appears, click OK.

3   Choose File > Place. In the Place dialog box, navigate to the ai05lessons folder and select the **ai0502.tif** file. Select the Template check box at the bottom of the Place dialog box to import the selected artwork as a template layer. Click Place. A faint outline of a truck appears in your document.

*Turn your artwork into a template before placing it in on the artboard.*

**4**  Select the Move tool (✛), and then click anywhere on the artboard to deselect the truck artwork.

**5**  In the Control panel, choose None (☒) from the Fill Color drop-down menu and choose the color black from the Stroke Color drop-down menu, if it isn't already selected. Choose 2 pt from the Stroke Weight drop-down menu.

*Set the attributes for the vector stroke.*

**6**  Select the Pen tool (✎) from the Tools panel. Position the cursor near label 1, then click and release to create the first anchor point of the path along the tracing template for the truck. If necessary, increase the magnification to see the template more clearly.

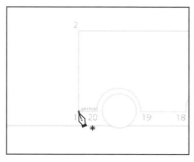

*Create the first anchor point of the truck.*

**7**  Press and hold the Shift key and click along the truck outline near label 2. Because you held down the Shift key, Illustrator creates a straight 90° line to the second anchor point.

**8**  Press and hold the Shift key, and click at label 3 to continue tracing the truck's outline.

**9**  Continue to press and hold the Shift key, and click along the truck body at labels 4, 5, 6, and 7.

**10**  The line between labels 7 and 8 is diagonal, and not on a 45° or 90° angle, so release the Shift key and click at label 8.

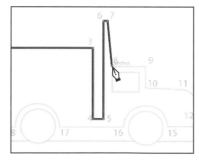

*Continue outlining the truck.*

**11**  Again, press and hold the Shift key, and click at labels 9 and 10.

**12**  Release the Shift key on the keyboard and click at label 11. Up to this point, the exercise has dealt entirely with creating straight lines and corner points; for the line between labels 11 and 12, you need to create a curved line.

Because the point created at label 11 is a corner point, the Pen tool automatically will default to creating a straight line between this anchor and the next anchor point. You will change this behavior by converting the anchor point from a corner to a curved anchor point.

**13**  Hover the Pen tool over the anchor point created at label 11, and look for the Convert Anchor Point symbol (∧) to appear next to the tool. Click and drag with the tool in the direction of the curve to create a new direction handle.

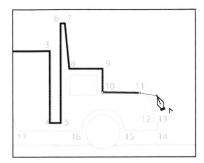

*As you drag to create the directional handle, the cursor has the appearance of an arrowhead without a stem.*

**14**  Click with the Pen tool at label 12 to create a smooth point and complete the line.

**15**  Press and hold the Shift key on the keyboard, and click labels 13, 14, then 15.

**16**  The half circle between labels 15 and 16 presents the same challenge that you faced previously. Again, hover the Pen tool over the anchor point you just created. While pressing and holding the Shift key, click and drag upward to create a constrained directional handle.

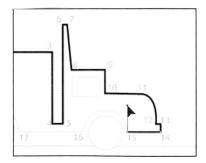

*Move the direction handle up to start another curve.*

**17**  At label 16, click and drag the cursor down to create a new smooth point and continue the line.

18 Position the cursor over the anchor point that you just created at label 16, and click it when you see the Convert Anchor Point symbol (⋀) appear next to the Pen tool. Press and hold the Shift key and click at label 17 to convert the curve point to a corner point.

19 Repeat the process, explained in step 18, until you reach the anchor point numbered 20. After you have collapsed the anchor point at label 20, position your cursor over label 1. A circle appears next to the Pen tool (◊), indicating that this action will close the path you have just drawn. Click the anchor point to complete the line and close the path.

20 Choose File > Save, then choose File > Close.

## Placing an image using Image Trace

Illustrator CC provides an Image Trace feature that converts raster images into editable vectors. Using the Image Trace feature, you choose from a number of presets to help you create the best conversion and achieve the results that you want.

When you place a bitmap image in your document, you can access Image Trace in two ways: using the default presets located in the Control panel or using the Image Trace panel.

*A.* Auto-Color. *B.* High Color *C.* Low Color.
*D.* Grayscale. *E.* Black and White. *F.* Outline.

Along the top of the Image Trace panel are six preset buttons: Auto-Color, High Color, Low Color, Grayscale, Black and White, and Outline. Select your image and choose one of the default presets. The preset you choose will preview live on the artboard.

To customize the results, you can fine-tune the trace manually using the options in the Image Trace panel. You can control the number of colors used, path and corner appearances, complexity of the tracing, and more.

## Image Trace Options

**Preset**: Specifies 11 types of tracing presets.

**View**: Specifies the view of the traced object. You can choose to view the tracing result, source image, outlines, and other options.

**Mode**: Specifies if the tracing result will be in color, grayscale or black-and-white.

**Palette**: Specifies the palette used to determine the number of colors in the tracing result. To let Illustrator determine the colors, select Automatic (this option is available only when the Mode is set to Color).

**Color settings**: Depending on what is selected for the Mode and Palette options, the following color settings are displayed:

**Colors**: The number of colors used in the tracing result (this option is available only when Mode is set to Color).

**Grays**: The number of grays used in the tracing result (this option is available only when Mode is set to Grayscale).

**Threshold**: Value for generating a black-and-white tracing result from the original image (this option is available only when Mode is set to Black and White).

**Paths**: Controls the distance between the traced path shape and the original path shape. The lower the value, the tighter the path fits; the higher the value, the looser the path fits.

**Corners**: Specifies the corner appearance. A higher value results in more corners.

**Noise**: Determines the pixel area that is ignored while tracing.

**Method**: Specifies a method for tracing:

> **Abutting**—This option creates paths that are cutout.

> **Overlapping**—This option creates paths that are stacked.

**Fills**: Creates filled regions in the tracing result.

**Strokes**: Creates stroked paths in the tracing result.

**Snap Curves To Lines**: Determines if curved lines are to be replaced with straight lines.

**Ignore White**: Specifies if White filled areas are to be replaced with no fills.

1   Choose File > Open. In the Open dialog box, select the **ai0503.ai** file and click
    Open. This Illustrator file consists of two images already placed for you on separate
    layers for this exercise. You will only see one image, the bananas, since the Target
    layer's visibility is turned off at this time.

2   Choose File > Save As. In the Save As dialog box, make sure that you are in the
    ai05lessons folder and name the file **ai0503_work.ai**, then click Save. When the
    Illustrator Options dialog box appears, click OK.

3   You will first work with a picture of bananas, converting it from a bitmap image to
    a vector image. Select the Zoom tool (🔍) in the Tools panel and click once on the
    center of the page to enlarge the view so you can see the tracing results better.

4   Using the Selection tool (▸), click the picture, then choose Window > Image Trace.
    The Image Trace panel appears. Position the panel to the side of your image so you
    can view both the panel and image at the same time.

*Click the picture and open the Image Trace panel.*

5   On the top of the panel are six preset options. Click the Auto-Color button. The Auto-Color preset previews live on the artboard.

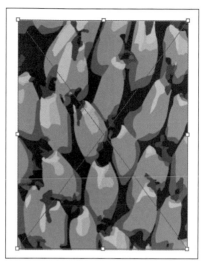

*Click the Auto-Color preset and preview the results on the artboard.*

6   The default preset gets you started, but you can fine-tune the tracing results before expanding the final image. If you do not see the Advanced options, click the arrow to the left of Advanced in the Image Trace panel to expand the advanced options.

**7**   From the Palette drop-down menu, select *Full Tone*. In the Advanced option section, type **25%** in the Paths, **50%** in the Corners and **70 px** in the Noise text fields, then press Enter (Windows) or Return (Mac OS). As you can see, these small adjustments produce a much better rendering of the original bitmap image.

*Make some custom adjustments to enhance the image tracing results.*

*To view your original image, click and hold the visibility icon located to the right of the View drop-down menu. Let go of the mouse button to turn off the preview and continue making adjustments.*

8   Once you are satisfied with the results, you can save your own preset to use again on other images. Click the Preset panel menu and select Save as New Preset. In the Save Image Trace Preset dialog box, type **Full Tone Image** then click OK.

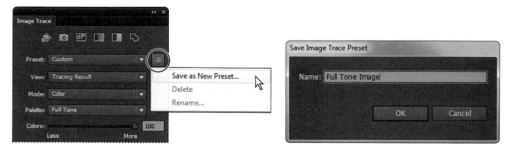

*Save your own custom preset.*

9   In the Control panel, click the Expand button to finalize the trace and expand your image into a fully editable vector image. Try using the Selection and Direct Selection tools to experiment with the results.

*Click Expand in the Control panel to complete the vector trace.*

10  Choose File > Save. Leave the file open for the next exercise.

## Working with the new Image Trace Method option

One of the new features worth experimenting with in the Image Trace panel is the Method option. There are 2 methods to choose from:

- **Abutting**—This option creates cutout paths.
- **Overlapping**—This option creates stacked paths.

To understand the difference between these two methods, perform the following steps:

1   If the Layers panel is not visible, choose Windows > Layers or click the Layers button (👁) in the dock on the right side of the workspace. In the Layers panel, click the visibility icon (👁) to the left of the Bananas layer to hide it, then click the visibility icon to the left of the Target layer to show it.

2   If the Image Trace panel is not visible, choose Windows > Image Trace. Using the Selection tool (▶), click the picture of the target to select it. In the Method section in the Image Trace panel, click the Abutting option. At the top of the panel, click the Auto-Color preset button (▦), then click the Expand button in the Control panel.

**3**  Click anywhere on the artboard to deselect the image. Select the Direct Selection tool (☈) from the Tools panel, then click and drag the outer red circle on the target slightly to the right. You will notice that by choosing the Abutting option, the paths are cut out in sections that you can move and edit easily.

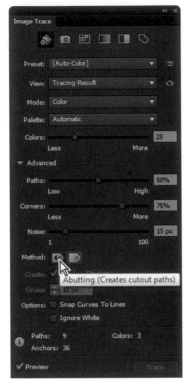

*Choose the Abutting method in the Image Trace panel.*

*The results.*

**4**  Now let's try the Overlapping method to see the difference. Choose Edit > Undo Move to reposition the red circle back into place, then choose Edit > Undo Expand Tracing to undo the tracing of the image and bring it back into its original bitmap state.

**5**  With the target still selected, click the Auto-Color preset button (▨) in the Image Trace panel, then select the Overlapping button for the Method. Click the Expand button in the Control panel.

**6** Click anywhere on the artboard to deselect the image. Select the Direct Selection tool (⇲) from the Tools panel, then click and drag the outer red circle on the target slightly to the right. By choosing the Overlapping method, the paths stack on top of each other.

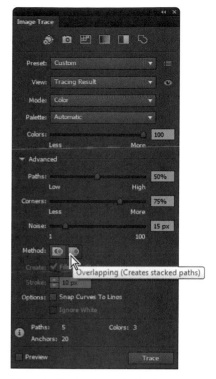

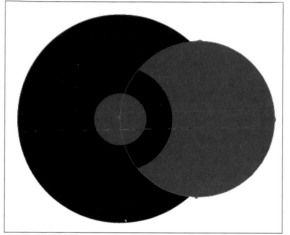

*Choose the Overlapping method in the Image Trace panel.*

*The results.*

**7** Choose File > Save, then File > Close.

There are many options to explore within the new Image Trace panel. Try placing your own bitmap image and experimenting with the various tracing results.

## Other drawing tools

While the Pen tool is definitely the most versatile drawing tool in the application, there are several other drawing tools that exist to fulfill specific functions.

### Using the Line Segment and Arc tools

As the tool names imply, the Line Segment and Arc tools create line segments and arcs. As you learned in the previous exercises, the Pen tool can also create lines and arcs. However, unlike the line segments and arcs that can be created with the Pen tool, each new line or arc is separate and unique from the previous one.

1   Choose File > Open. In the Open dialog box, navigate to the ai05lessons folder and select the **ai0504.ai** file. Click Open.

This is a practice file containing several different line templates that you will work through in the following exercises. Choose File > Save As. In the Save As dialog box, navigate to the ai05lessons folder, and type **ai0504_work.ai** in the File name text field. Click Save. In the resulting Illustrator Options dialog box, click OK to accept the default settings.

2   In the Control panel, choose None (◪) from the Fill Color drop-down menu and choose the color black from the Stroke Color drop-down menu, if it isn't already selected. Choose 2 pt from the Stroke Weight drop-down menu.

3   Select the Line Segment tool (╱) from the Tools panel on the left, and locate the template labeled Exercise 1. Hold the Line Segment tool over the start of the first line (labeled 1). Click and drag with your mouse from label 1 to label 2 to create a line segment.

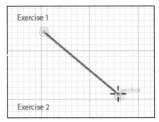

*Using the Line Segment tool.*

4   Position the cursor over label 3. While pressing and holding the Shift key, click and drag the mouse from label 3 to label 4. The Shift key is used to constrain the Line Segment tool to perfectly horizontal, vertical, or diagonal (45-degree) lines.

5   Position the cursor over label 5. While pressing and holding the Shift key, click and drag the mouse from label 5 to label 6.

**6**    Click and hold the Line Segment tool to view the hidden tools. Select the Arc tool ($\frown$) and locate the template labeled Exercise 2. Hold the Arc tool over the start of the first line (labeled 1). Click and drag with your mouse from label 1 to label 2. This creates an arc.

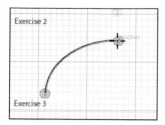

*Create an arc path.*

**7**    Position the cursor over label 3. While pressing and holding the Shift key, click and drag the mouse from label 3 to label 4. The Shift key constrains the created arc.

**8**    Position the cursor over label 5. Click and drag to label 6. Continue pressing down the mouse button, and notice that the arc is very similar to the others you have previously created. While still pressing and holding the mouse button, press **F** on the keyboard and release it to reverse the direction of the arc.

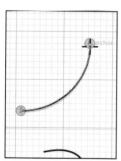

*Press F while creating an arc
to reverse the curve's direction.*

*While drawing an arc, press the up and down-arrow keys on the keyboard to change the angle of the arc.*

**9**    Choose File > Save to save your work, and then choose Select > Deselect.

## Using the Pencil, Smooth, and Path Eraser tools

While the Pen tool exists for precise line work, the Pencil tool creates freeform lines. In addition to being able to draw lines, the Pencil tool can also be used to refine existing lines. You will now complete Exercise 3.

**1** Select the Pencil tool (✐) from the Tools panel and locate the template labeled Exercise 3. Hold the Pencil tool over the start of the first line (labeled 1).

**2** Click and drag with your mouse from label 1 to label 2 to replicate the looping line shown in the template. Don't worry if your path doesn't follow the path exactly. The freeform nature of the Pencil tool makes this difficult for even experienced users.

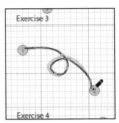

*Create a line using the Pencil tool.*

**3** Choose the Selection tool (▸) and select the line between labels 3 and 4. Select the Pencil tool, then click and drag along the guideline between labels 3 and 4. The line adjusts to fit the new path you have created.

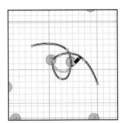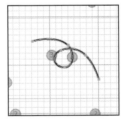

*Select, and then redraw a part of the path.*

**4** Choose the Selection tool again and select the line between labels 5 and 6. Click and hold the Pencil tool in the Tools panel, and choose the Smooth tool (✐).

**5**    Beginning at label 5, click and drag the Smooth tool back and forth across the jagged part of the line to label 6. This smooths out the jagged line. Depending upon the magnification at which you are viewing the page, you might have to repeat this process several times to match the example. When viewing the page at a higher magnification level, you will need more passes across the artwork with the Smooth tool.

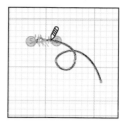 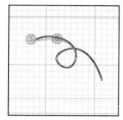

*Smooth the path using the Smooth tool.*

**6**    With the Selection tool, select the line between labels 7 and 8. Click and hold the Smooth tool in the Tools panel and choose the Path Eraser tool (✐).

**7**    Beginning at label 7, click and drag the Path Eraser tool back and forth across the selected line to erase it. Be sure to thoroughly overlap the line or you might leave stray segments intact.

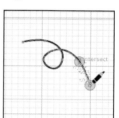 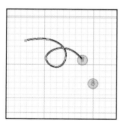

*Using the Path Eraser tool, erase the path between labels 7 and 8.*

**8**    Choose File > Save to save your work.

## Using the Eraser tool

The Eraser tool can erase vector objects in much the same fashion as a real-world eraser. This opens the door to the creation of a wide range of organic shapes in a very intuitive way.

1   Using the Selection tool (⬧), select the black circle in Exercise 4, then choose the Eraser tool (✐) in the Tools panel.

2   Click and drag from label 1 to label 2 in a pattern similar to the one in the template to the left of it. The Eraser tool bisects the circle, forming two separate shapes. Be certain to start outside the shape before clicking and dragging.

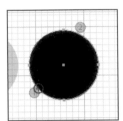

*Use the Eraser tool to bisect the circle.*

3   Choose the Selection tool and select the black line located between labels 3 and 4. Choose the Eraser tool and drag over the line between labels 3 and 4 to sever it.

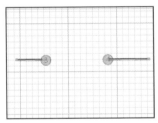

*Use the Eraser tool to remove a section of the path.*

4   Choose File > Save to save your work.

## Editing existing paths

In addition to creating lines and shapes, the tools in Illustrator provide the ability to modify paths that you have already created. The two main ways to do this are by adding or removing anchor points to a path, and converting anchor points from smooth to corner points, or vice versa.

### Adding and removing points

The best way to modify paths in your artwork is to add or remove anchor points from an existing path. Both the Pen tool and the Control Panel can be used to modify the anchor points. You will now complete Exercise 5.

1   Using the Selection tool (▶), select the first path in Exercise 5 to highlight it, then choose the Pen tool (✍) from the Tools panel.

2   Place the Pen tool over the portion of the path at label 1. The new cursor (✍.) indicates that clicking with the Pen tool will create an anchor point on the line segment. Click the line segment to create a new anchor point.

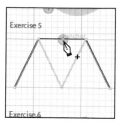

*Create a new anchor point.*

3   The anchor point that was just created is automatically highlighted. Use the arrow keys on your keyboard to move this anchor point into position to match the template.

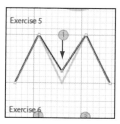

*Move the anchor point using the arrow keys on the keyboard.*

4   Now you'll move to the next template. Choose the Direct Selection tool (▷) from the Tools panel, and draw a selection marquee around the anchor point at label 2 to highlight it.

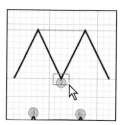

*Select the anchor point.*

**5** Click the Remove Selected Anchor Points button () in the Control panel to remove the highlighted anchor point from the line and make it match the template.

*When the path is selected, you can also use the Pen tool to remove an anchor point. The only disadvantage to using the Pen tool to remove anchor points is that it cannot remove points from the beginning or end of a line.*

**6** Choose File > Save to save your work.

## Refining a curve

You will now experiment with curved paths by completing Exercise 5 in the **ai0504_work.ai** lesson file.

**1** Locate the third and final path in Exercise 5. Using the Direct Selection tool (), draw a selection marquee around the anchor point at label 3.

**2** Click the Convert Selected Anchor Point to Corner button () in the Control panel to change the smooth point into a corner point. This changes the curvature of the preceding line segment.

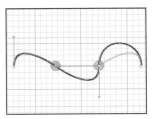

*The curve changes.*

**3** With the line still selected, click and hold the Pen tool () in the Tools panel, then select the Convert Anchor Point tool ().

**4** Select the anchor point at label 4 to convert it from a smooth point to a corner point.

*If you want to convert a corner point to a smooth point, you can do so either from the Control panel or by clicking and dragging on a corner point with the Convert Anchor Point tool.*

**5** Press Ctrl+Shift+A (Windows) or Command+Shift+A (Mac OS) to deselect everything on the artboard. Choose File > Save to save your work.

## Cutting and joining paths

One of Illustrator's very helpful features is the ability to cut and join paths. Paths can be cut either at anchor points or line segments, but they can only be joined by connecting two adjacent anchor points, called end points. You will now complete Exercise 6.

**1** Select the Direct Selection tool (⬉) from the Tools panel, and draw a selection marquee around the anchor point at label 1.

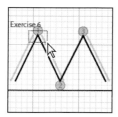

*Draw a marquee around the anchor point.*

**2** Click the Cut Path at Selected Anchor Points button (⬛) in the Control panel to sever the path at this point. Repeat this step for the anchor point at label 2.

**3** Click and hold the Eraser tool (⬛) in the Tools panel to reveal and select the Scissors tool (✂). Click the anchor point at label 3. This tool performs the same function as the Cut Path at Selected Anchor Point button in the Control panel.

*If you miss the anchor point even by a little, the Scissors tool displays an error message and you have to try again.*

**4** Choose the Selection tool (▶) in the Tools panel, and use it to move the individual line segments apart to the positions of the blue lines in the template.

**5** Select the Direct Selection tool and draw a selection marquee around the two end points located at label 4. Zoom in if necessary to confirm that these end points are not connected.

**6** Click the Connect Selected End Points button (⌢) in the Control panel. This merges the two anchor points into one.

7    Select the Direct Selection tool and draw a selection marquee around the two end points located at label 5. Zoom in if necessary to confirm that these end points are not connected. Select Object > Path > Join. If a Join dialog box appears, select Corner and click OK.

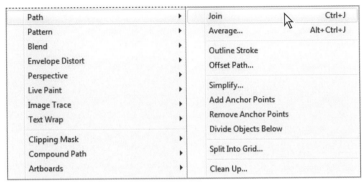

*Select Object > Path > Join.*

8    Select the two end points located at label 6 by clicking and dragging to create a marquee containing both points, then right-click (Windows) or Ctrl+click (Mac OS) on the page and choose Join from the context menu.

9    Select the two end points located at labels 7 and 8 by drawing a selection marquee using the Direct Selection tool.

10   Click the Connect Selected End Points button ( ⌒ ) in the Control panel. A line connecting the two selected end points is created.

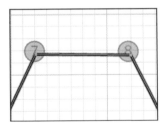

*The two end points are connected.*

*You can select two end points and press Ctrl+J (Windows) or Command+J (Mac OS) to create a connecting path to each end point. If you want to move the end points to meet (not create a new path) you can select both end points and press Shift+Ctrl+Alt+J (Windows) or Shift+Command+Option+J (Mac OS).*

11   Choose File > Save, then choose File > Close.

# Combining shapes using the Shape Builder tool

In this section, you have the opportunity to create an illustration using a drawing feature called the Shape Builder tool (). By using the Shape Builder tool, you can create unique shapes by adding, subtracting, and intersecting one shape from another.

1 Choose File > Browse in Bridge. When Bridge comes forward, navigate to the ai05lessons folder and double-click the file named **ai0505_done**. An image of a fish appears. You will create this shape by using the Shape Builder tool.

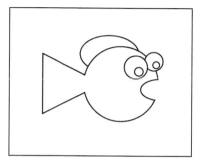

*The completed artwork.*

2 Choose File > Close to close this file, or keep it open for reference.

You will start out by creating the fundamental shapes that will be used to create the fish in the illustration.

3 Create a new Illustrator document by choosing File > New. In the New Document dialog box, type **ai0505_work** in the File name text field. Choose Print from the New Document Profile drop-down menu. Choose Letter from the Size drop-down menu, if it is not already selected, and set the Units to Inches. Click OK.

4 Select File > Save. Make sure that you are in the ai05lessons folder, and keep the type Adobe Illustrator. When the Illustrator Options dialog box appears, click OK.

5 Press **D** to confirm that the fill and stroke are set at the default of white and black, respectively.

6 Click and hold the Rectangle tool and select the hidden Ellipse tool.

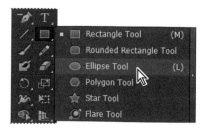

*Select the hidden Ellipse tool.*

**7** Click anywhere on the artboard (don't click and drag). If you inadvertently create an ellipse, press Ctrl+Z (Windows) or Command+Z (Mac OS) to undo your last step. Then click once on the artboard. The Ellipse dialog box appears.

**8** Type the value of **1 in** into the Width text field, and then press tab and enter **1** in into the Height text field. Click OK.

This circle will serve as the body of your fish.

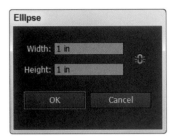

*Click once on the artboard to open the Ellipse dialog box.*

**9** Zoom in so the fish's body fills your window, click and hold the Ellipse tool (○), and select the hidden Polygon tool (○). Click and drag to create a polygon shape, but do not release it. Instead press the down-arrow on your keyboard several times until the polygon is a triangle. Release the mouse when you have a triangle shape. Do not be concerned with the angle or size for now.

*Press the down-arrow (while creating the shape) to reduce sides on the polygon.*

**10** Choose the Selection tool (▸) and notice that a bounding box appears around the triangle. If the bounding box is not visible, make sure that you are on the Selection tool and choose View > Show Bounding Box.

**11** Position your mouse around an outside corner, and when you see the curved arrow cursor, click and drag to rotate the triangle. Position your triangle so that it creates the shape of a fish tail.

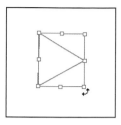

*Click and drag to rotate the triangle.*

**12** With the Selection tool still active, position your mouse on a corner point and click and drag to scale the triangle either up or down; you are now visually resizing the triangle. Resize the triangle until you think it would make a good fit as a fish tail. In our example, the tail is approximately .8 inches.

If you would rather enter an exact amount, choose Window > Transform; the Transform panel appears. With the triangle selected, type **.8 in** into the W: (Width) text field, then press Tab and type **.8 in** into the H: (Height) text field.

*Enter an exact measurement in the Transform panel.*

**13** Using the Selection tool, click and drag to position the triangle so that it is on the left side of the ellipse, making sure it overlaps slightly.

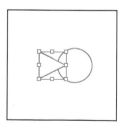

*Position the triangle so that it is slightly overlapping the ellipse on the left side.*

**14** Choose File > Save or press Ctrl+S (Windows) or Command+S (Mac OS) to save your file. Keep it open for the next part of this lesson.

## Combining the shapes

You will now start the process of combining your shapes.

1   Using the Selection tool (▶), click the triangle shape if it is not selected, then Shift+click the ellipse.

2   Select the Shape Builder tool (◉) in the Tools panel. Click and drag from one shape to another. The triangle and ellipse are combined into one shape.

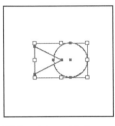  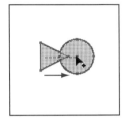

*Click and drag with the*          *The resulting combined shape.*
*Shape Builder tool.*

## Subtracting with the Shape Builder tool

You will now create what will soon be the mouth shape (when it is subtracted from your ellipse shape).

1   Click and hold the Polygon tool (○) in the Tools panel to select the hidden Ellipse tool (○).

2   Choose View > Snap to Point to uncheck that feature. When creating small shapes, the Snap to Point feature can prevent you from forming the correct shape.

3   Click and drag a small ellipse over the right side of the newly created shape. Keep in mind that the ellipse will be subtracted from the combined shape to form the mouth.

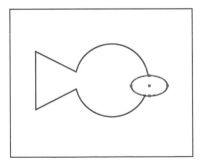

*Create the shape that will be subtracted to form a mouth.*

4   Switch back to the Selection tool and Shift+click the combined shape to activate both the ellipse and combined shape at the same time.

5   Select the Shape Builder tool and press and hold the Alt (Windows) or Option (Mac OS) key. The cursor now shows a minus sign in the lower-right.

**6**  With the Alt/Option key still being held down, click and drag from the inside-right edge of the ellipse into the left edge. When you release, the ellipse shape is subtracted from the combined shape, forming a mouth.

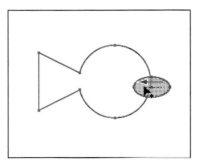
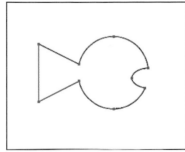

*Select both shapes.*    *Press and hold the Alt/Opt key and drag within the ellipse shape to subtract it.*

You will use the Shape Builder tool for one last time to add a shape (on top of the fish) to create the fin.

**7**  Select the Ellipse tool, then click and drag to create an oval shape that intersects across the top of the combined shape. Again, there is no exact size or position required for this shape.

In the next step, you will take advantage of a shortcut that allows you to activate the Selection tool temporarily, helping you to avoid switching tools.

**8**  Press and hold the Ctrl (Windows) or Command (Mac OS) key and notice that, even though you are on the Ellipse tool, the cursor has changed into the Selection cursor. With the Selection cursor, click and drag a marquee that touches both the ellipse and the fish body shape to activate both shapes.

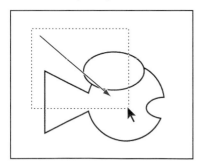

*Press and hold the Ctrl/Command key to temporarily access the Selection tool.*

**9**   With both shapes selected, select the Shape Builder tool and click and drag from the area where the ellipse and the fish body shape meet into the fish shape. The intersected area is added to the fish body shape.

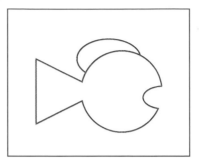

Click and drag from within the intersected shape into the fish body shape.   The result.

**10**   Choose File > Save or press Ctrl+S (Windows) or Command+S (Mac OS) to save your file. Keep it open for the next part of this lesson.

## Creating the fish eyes

In this section, you add an eye to the fish illustration.

**1**   Select the Ellipse tool (○) and then click and drag a circle that will serve as the outside of the fish eye. In our example, the size was approximately .25 in.

If you want your circle to match our example, you can type the value of **.25 in** into the Width and Height text fields in the Transform panel.

**2**   Using the Selection tool (⬉), reposition the circle so that it is approximately the correct position for the eye that is furthest away.

**3**   Select the Ellipse tool, and pressing and holding the Shift key, draw a smaller circle to act as the iris in the eye.

**4**   Using the Selection tool reposition the iris, if necessary.

Create the eye for the fish.

**5**   With the Selection tool, select both parts of the eye and then press and hold the Alt (Windows) or Option (Mac OS) and drag the eye to the left. This clones the original eye, you now have two eyes.

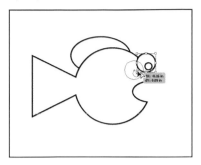

*Press and hold Alt/Option and drag to clone a selected object.*

**6**   Make sure that the newly cloned eye is selected then position your cursor on a corner of the bounding box.

**7**   When the cursor changes to a double-arrow, click and drag outward to enlarge the eye slightly.

*The illustration with the eyes added.*

**8**   Choose File > Save, and choose File > Close to close the file.

## Self study

Experiment with color and shapes by coloring the fish image you just created named **ai0505_work.ai**.

Create you own custom shapes using the Shape Builder tool. You can create multiple overlapping shapes and click and drag across selected objects to combine them into one shape. Experiment with subtracting shapes from others by pressing and holding the Alt (Windows) or Option (Mac OS) key when clicking and dragging with the Shape Builder tool. Here are some examples of shapes that you can practice creating:

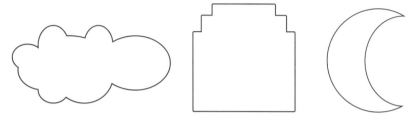

*Examples of shapes you can create with the Shape Builder tool.*

## Review

### Questions

**1**   When drawing with the Pen tool, how does creating the first point of a straight line differ from creating the first point of a curved line?

**2**   How do you import a bitmap image that you want to trace in Illustrator?

**3**   What key do you press and hold when you want to remove one shape from another using the Shape Builder tool?

### Answers

**1**   To create the first point for a straight line, you must click and release the Pen tool. When creating a curved line, you should click and drag the Pen tool in the direction of the curve you want to create.

**2**   Use the File > Place command and check the *Template* option in the Place dialog box. While the Template option is not required, it is helpful for tracing scanned artwork.

**3**   You can press and hold the Alt (Windows) or Option (Mac OS) to remove one shape from another using the Shape Builder tool.

## What you'll learn in this lesson:

- Adding tonal variations with gradients
- Saving custom swatches
- Creating and using patterns
- Using the Color Guide
- Creating a color group

# Exploring Additional Color Options

*Adobe Illustrator offers an expansive amount of features that allow you to create original fill colors and strokes. In this lesson, you find out how to create and use patterns, and to take advantage of gradients. You also learn how to explore more color opportunities with the Color Guide.*

## Starting up

Before starting, make sure that your tools and panels are consistent by resetting your workspace. See "Resetting Adobe Illustrator CC Preferences" in the Starting up section of this book.

You will work with several files from the ai06lessons folder in this lesson. Make sure that you have loaded the ailessons folder onto your hard drive from the supplied DVD. See "Loading lesson files" in the Starting up section of this book.

**See Lesson 6 in action!**

*Use the accompanying video to gain a better understanding of how to use some of the features shown in this lesson. You can find the video tutorial for this lesson on the included DVD.*

## Taking a look at the finished illustration

In this lesson, you will take a black-and-white illustration and liven it up with gradients and patterns. You will then discover how to build interesting combinations of color together using the Color Guide.

1  To view the completed illustration, choose File > Browse in Bridge, and using the Favorites tab, click Desktop.

2  Once at the Desktop, double-click the ai06lessons folder that you dragged from the DVD, and double-click the file named **ai0601_done.ai**. An illustration of a boy holding a gift appears.

*The completed illustration.*

3  After examining the finished file, choose File > Close to close the file, or keep it open for reference throughout this lesson.

**4**   Choose File > Browse in Bridge, in the ai06lessons folder double-click the file named **ai0601_start.ai**; a black-and-white illustration appears.

*The black-and-white start file.*

**5**   Choose File > Save As. In the Save As dialog box, navigate to the ai06lessons folder and type **ai0601_work.ai** into the Name text field, then click Save. In the Illustrator Options dialog box, click OK to accept the default settings. Keep the file open for the next part of this lesson.

# Adding tonal values with gradients

Gradients are used to add tonal shading to illustrations. In this lesson, you discover how to use existing gradients, and take advantage of the Gradient panel and Gradient tool. You also find out how to create your own custom gradients and store them for repeated use.

You will start by using an existing gradient, from the Swatches panel, to color the ribbons.

1   Zoom in on the area of the top portion of the box and ribbon, then using the Selection tool (▶), click and drag a marquee around the top ribbon to select most of the ribbon parts. Don't worry about crossing over the rectangle in the background, since it is on a locked layer and will not become selected.

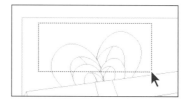

*Click and drag a marquee with the Selection tool.*

2   Now, press and hold the Shift key and click the two remaining pieces of ribbon.

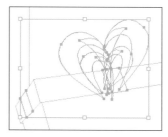

*Shift-click the two remaining pieces of ribbon.*

In order to save yourself time later, you will save this selection. By saving the selection, you can avoid having to reselect over and over again. Anytime that you inadvertently deselect the ribbon, you can reselect by selecting Select > Ribbon.

3   With the ribbon selection active, choose Select > Save Selection. When the Save Selection dialog box appears, type **Ribbon** into the Name text field, then click OK.

*Save your selection for future use.*

**4**    Click the Fill box at the bottom of the Tool bar to make sure that the Fill is selected instead of the Stroke. If the Swatches panel is not visible, choose Window > Swatches. With the ribbon selected, choose the Summer Red Radial gradient swatch. The ribbon now has the gradient applied.

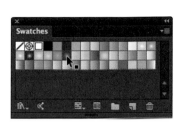
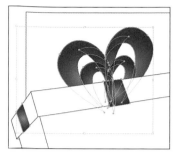

*Apply the Summer Red Radial gradient to the ribbon.*

Notice that the radial gradient starts and stops in every shape that the gradient was applied to. You will now use the Gradient tool to change how the radial gradient is applied to these shapes.

**5**    With the ribbon still selected, choose the Gradient tool (◼) from the Tools panel.

**6**    With the Gradient tool selected, ignore the gradient ramp that appears on the ribbon and click and drag down and to the left from the center of the selected ribbon outward. This directs the radial gradient to start from the center. Note that the gradient is now continuing throughout all of the shapes instead of starting individual radial gradients in each shape.

*The radial gradient.*    *Using the Gradient tool, pull from the center creating the ramp.*    *The gradient after using the Gradient tool.*

**7**    Choose File > Save to save this file, keep the file open for the next part of this lesson.

## Customizing an existing gradient

You will now have the opportunity to customize the existing gradient.

**1**    If the ribbon is not selected, choose Select > Ribbon to reactivate the selection. If you do not have the Ribbon as an option under the Select menu, refer back to step 3 in the previous exercise of this lesson.

**2**    With the Gradient tool active, cross over the gradient annotator (or gradient ramp) that appears on the Ribbon selection with your cursor. If you do not see the color stops, click back on the Summer Red Radius swatch again. There are three color stops on this gradient, indicating that the gradient has three colors that are being blended. You will now select one of the stops and make it darker.

**3**    Double-click the gradient stop on the far right; the Colors panel appears.

**4**    Click and drag the Magenta slider to the value of 100%, or enter **100** into the Magenta text field.

**5**    Click and drag the Black value to 50%, or enter **50** into the Black (K) text field. Press the Return or Enter key to exit the Colors panel. The color value is changed.

**6**    With the Ribbon selection still active, and the Gradient tool still selected, click and drag up to change the look of the gradient. You can click and drag as many times as you like until you get the look you like.

Keep in mind that the gradient will create a more gradual blending effect from one color to another with a longer ramp than if you pull the gradient ramp a shorter distance. You can also click the gradient ramp and relocate it to another location.

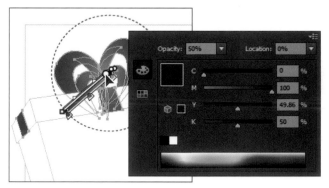

*Change a color stop.*

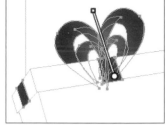

*Drag the gradient in a different direction.*

*You can enter an exact angle for your gradient by choosing Window > Gradient, and entering a value into the Angle text field.*

You will now remove a color stop from the gradient.

**7**  With the gradient ramp still selected, click the center color stop and click and drag it off the ramp (any direction), it is now removed from the gradient.

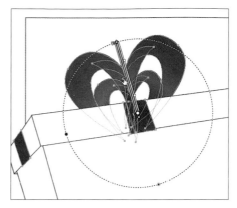

*Easily remove color stops by dragging them off the ramp.*

## Saving the gradient

Now that you spent a fair amount of time creating your own custom gradient, you will save it for future use.

**1**  Using the Selection tool (➤), click anywhere on the scratch area to deselect the ribbon, then click any one of the ribbon sections to activate a single selection. The new gradient fill you created is now in the Fill box at the bottom of the Tools panel.

**2**  If the Swatches panel is not visible, choose Windows > Swatches, then click the New Swatch button (⬚).

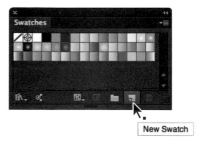

*Click the New Swatch button.*

3   When the New Swatch dialog box appears, type **my red gradient** in the Swatch
Name text field and click OK. The new gradient is added to your Swatches panel.

*Save the gradient.*

## Applying a second instance of the gradient

You can apply the same gradient over and over again to separate objects in an illustration.
Each instance can look very different based upon how you use the Gradient tool.

1   Select the Direct Selection tool ( ), and while pressing and holding the Shift key, click
all four parts of the inside of the ribbon (see figure below).

2   If necessary, click the *my red gradient* swatch in the Swatches panel to make sure that it
is applied.

3   Select Window > Gradient, the Gradient panel appears. You can use the Gradient
panel to change colors in the gradient, as well as the angle and type of gradient.

4   Click and hold Radial to change the type of gradient to Linear. Several gradient
annotators appear.

5   Select the Gradient tool, then click and drag up from the bottom of the Ribbon
selection.

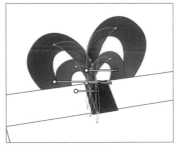

*In the Gradient panel change
from Radial to Linear.*

*Multiple annotators will appear.*

*With just the inside of the ribbon selected,
change the direction of the gradient.*

6   With the shapes still selected, click the New Swatch icon in the Swatches panel. When
the New Swatch dialog box appears, type the name **red linear gradient**, and click OK.

7   Choose File > Save to save this file, keep it open for the next part of this lesson.

## Using the Gradient panel

In the previous exercise, you edited an existing gradient using the gradient annotator. In this next part of the lesson, you will use the Gradient panel to create another custom gray gradient.

**1** Choose View > Fit Artboard in Window, then using the Selection tool (▸), click the large front panel of the box.

**2** Choose Window > Gradient. The Gradient panel appears, and the last used gradient appears in the panel. Click and drag the Gradient tab to undock the Gradient panel from the docking area.

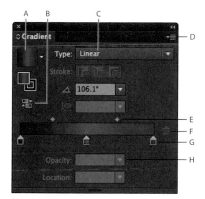

*A. Gradient Fill box. **B**. Reverse Gradient. **C**. Gradient Type drop-down menu. **D**. Panel menu. **E**. Midpoints. **F**. Delete stop. **G**. Color stop. **H**. Opacity.*

**3** If the Swatches panel is not open, choose Window > Swatches. When the Swatches panel appears, click and drag the tab in order to undock the Swatches panel.

**4** With the front panel selected, click anywhere on the gradient ramp. The front panel is filled with the red gradient.

**5** In the Gradient panel, click the center color stop, then click and drag it off the ramp to remove it from the gradient.

**6**    In the Swatches panel, click and drag the black swatch to the left color stop in the Gradients panel. The red color is replaced with the black swatch.

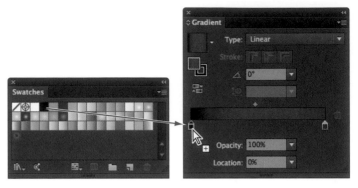

*Click and drag the black color swatch to the first color stop.*

**7**    Now, double-click the black color stop. When the Color panel appears, change the black value to **50**, then press Enter or Return.

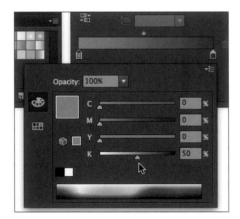

*Double-click the color stop and change the value to 50% black.*

**8**    Click and drag the White Swatch (in the Swatches panel) to the right color stop in the Gradient panel. The gradient now blends from black to white.

**9**  Using the Gradient tool (▣), click and drag from the top of the gift to the bottom in the front panel.

*Click and drag from top to bottom.*

**10**  Save the new gradient by clicking the New Swatch button (▣) at the bottom of the Swatches panel. When the New Swatch dialog box appears, type **gray gradient** into the Swatch Name text field and click OK.

**11**    Switch to the Selection tool, click the side panel, and then Shift+click the two lid panels.

*Select the other three panels.*

**12**    Click the newly saved gray gradient in the swatches panel to apply it to the other three panels.

*The gradient applied to the other panels.*

**13**    Chose File > Save. Keep this file open for the next part of this lesson.

## Updating a gradient

You can easily update a saved gradient swatch and replace all instances. In this part of the lesson, you will open a swatch library and then you will change the gray gradient stop to a yellow gradient stop.

1   Select the front panel, and make sure the Gradient panel and Swatches panel are still undocked and visible in your workspace.

2   From the Swatches panel menu (·≡), select Open Swatch Library > Celebration. A separate panel appears with additional colors you can use to color your artwork.

3   Select the yellow color named with the values C=**0**, M=**20**, Y=**100**, K=**0**, and drag the swatch to the gray color stop on the gradient ramp. The gray gradient is replaced with yellow.

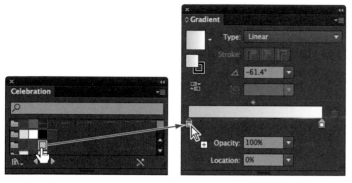

*Select the yellow color in the*          *Drag the yellow to the gradient ramp to*
*Celebrations swatches.*                      *replace the gray color stop.*

4   While pressing and holding the Alt (Windows) or Option (Mac OS) key, click the gradient preview in the Gradient panel and drag it on top of the same gray gradient swatch in the Swatches panel. By pressing and holding the Alt/Option key, you replace all instance of that gradient. If you did not press and hold the Alt/Option key, a new swatch would be created.

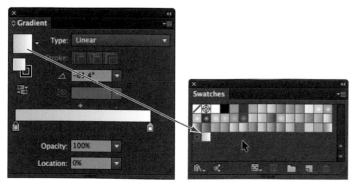

*Press and hold the Alt/Option key while dragging a replacement gradient on top of another.*

# Creating and using patterns

Using Adobe Illustrator, you can create reusable patterns quickly and easily. In this next part of the lesson, you create several patterns to be used in the illustration. You will also discover keyboard shortcuts to rotate and resize patterns, as well as other tips and tricks to customize your patterns.

1   With the **ai0601_work** file open, select the Polygon tool (○) that is hidden underneath the Rectangle tool (□).

2   Click and drag out on the artboard (away from any other artwork), but do not release the mouse. While dragging, press the arrow key down twice. This reduces the number of sides from 6 to 4. Try to angle the polygon so that it is a diamond shape. The shape is created, and automatically filled with the last-used yellow gradient.

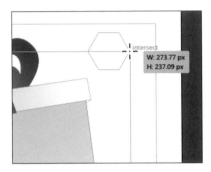 

*Create a diamond shape using the Polygon tool.*

3   Angle your polygon to appear as a diamond by choosing the Selection tool (▶) and clicking and dragging any corner (of the bounding box) repositioning the shape.

4   With the Selection tool still active, position your cursor over the diamond shape. Clone the diamond by pressing and holding the Alt (Windows) or Option (Mac OS) key and dragging to another location near to the original. No exact position is necessary.

5   Repeat the cloning of the diamond shape one more time. You will then have a total of three diamonds.

6   With the Selection tool, change the angle of the two newly cloned diamonds so that no diamonds are at the same angle.

7   Click any one of the diamond shapes, then click the Purple Radial Swatch in the Swatches panel. You can close the Celebration swatch panel to tidy up your workspace.

**8**  Click another diamond shape and then click the Summer Red Radial swatch in the
Swatches panel.

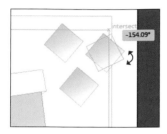 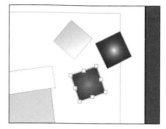

*Change the angle of the diamonds.*      *Apply new swatch colors.*

**9**  Choose File > Save. Keep the file open for the next part of this lesson.

## Creating a bounding box

In this next section, you create a bounding box that will determine how your pattern
will repeat. It is not necessary to create a bounding box, but if you do not, your pattern is
automatically defined by the edge of your objects. Once the bounding box is created, you
will turn your shapes into a repeatable pattern.

**1**  Since you want to make sure the bounding box is the backmost object, select the
Draw Behind button at the bottom of the Tools panel.

*Click the Draw Behind button.*

**2**  Select the Rectangle tool (☐) and click and drag to surround your diamond shapes.
Keep in mind that you are creating a repeatable tile, so that if you have lots of space
around the diamond shapes, you will have more space between the repeat.

**3**  With the backmost shape still selected, choose Stroke from the Control panel and
select None.

**4**  Click Fill in the Control panel and select the White swatch. The white bounding box
you created is now behind the shapes.

*Create a white bounding
box behind the shapes.*

5   If necessary, adjust the sizing of the bounding box using the Selection tool.

Now you will create the pattern swatch.

6   Using the Selection tool, click and drag to create a marquee around the diamond shapes and the bounding box to select all four objects.

7   Make sure that the Swatches panel is still visible, and then click and drag the objects right into the Swatches panel and release. The pattern is now added as a swatch to the Swatches panel.

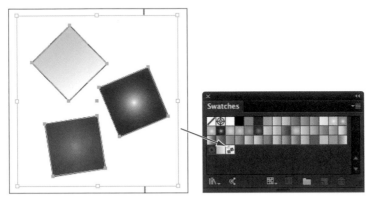

*Drag your bounding box and new shapes to the Swatches panel.*

## Applying the pattern

You will now apply the pattern to your illustration. Before doing that, you will delete the original artwork that created the pattern and unlock a layer.

1   Check to see that the elements used to create the pattern (three diamonds and the bounding box) are selected and then choose Edit > Clear. The objects are deleted.

2   Choose Window > Layers to show the Layers panel, and then click the padlock icon to the left of the background layer. This unlocks the elements on this layer.

3   Click the background layer to make it active.

*Unlock the background layer.*

**4**   Make sure the Draw Behind button (at the bottom of the Tools panel) is selected, then select the Rectangle tool and draw a rectangle that fills the entire artboard, from edge to edge. If necessary, use the Selection tool to resize this rectangle.

**5**   When the rectangle is completed, make sure that Fill is forward (in the Tools panel) and then click the new pattern swatch you created. The pattern is applied to the rectangle's fill.

*Create a rectangle behind the existing shape.*    *Fill with your pattern.*

**6**   Choose File > Save to save this file. Keep it open for the next part of this lesson.

## Editing a pattern fill

There are many ways that you can edit a pattern. In this next part of the lesson, you will change the size and rotation of the pattern.

**1**   Select the large rectangle shape that has the pattern fill, and then double-click the Scale tool (⬚) in the Tools panel. The Scale dialog box appears.

**2**   Change the Uniform scale to **50%**, uncheck Transform Objects, and check Preview. By unchecking Objects you scale only the pattern, not the shape that contains the pattern.

Note that you can pick a more appropriate value as there was not a specific size requested for the original pattern shapes. Click OK.

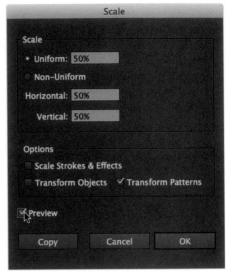

*Select to scale only the pattern.*        *The result.*

**3**    Now select the Rotate tool (○).

Even though you can double-click and enter an exact value with the Rotate tool, you will take advantage of a more visual method for rotating your pattern within the rectangle.

**4**    Press and hold the Tilde (~) key and click and drag. The Tilde (~) key is a shortcut key for rotating the pattern fill in an object. This also works with scale, but is a little difficult to control.

*Use a keyboard shortcut to rotate the pattern only, in an object.    The Result. Your pattern has been rotated.*

**5**    Using the Selection tool, click the white rectangle that is in front of your pattern.

6    Click the Purple Radial swatch in the Swatches panel. The pattern fills the rectangle.

*Finish the background by applying a gradient.*

*A Pattern Options dialog box has been added for Illustrator CC to allow you to more easily create and edit seamless tiled vector patterns. Read more about this new feature in Lesson 14, "Adobe Illustrator CC New Features."*

## Locating existing patterns

You can also take advantage of existing patterns. In this lesson, you find a pattern in the swatches library, and then edit it.

**1** From the Swatches panel menu (•≡), choose Open Swatch Library > Patterns > Basic Graphics > Basic Graphics Dots. A Basic Graphics Dots panel appears.

**2** Select the hat of the boy holding the present, then choose the dot pattern labeled 6 dpi 50% (for those from the print environment, this represents a 6 lines per inch dot pattern, at a 50% tint). The pattern is applied to the hat.

 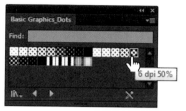

*Select the 6 dpi 50% pattern swatch.*      *It is applied to the selected hat.*

**3** Click the shirt of the boy and apply the 6 dpi 50% pattern.

You will now edit this pattern and resize it.

**4** Once you choose to use a pattern it is added to the Swatches panel. Click and drag the new dot pattern from the Swatches panel to the pasteboard. The original artwork that created the pattern is now able to be edited.

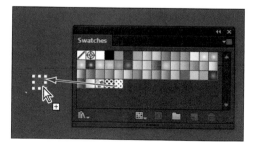

*Click and drag the swatch from the Swatches panel to the pasteboard.*

5    Select the Zoom tool (🔍), then click and drag around the pattern to zoom into the pattern.

*Click and drag with the Zoom tool.*     *The result.*

6    In the Tool bar, click and hold the Direct Selection tool and select the Group Selection tool (↖), then click and drag a marquee around the pattern artwork. Notice that the bounding box is also included in this selection.

7    Press and hold the Shift key and click the border of the bounding box to deselect it.

8    With the dots selected, click the swatch you created earlier named *my red gradient*.

*Select the dots.*     *Apply your custom gradient.*

9    Switch to the Selection tool (▸) and click and drag a marquee around all the pattern elements to make a selection that includes all of the dots and the bounding box.

**10** Press and hold the Alt (Windows) or Option (Mac OS) key and drag the new pattern on top of the existing black-and-white 6 dpi 50% pattern (in the Swatches panel). Just like with the gradient, you have replaced all instances of that pattern with a new one.

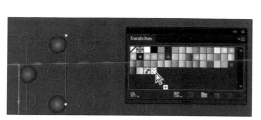

*Alt/Option new pattern on top of existing pattern.*          *Instances of pattern are replaced.*

**11** You can now delete the artwork creating the pattern that is on your pasteboard. Don't forget that you can access the original artwork of any pattern by dragging it to the pasteboard at any time.

**12** Using the Selection tool, select the shirt and hat and then double-click the Scale tool. Type **300** into the Uniform Scale text field. Make sure that Transform Objects is unchecked, and Preview is on, and click OK.

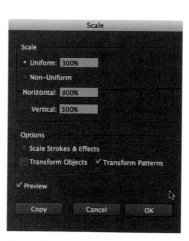

*Change the scale of the dots.*          *The result.*

**13** Choose File > Save to save this file. Keep it open for the next part of this lesson.

## Finishing up the illustration

In this next part of the lesson, you have some freedom to choose various fills. You can either use our suggestions, or pick your own. We have saved views in this file to make it easy for you to zoom into certain areas.

**1**   Choose View > Eyes. You are zoomed into the eye area.

*You can save views too. All you need to do is choose View > New View when you are in a view you would like to save.*

**2**   Using the Group Selection tool (  ), Shift+click the two large circles creating the irises of the eyes, and then choose the swatch Purple Radial.

*Color the iris of the eye.*

**3**   Now press Ctrl+0 (zero) (Windows) or Command+0 (zero) (Mac OS) to fit the artboard to the window.

**4**   Using the Group Selection tool select the face, arm, belly, and three fingers (on the left side of the gift).

**5** Select the color named Skintone 7 from Fill in the Control panel, or the Swatches panel.

*Add skin color to the boy holding the gift.*

**6** Choose View > Shoes. The saved Shoes view is applied.

**7** Apply colors that you like to the shoes, pants and shoelaces.

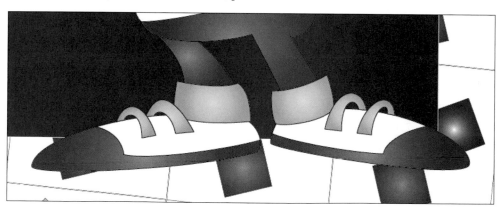

*Choose colors for the shoes and pants.*

## Altering an object in Isolation Mode

You might find that when attempting to color the front part of the shoes, the individual shapes are not available for editing. This is because they were created with what is known as a Clipping Mask; covered in more detail in Lesson 9, "Organizing your Illustrations with Layers." The easiest method to edit shapes included in a Clipping Mask is to enter something called the Isolation mode.

To enter into Isolation Mode double-click one of the shoes. Note that the shape you double-clicked on editiable, while all other objects dim. Also notice that an arrow appears, at the top of your work area,this is called the Isolation Mode Border.

*Arrow and pathway indicating Isolation Mode.*

Once you've isolated the shape you can edit it by changing the color.

To exit this Isolation mode, click the left facing arrow in the Isolation Mode Border.

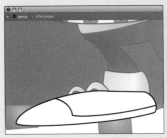

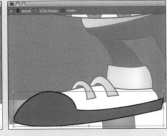

*Double-click the object revealing the Isolation Mode Border.*  *Further clicking isolates the object for editing.*  *Recolor your object.*

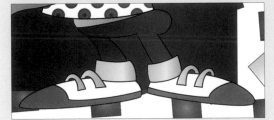

*The result.*

8   Select View > Face. The face is now zoomed into.

9   Using the Group Selection tool, select the tassel on the hat and change it to *my red gradient*.

**10** Using the Group Selection tool, select the hair and eyebrows, and then select the swatch named *Autumn Dark Gold*.

*Change the color of the hair, eyebrows, tongue, and tassel.*

**11** Finish off the illustration by selecting the tongue and changing its fill to the red linear gradient.

**12** Choose File > Save. Keep this file open for the next part of this lesson.

## Creating a color group

In this part of the lesson, you will store all your used colors into a color group. By creating a color group, you can easily reference colors and apply them to other artwork. First of all, you will save a new version of your illustration.

**1** Choose File > Save As. If necessary, browse to save your file in the ai06lessons folder. In the File Name text field, type **ai0601_colorguide.ai**, and then click Save. When the Illustrator Options dialog box appears, click OK.

**2** With the Selection tool (k), press Ctrl+A (Windows) or Command+A (Mac OS) to select all the objects in the illustration.

**3** From the Swatches panel menu (·≡), choose New Color Group. The New Color Group dialog box appears.

4 Type **Party Colors**. Make sure that Selected Artwork is selected, and that the two options below are selected. Click OK. A color group has been added to the Swatches panel.

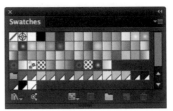

Select the colors you want to create a color group.          The result.

## Using the Color Guide

Now that you have stored your original colors in the Swatches panel, you will reduce the illustration to one color using the Color Guide.

The Color Guide provides you with inspiration as you apply color to your artwork. It suggests harmonious colors based on the color that is active in the Tools panel. You can change the suggested colors by changing the harmony rule, which is the method by which the Color Guide panel makes its color suggestions. Let's see how you can use the Color Guide panel to translate your artwork into one color.

1 Choose Select > All to select the illustration.

2 Choose Window > Color Guide to open the Color Guide panel.

**3**   Click the Edit or Apply Colors button at the bottom of the Color Guide panel. The Recolor Artwork dialog box appears. If you have Recolor artwork checked in the lower-left corner, the artwork is automatically recolored, based upon the default selection in the Harmony Rules drop-down menu.

*Choose to recolor the artwork.*

## The Recolor dialog box

The Recolor dialog box offers many options, but there are basically three main areas that you should be aware of:

**Edit**: Use the Edit tab to create new color groups or edit existing color groups. Use the Harmony Rules menu and the color wheel to experiment with color harmonies.

**Assign**: Use the Assign tab to view and control how colors from a color group replace original colors in your artwork. You can assign colors only if you have artwork selected in the document.

**Color Groups**: Lists all saved color groups for the open document (these same color groups appear in the Swatches panel). While in the dialog box, you can edit, delete, and create new color groups using the Color Groups list. All your changes are reflected in the Swatches panel.

4   Choose different options from the Harmony Rules dialog box to experiment with color and your illustration.

5   Click Edit to see the color wheel and click and drag to make additional color selections.

6   When you are finished experimenting, click back on Assign, then choose 1 from the Colors drop-down menu. All colors are assigned (as tints) to one color.

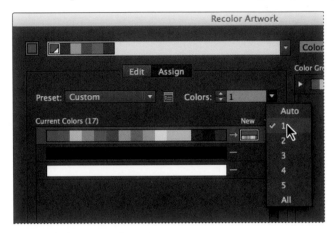

*Convert all colors to tints of one color.*

Next, you will change that color.

7   Select the blue color that appears in your original colors and drag it on top of the assigned color (on the right). The illustration is now created from tints of your blue color. Click OK. If a dialog box opens asking you if you want to save changes to your swatch group, click Yes.

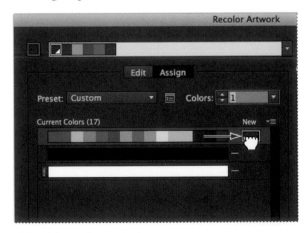

*Click and drag a color to assign it.*

**8**    Choose File > Save to save your file.

*The completed illustration.*

## Self study

Return to the **0601_work.ai** file (Save another version if you like), and make these changes to it:

1  Explore the possibilities with transparent gradients by changing the opacity on the selected gradient stopper. You can also use gradients on strokes.

2  Create a new pattern to use in the background, and replace the existing one.

3  Bring the Illustration down to four colors using the Recolor artwork dialog box.

   Have fun, make changes, and save multiple versions if you are afraid of destroying your artwork.

## Review

### Questions

1  What key do you press and hold when replacing a gradient or pattern swatch?

2  What are two methods you can use to change the angle of a gradient?

3  How do you create a pattern?

4  How can you extract all the colors that you used in an illustration?

5  How do you edit an existing pattern?

### Answers

1  To replace a gradient or pattern swatch, press and hold the Alt/Option key as you drag a new swatch version on top of the original.

2  You can change the angle of a gradient by clicking and dragging over a selected object (that has a gradient applied to it) with the Gradient tool, or you can input an angle into the Angle text field in the Gradient panel.

3  To create a pattern, you can create the artwork that you want to repeat and then drag it into the Swatches panel. If you want a tile to repeat, you can create a bounding box behind the artwork. Note that if the bounding box has a stroke applied, it will be visible in the repeat.

4  You can save used colors by selecting the illustration, then selecting New Color Group from the Swatches panel.

5  You can edit an existing pattern by dragging it from the Swatches panel to the pasteboard. Make the changes that you want and then Alt/Option drag it back on top of the original pattern (in the Swatches panel).

## What you'll learn in this lesson:

- How to create a pattern
- Editing a pattern
- Using the Pattern Options panel

# Using Patterns

*You can easily create patterns in Illustrator and with some simple tweaking, you can rotate, scale, and reposition your patterns. In this lesson, you are introduced to the Pattern Options panel.*

## Starting up

Before starting, make sure that your tools and panels are consistent by resetting your workspace. See "Resetting Adobe Illustrator CC Preferences" in the Starting up section of this book.

You will work with several files from the ai07lessons folder in this lesson. Make sure that you have loaded the ailessons folder onto your hard drive from the included DVD. See "Loading lesson files" in the Starting up section of this book.

**See Lesson 7 in action!**

*Use the accompanying video to gain a better understanding of how to use some of the features shown in this lesson. You can find the video tutorial for this lesson on the included DVD.*

## The Pattern Options panel makes creating patterns more manageable

Many designers and illustrators create patterns in Illustrator on a daily basis, but working with them in previous versions of the program was cumbersome at best. It was easy enough to create your objects, define the pattern, and then apply the pattern swatch to your illustration. But if you wanted to to edit the pattern it was difficult, and lining up a tiled repeat using a pattern swatch was often frustrating. In this lesson, you create a pattern and then edit it using the Pattern Options panel.

## Creating a pattern

The Pattern Options panel offers a much greater level of control over your patterns. You can change the tile type, spacing, copies and more, depending on the settings you've chosen. You can dim copies of repeats (using a slider and percentage field) as you're working on it, so you know you're working on the original object. You can even interactively tweak the tiling using the Pattern Tile tool, which is accessible from within the panel itself.

To create a pattern in Illustrator:

1   Choose File > Open, and open **Pattern_start.ai** from the ai07lessons folder. You create and apply a pattern to the jacket illustration in this exercise.

2   Choose File > Save As and save your file in the ai07lessons folder as **Pattern_work.ai**.

3   In the Save As dialog box, leave the file format set to Adobe Illustrator and click Save. When the Illustrator Options dialog box appears, click OK to keep all options at their default settings.

Typically you might use Illustrator's drawing tools to create a pattern tile. For this lesson one has been created for you and stored in the upper left corner of the artboard.

4   Zoom in if necessary, and use the Selection tool to select all four pieces of the pattern tile.

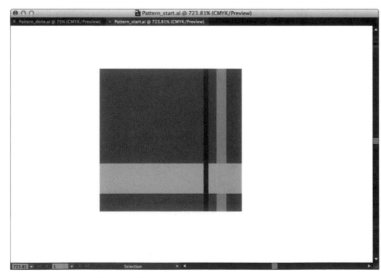

*Create a new pattern tile using Illustrator's drawing tools.*

**5**   To create the pattern swatch, choose Object > Pattern > Make.

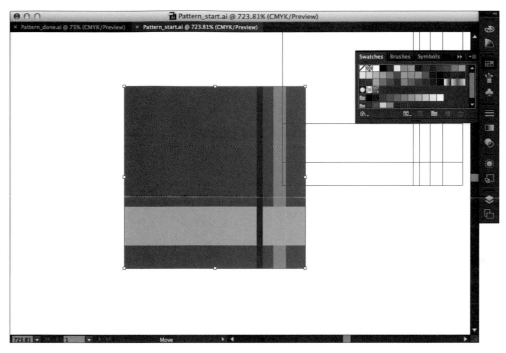

*Make a new pattern swatch from the tile using Object > Pattern > Make, or by dragging it into your Swatches.*

**6**   Your pattern is now ready to be applied to the jacket.

*You can't create a pattern tile from objects to which a pattern has already been applied. These objects will be rejected by the Swatches panel.*

## Applying a pattern

Once you've successfully created a pattern swatch from the tile you've created, you can use Illustrator's Live Paint feature to easily apply it to your illustration.

To apply a pattern:

**1**   Choose View > Fit Artboard in Window to see the entire illustration, and click the jacket with the Selection tool to select it.

**2**   Select the Live Paint Bucket (▨) from the Tools panel hidden beneath the Shape Builder tool.

**3**   In the Swatches panel, choose your newly-created pattern swatch by clicking it.

**4**   Move your cursor over the jacket, and when prompted, click once to create a Live Paint Group. The tiled pattern applies to the area of the jacket you've clicked on.

**5** Continue to click with the Live Paint Bucket until all areas of the jacket are filled with your pattern. Note that the point of impact is the tip of the tool, not where the paint is dripping out of the bucket (as it was with earlier versions of Illustrator). Be careful not to click the strokes instead of the fills.

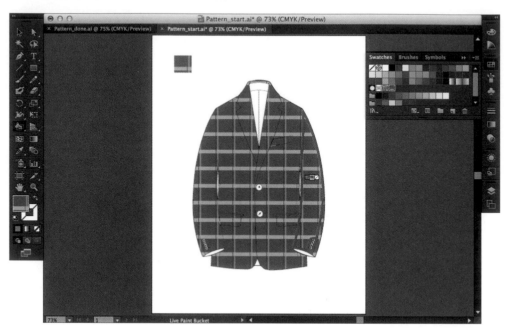

*Apply your pattern to the illustration using the Live Paint Bucket tool.*

**6** Choose File > Save and keep this file open for the next part of the lesson.

*Be very careful not to click the strokes with the Live Paint Bucket tool. Zoom in very tight to avoid this common pitfall. You can undo any mistakes.*

## Editing a pattern swatch

Up to this point, the process you've used for creating and applying your pattern has been essentially the same as in previous versions. Unfortunately, the pattern swatch you've applied is much too large for the illustration, and needs to be edited. This is where you'll start to see the benefits of using the Pattern Options panel.

To edit a pattern:

1   Double-click the pattern swatch you've created in the Swatches panel to access the Pattern Options panel, and to launch Isolated Pattern mode. You can also access these features by choosing Window > Pattern Options with your pattern swatch selected.

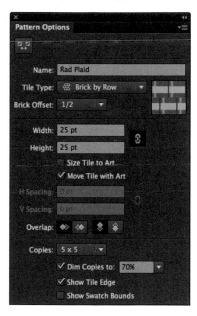

*Experiment with different offsets and edit pattern contents with Pattern Options and Isolated Pattern mode.*

2   Inside the Pattern Options panel, type **Rad Plaid** into the Name field.

3   In the Tile Type pull-down, choose Brick by Row. The Tile Type options allow you to offset the position of your pattern tiles horizontally, vertically, or hexagonally. Choose 1/2 as the Brick Offset amount by row.

4  Click the Maintain Height and Width Proportions () button to lock the width and height fields together proportionally. Then, in the Width field, type **25 pt**, and press Tab to repeat the setting in the Height field. These settings will reduce the size of the objects within the pattern tile.

*If the Width and Height fields are unavailable, uncheck the Size Tile to Art check box to allow customized sizing of the pattern tile's contents. Activating Size Tile to Art will allow you to control horizontal and vertical spacing between the pattern tiles.*

5  Alternatively, click the Pattern Tile Tool at the top of the panel (🔡), and drag the pattern tile's bounding handles to size the tile objects. Pressing and holding the Shift key will constrain the proportions as you drag.

6  If your settings have caused an overlap of the pattern tiles, you can control this with the Overlap buttons below the Spacing fields. Leave this option at its default for this exercise.

7  Use the Copies pull-down to add repeats to your sample. Additional settings in this area control the visibility (dimming, edges and bounds) of these repeats. Again, leave these settings at their defaults for this exercise.

8  Accept your Pattern Options by clicking the Done button near the top of your document window. You will leave Isolated Pattern mode and return to your illustration, where you can see that your edits have been applied to the jacket illustration.

### Editing a pattern in an object

The pattern swatch you've applied is a little too large for the parts of the illustration, and needs to be edited. To fix this you will use the Pattern Options panel.

To edit a pattern's application numerically:

1  Use the Direct Selection tool to select the patterned fill of the jacket's left lapel.

2  In the Tools panel, double-click the Rotate tool (⟳) to access the Rotate dialog box.

3  Make sure that only the Transform Patterns check box (not Transform Objects) is checked, and check the Preview check box.

*Transform the applied pattern numerically using the Rotate dialog box.*

**4**    Enter **160** into the Angle field and click OK. You have rotated the pattern to match the angle of the lapel.

**5**    Repeat steps 1–5 to change the angle of the other lapel and the three pockets in the jacket illustration.

## Editing a pattern's application visually

**1**    Using the Direct Selection tool, drag a marquee around the jacket to select it.

**2**    In the Tools panel, select the Scale tool (⬒).

**3**    Press and hold the Tilde (~) and the Shift keys, and then drag from outside the illustration toward its center. The Tilde key restricts the scale transformation to the pattern, and the Shift key keeps the scaling proportional.

*Pressing and holding the Tilde (~) key while dragging restricts any transformation to the pattern only.*

**4**    Repeat step 3 until you are satisfied with the pattern scaling. For this example, the pattern was scaled down an additional 80%.

**5**    Choose File > Save and File > Close to save and close this file.

## Self study

Experiment with some of the free patterns that come with Illustrator CC. Additional pattern swatches are available when you select the Swatch libraries button in the lower-left corner of the Swatches panel. Choose Patterns and then select from the listed sets.

Apply a new pattern to the jacket, and then experiment with changing the size and angle of your pattern. Also, open the Pattern Options panel and experiment with different designs and repeats.

## Review

### Questions

1  How can you easily create a pattern swatch?

2  What is one item that cannot be a pattern swatch?

3  What key can you press and hold to scale a pattern?

### Answers

1  You can create a pattern swatch by clicking and dragging selected artwork into the Swatches panel.

2  You cannot make a pattern swatch from another pattern swatch.

3  You can press and hold the Tilde (~) key to scale your pattern and not affect the scale of the object that it is in.

# Lesson 8

## What you'll learn in this lesson:

- Importing text from an external file
- Changing text formatting
- Saving character and paragraph styles
- Setting type on a curved path
- Applying text wrap to an object

# Working with and Formatting Text

*Adobe Illustrator CC boasts extensive text handling features. In this lesson, you'll discover how Illustrator provides you with the tools and flexibility you need to work with text.*

## Starting up

Before starting, make sure that your tools and panels are consistent by resetting your workspace. See "Resetting Adobe Illustrator CC Preferences" in the Starting up section of this book.

You will work with several files from the ai08lessons folder in this lesson. Make sure that you have loaded the ailessons folder onto your hard drive from the supplied DVD. See "Loading lesson files" in the Starting up section of this book.

### See Lesson 8 in action!

*Use the accompanying video to gain a better understanding of how to use some of the features shown in this lesson. You can find the video tutorial for this lesson on the included DVD.*

# Formatting type

Adobe Illustrator provides several options for formatting type in your document. Depending on your desired result, you might want to set some of these options that change the overall appearance of the type. Let's explore the different options that are available to you.

1   Launch Adobe Illustrator CC.

2   Choose File > Browse in Bridge or click the Go to Bridge button (Br) in the Application bar.

3   Navigate to the ai08lessons folder within Bridge, and double-click the file named **ai0801_done.ai**. The file opens in Adobe Illustrator.

4   This is the completed file. You can investigate the finished file and then choose File > Close, or you can keep it open throughout the lesson for reference.

*The final version.*

5   Navigate to the ai08lessons folder within Bridge, and double-click the file named **ai0801.ai**. The file opens in Adobe Illustrator.

6   In Illustrator, choose File > Save As. In the Save As dialog box, navigate to the ai08lessons folder and type **ai0801_work.ai** in the File name text field. Click Save. If a dialog box appears stating that changing a used spot color to a process color can generate unexpected results, click Continue. In the Illustrator Options dialog box, leave the settings at their defaults and click OK.

7   To be sure that all the panels and tools are easy to find, choose Window > Workspace > Essentials, then choose Window > Workspace > Reset Essentials. This resets your tools and panels to their default locations.

**8**    This document was created using layers, so before you begin working, open the Layers panel, either by clicking the Layers button (⬛) in the dock on the right side of the workspace, or by choosing Window > Layers. Click the Artwork layer, the second layer listed in the Layers panel, to make it active.

### A word on legacy text

Type objects that were created in Illustrator 10 and earlier cannot be edited in Illustrator CC until they are updated. You will encounter legacy text only if you open or copy and paste text from an Illustrator document that was created in version 10 and earlier.

Upon opening the file from a previous version of Illustrator, you see a dialog box asking you if you would like to convert the type. Choose No. The reason for this dialog box is that type can shift during the updating of legacy text to a new version of Illustrator, causing reflow and other physical changes.

Once the document opens, select the text that needs to be converted and choose Type > Legacy Text > Update Selected Legacy Text. This allows you to see any adjustments as the text is updated. Once updated, the text can be edited and adjusted as needed.

It isn't mandatory that legacy text be updated. If you need to open a document that contains legacy text, you can choose not to update the text. You can still view the text on-screen and print your artwork as needed; you just can't edit text that hasn't been updated.

**9**    Activate the Type tool (T) in the Tools panel, then click once in the upper-left corner of the box's left panel, which has an image of a biker on it.

Clicking once anywhere on the artboard with the Type tool creates point type. Point type allows you to type text wherever you click with the cursor. Point type is generally used when setting a single line of copy or a headline. Later in this lesson, you'll learn about another method of setting text, called area, and ways you can convert text from one to the other.

A blinking cursor appears where you clicked. To more closely see the cursor and the text, zoom in on the document by pressing Ctrl+(plus sign) (Windows) or Command+(plus sign) (Mac OS) a few times. If you need to reposition the artboard after increasing the page magnification, use the Hand tool (✋).

**10**    Type **Nutz provides energy to get you through the day!**

**11**    With the Type tool still selected, triple-click anywhere within the type you just created to select the whole line of type.

**12** Click the Character link in the Control panel at the top of the workspace to open the Character panel. Change the font to Myriad Pro Bold Italic and set the font size to 18 pt, then press Enter or Return.

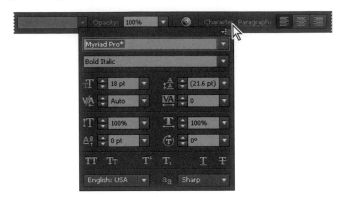

*The Character panel allows you to change the attributes of the selected type.*

*Some character formatting options are available directly within the Control panel. Character formatting can also be accomplished by choosing Window > Type > Character.*

**13** To make the type more readable, change the color of the selected type to white by clicking the Fill color swatch in the Control panel and choosing the white swatch from the Swatches panel that appears.

The word *Nutz* is the name of the fictional company that sells the box of mixed nuts you are creating. Because it is a company name, it should have an ® symbol next to it, indicating that the name is a registered trademark.

**14** Click once to the immediate right of the word *Nutz* and choose Type > Glyphs to open the Glyphs panel. The Glyphs panel displays every symbol available in the currently chosen font. Scroll through the Glyphs panel, locate the ® symbol, and double-click it to insert that symbol at the location of your cursor. Close the Glyphs panel.

*The Glyphs panel displayed.*

**15** Press Ctrl+Shift+A (Windows) or Command+Shift+A (Mac OS) to deselect everything in your document. Choose File > Save to save your work.

## OpenType fonts

OpenType is a font format that has a number of advantages over other formats. OpenType fonts are cross-platform, which means they can be used on the Windows and Mac OS platforms alike. In addition, OpenType fonts are composed of a single file, unlike older Postscript fonts, which require a separate screen and printer font file in order to work properly. OpenType fonts support expanded character sets and layout features that provide richer linguistic support and advanced typographic control. Most of the large font foundries are now releasing fonts in the OpenType format, and many OpenType fonts are based upon PostScript, allowing them to be used for high-resolution imaging and printing.

Adobe Illustrator takes full advantage of the features available with OpenType fonts. In fact, Illustrator has dedicated an entire panel within the application to controlling the features of OpenType. You can open this panel by choosing Window > Type > OpenType.

### Paragraph formatting

Unlike character formatting, paragraph formatting can only be applied to one or more paragraphs at a time. You can't apply a paragraph formatting attribute to a word, for instance; it's the whole paragraph or nothing. The key factor with paragraph formatting is a hidden character within a body of text that defines the end of one paragraph and the beginning of another—the paragraph return, which is created when you press Enter (Windows) or Return (Mac OS) on your keyboard. Let's apply some paragraph formatting to the text in your artwork.

**1** Press Ctrl+0 (Windows) or Command+0 (Mac OS) to see the entire project, then select the Zoom tool from the Tools panel and zoom in on the area below the nutrition facts.

*The Zoom tool can also be accessed by pressing and holding Ctrl+spacebar (Windows) or Command+spacebar (Mac OS), then clicking the area you want to magnify while still pressing and holding the key combination.*

**2**    Using the Type tool (T), click and drag to create a type area beneath the nutrition facts. To be certain that you create a new area for text, confirm that the cursor icon displays the I-beam with a dotted frame around the edges (⌶) before clicking and dragging. A blinking cursor appears in the upper-left corner of the frame that you just drew.

*Using the Type tool, click and drag to create a text area.*

*By clicking and dragging with the Type tool, you create area type. Area type differs from point type in that it acts as a text container and allows you to resize the frame while the text reflows within it. Point type doesn't work this way; if you resize a point type frame, you scale the text within it.*

**3**    Choose File > Place. In the Place dialog box, navigate to the Text folder inside the ai08lessons folder. Select the ingredients.txt file and check the Replace check box located in the lower portion of the Place dialog box. Select Place. In the Text Import Options dialog box that appears, leave the settings at their defaults and click OK.

*Illustrator CC offers a new feature that allows you to convert your text from area type to point type, and vice versa. Once type is established, select the text box with the Selection tool (▸) and select Type > Convert to Area Type or Convert to Point Type. To toggle between area and point type, double-click the extended handle to the right of the text bounding box.*

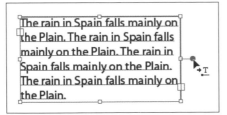

*Double-clicking the extended handle converts your text.*

**4**    Press Ctrl+A (Windows) or Command+A (Mac OS) to select all the text you just placed. In the Control panel, set the font to Myriad Pro Bold Condensed, and the size to **8 pt**.

**5**    Click the Fill color swatch in the Control panel and choose the White swatch from the swatch options to turn the text white. Choose Type > Change Case > UPPERCASE to make all the text uppercase.

**6**    Click once within the ingredients text, then click the Paragraph link in the Control panel at the top of your screen to reveal the Paragraph panel. Click the Justify with last line aligned left button at the top of the Paragraph panel to change the alignment of the text. Deselect the Hyphenation button.

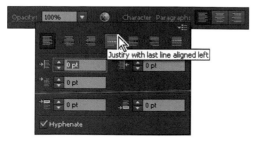

*The Paragraph panel allows you to change paragraph-level attributes.*

**7**    After formatting, the type might not fill the frame. To tidy things up, switch to the Selection tool (🡒) and drag the center frame handle at the bottom of the frame upward to reduce the frame's size.

*Resize the text frame by dragging one of the frame handles.*

**8**    Choose File > Save to save your work. Keep the file open.

## Formatting imported type

Next, you'll import some additional text that will appear on the back of the box, and apply additional paragraph formatting to the text.

**1**    Choose View > Fit Artboard in Window, or press Ctrl+0 (Windows)/Command+0 (Mac OS) to see the entire spread.

**2**    Choose the Type tool (T) from the Tools panel, then click and drag to create a large type area on the back of the box (the box panel on the right side of your screen.) As you did in the previous exercise, be certain that you create a new area for text by confirming that the cursor icon displays the I-beam with a dotted frame around the edges (⌶) before clicking and dragging.

**3** To precisely position the text area, open the Transform panel by clicking the Transform link on the far right side of the Control panel. Due to varying monitor resolutions, you might not see the Transform link. If you do not see this option, click the Panel Menu button in the Control panel and choose Transform to see the text or choose Window > Transform to open the Transform panel. Click in the center of the reference point locator (▦) to determine that all transformations are made relative to the center of the text area. Type **1148 pt** into the X text field, **425 pt** into the Y text field, **450 pt** into the W text field, and **550 pt** into the H text field.

*If you do not have the units of measurement set up for points (pts), the input measurement automatically converts to the equivalent value in the units that were last used.*

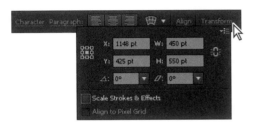

*The Transform panel allows you to precisely position and size objects in your document.*

**4**    Choose Type > Area Type Options. In the Columns area of the Area Type Options
dialog box, type **2** for the number of columns, **3 in** in the Span text field, and **.25 in**
for the gutter. Click OK.

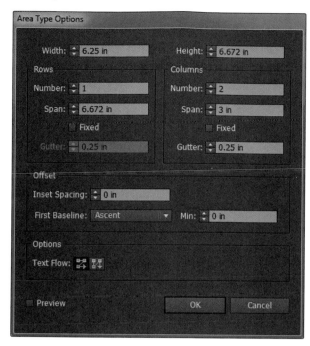

*The Area Type Options dialog box allows you create columns.*

**5**    Click in the top-left corner of the text area with your Type tool to place the cursor
within the frame. Choose File > Place. In the Place dialog box, navigate to the Text
folder within the ai08lessons folder and select the **nuts.txt** file. Make sure to check the
Replace check box and then click Place. In the Text Import Options dialog box, leave
the settings at their defaults and click OK. The text from the file appears within the
text area, displayed in two columns.

**6**    Place the cursor anywhere within the text and press Ctrl+A (Windows) or
Command+A (Mac OS) to select all the text. In the Control Panel, change the font to
Myriad Pro Regular 12 pt. Click the Fill color swatch in the Control panel and choose
White from the Swatches panel. This is just a temporary fix so that you can see the
selected text against the dark background.

**7**    Press Ctrl+(plus sign) (Windows) or Command+(plus sign) (Mac OS) twice to better
see the text. Highlight the first line of type in the text area (which reads, *The Benefits
of Nuts),* and in the Control panel, change the font to Myriad Pro Bold and the size to
18 pt, then press Enter or Return. Now the heading, *The Benefits of Nuts,* stands out
from the accompanying body text. In a later exercise, you will take these attributes
and turn them into a general style for headings.

**8**   Click within the first full paragraph of text which begins with, *Most people that you talk to...* Click the Paragraph link in the Control panel, and set the alignment to Justify with last line aligned left. Set the spacing after the paragraph to 8 pt, then press Enter (Windows) or Return (Mac).

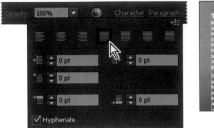 

*Adding space after a paragraph adds space without using an empty hard return in the copy.*

**9**   Choose File > Save to save your work. Keep it open for the next part of the lesson.

You have now formatted some of the text. In the next section, you'll create styles to streamline the formatting of additional text in your project.

## Space before and after

In the days of the typewriter, the method used to create additional space between paragraphs of text was to press the Enter or Return key twice; this was called a double-return. With a typewriter, a double-return is really the only way to accomplish this effect and might seem antiquated, but this practice is still in use to this day, even though there is a much better way.

You might be wondering why (and whether) it matters how you add space between paragraphs. The problem with using a double-return is that doing so completely limits the control that you have over the space between paragraphs. And if you need to adjust the spacing between paragraphs for any reason, the only option you have is to manually adjust that return by changing the leading and or point size of the return. This can be very time-consuming. The solution: space before and after. Using the space before and after options allows you to add space before and/or after a paragraph without adding empty returns between paragraphs. What's more, by including that spacing in a paragraph style, you can control the space between all paragraphs in your document with just a few clicks. It's the difference between a 30-second type change and a 30-minute type change.

### Paragraph and character styles

Illustrator allows you to save the formatting applied to text as a style. A style is a way to apply consistent formatting to text without having to do it manually. There are two types of styles that can be created in Illustrator: paragraph styles and character styles. As their names imply, paragraph styles can only be applied to an entire paragraph, while character styles can be applied to a single character or a range of characters in your text. Let's see how you can use these styles in your project.

1   With your **ai0801_work.ai** file still open, click once within the first line of text in the text area on the back of the box (*The Benefits of Nuts*). Choose Window > Type > Paragraph Styles to open the Paragraph Styles panel.

2   Click the panel menu button (⁃≡) in the upper-right corner of the Paragraph Styles panel. Choose New Paragraph Style. In the New Paragraph Style dialog box, type **Subhead** in the Style Name text field. Click OK. The new style you created appears in the Paragraph Styles panel.

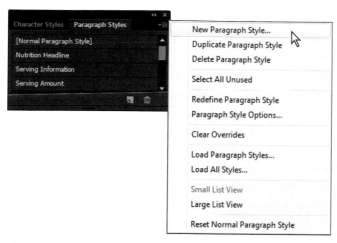

*Choose New Paragraph Style from the Paragraph Styles panel menu, and all the attributes of the text are automatically added to the style.*

3   Highlight the first line (*The Benefits of Nuts*) with your Type tool (T), and click Subhead in your Paragraph Styles panel to apply this style to the selected text. If a plus sign appears next to the Subhead style name, with the text still highlighted, Alt+click (Windows) or Option+click (Mac OS) again on the Subhead style.

*When you apply styles to text, if you see a plus sign (+) to the right of the style name, you might need to click the name of the style once more to clear that plus sign, or Alt | click (Windows) or Option+click (Mac OS) as you apply the style to cause your text to appear properly. A plus sign next to a style name indicates that the text contains overrides or doesn't match the definition of the style.*

4   Repeat steps 2 and 3, this time clicking inside the first full paragraph of text (beginning with *Most people...*) and naming the style **Body**. Don't forget to apply the Body style to the paragraph after you create it.

5   Finish styling the rest of the copy on the back of the box, applying the Body style to all the paragraphs and the Subhead style to the *Nuts Nuts Nuts* and *Only the Best!* headers.

*Don't worry about any misspelled words you see, you will address them later in this lesson.*

**6**    Click the Character Styles tab next to the Paragraph Styles panel to reveal the Character Styles panel. Find the line in the second full paragraph which starts with *In 2002...* and highlight the phrase *Physician's Health Study*. In the Control panel, change the font to Myriad Pro Bold Italic.

**7**    With the text still selected, click the panel menu button in the Character Styles panel, then choose New Character Style. In the New Character Styles dialog box, type **Body Italic** in the Style Name text field and click OK.

*Create a new character style named*
*Body Italic.*

**8**    Apply the Body Italic character style to the selected text by clicking the Body Italic entry in the Character Styles panel.

**9**    Now navigate to the bottom of the first column of text, highlight the word *FDA*, and apply the Body Italic character style to it as well. Repeat this process for the following sentence (which begins with *Scientific evidence...*).

*Apply the Body Italic character*
*style.*

**10**    Choose File > Save to save your work. Keep the file open for the next part of the lesson.

Now that your copy has been styled, maybe the subheads would look better in a different color. You could manually select each subhead and change its color, but it is much more efficient to edit the style now that all the subheads have been styled using a paragraph style.

## Editing styles

Styles can be edited directly from the Paragraph Styles or Character Styles panels.

**1**  Choose Select > Deselect, or press Ctrl+Shift+A (Windows) or Command+Shift+A (Mac OS), to deselect all the items in your document.

**2**  Click the Paragraph Styles tab next to the Character Styles panel to bring the Paragraph Styles panel forward. Double-click the Subhead style in the Paragraph Styles panel.

**3**  In the resulting Paragraph Styles Options dialog box, make sure the Preview check box in the lower-left corner is checked so that you can see the changes before you click OK. Click the Character Color entry on the left side of the dialog box and select the red swatch, named Die Tracing, from the list of swatches. You might need to reposition the Paragraph Style Options dialog box so that you can see the change in your artwork. Click OK.

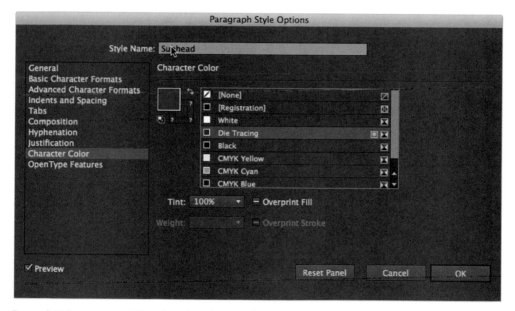

*Paragraph Styles are automatically updated throughout your document.*

**4**  Choose Select > Deselect, or press Ctrl+Shift+A (Windows) or Command+Shift+A (Mac OS), to deselect all the items in your document.

**5**  Double-click the Body style in the Paragraph Styles panel.

**6**   Click the Basic Character Formats entry on the left side of the dialog box. Choose Minion Pro from the Font Family drop-down menu and Regular from the Font Style drop-down menu. Click OK. This adjusts the style settings and all the fonts throughout the document to which the style is applied.

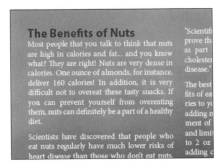

*The finished styles for body and headers.*

**7**   Press Ctrl+S (Windows) or Command+S (Mac OS) to save your work. Keep the file open.

## Loading styles

Styles can also be imported from other Illustrator documents. This not only allows you to maintain consistency across multiple related documents, but also saves you the time and hassle of recreating styles manually. In the following steps, you will import a style from another Illustrator file to reuse in your project.

**1**   From the Paragraph Styles panel menu (≡), choose Load Paragraph Styles. The Select a File to Import dialog box appears. Navigate to the ai08lessons folder and select the **styles.ai** file. Click Open and notice that a new style, called Vitamins, has been added to the Paragraph Styles panel.

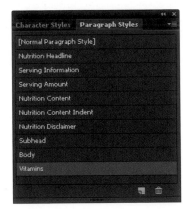

*By creating a paragraph style, you can efficiently apply character-based formatting to your text.*

**2**  Choose View > Fit All in Window, then zoom in on the lower-left corner of the front of the Nutz box, where there are vitamins and minerals listed in white text. Apply the Subhead paragraph style to the words *Vitamins* and *Minerals*. Apply the Vitamins paragraph style to the remainder of the text. If you see a plus sign next to the style after applying the style, highlight the word, then Alt+click (Windows) or Option+click (Mac OS) the style to remove the plus sign.

**3**  Choose File > Save to save your work.

## Text wrap

Illustrator allows your text, images, and objects to interact with each other by applying text wrap to objects, which causes the text to wrap around other objects in your Illustrator document. In the following steps, you'll apply text wrap to an image that is already in your document.

**1**  Press Ctrl+0 (Windows) or Command+0 (Mac OS) to fit the entire spread in the window, then press Ctrl+(minus sign) (Windows) or Command+(minus sign) (Mac OS) twice, at which point you'll see a single almond below and to the right of the spread.

*When you place an image in Illustrator, it is typically a square. The almond image is being silhouetted using a clipping mask, which gives it the proper shape of an almond.*

**2**  Activate the Selection tool (⬆) from the Tools panel. Drag the image of the almond so that it is on top of the two-column text on the back of the box (on your right). Resize the almond to approximately 50% by dragging a corner handle while pressing and holding the Shift key to keep its proportions intact.

**3**  Once the image is in the desired position and size, right-click (Windows) or Ctrl+click (Mac OS) on the almond image and choose Arrange > Bring to Front. Leave the image selected and choose Object > Text Wrap > Make. This applies text wrap to the selected image.

**4**  Press Ctrl+(plus sign) (Windows) or Command+(plus sign) (Mac OS) to zoom in on the almond image.

**5**    To adjust how closely the text wraps around the image, make sure that the image is still selected and choose Object > Text Wrap > Text Wrap Options. In the Text Wrap Options dialog box, check the Preview check box and increase the offset amount to 10 pt. Click OK.

*The Text Wrap Options dialog box allows you to adjust the distance that the text is offset from the edge of the image.*

**6**    Choose File > Save. Keep the document open for the next part of the lesson.

## Advanced techniques with text

Adobe Illustrator offers a variety of advanced tools for working with text. Let's explore some of those techniques now.

### Text on a path

In Illustrator, type can be applied to a path of just about any shape. You can use the Pen tool (✥), the Pencil tool (✐), or any of the shape tools to draw a path on which type can be applied. In the following steps, you'll add some text to a path that already exists on the box for a creative effect.

**1**    With your **ai0801_work.ai** file still open, zoom in on the curved path in the lower-right corner of the back of the box.

**2**    Click and hold the Type tool (T) in the Tools panel and choose the Type on a Path tool ( ). Click the far-left side of the path; this converts the existing path to a type path and allows you to enter and edit text on the path.

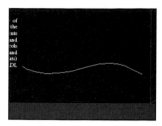

*Place your Type on a Path cursor at the end of the curved line to type along it.*

**3**    In the Control panel, click the Fill color swatch and select the white color from the Swatches panel. Change the font to Myriad Pro Bold Condensed, then type **17** in the Size text field, then press Enter or Return.

**4**    Type **Contains 14 Essential Vitamins and Minerals**. If the text does not fit completely on the path, choose Edit > Undo to remove the text and Edit > Undo again to remove the insertion point on the path. Repeat steps 2, 3, and 4.

*The text you entered.*

**5**    Press Ctrl+S (Windows) or Command+S (Mac OS) to save your work.

## Warping text

One of the great features of Adobe Illustrator CC is its ability to apply effects that distort and transform type in many ways, while keeping the text editable. This is advantageous in that it makes the process of editing or modifying text very efficient. Let's apply an effect to the NUTZ logo to enhance its appearance.

**1**    Press Ctrl+Shift+A (Windows) or Command+Shift+A (Mac OS) to deselect all objects in your document. Choose View > Fit in Window to see the entire box. Activate the Selection tool ( ) and click the word *NUTZ* on the front cover of the box.

**2**    Choose Effect > Warp > Bulge.

3   In the Warp Options dialog box, turn on the Preview check box so that you can see the changes to your artwork as you adjust the values in the dialog box. Make sure the Horizontal option button is selected and set the Bend to **75** percent. Click OK.

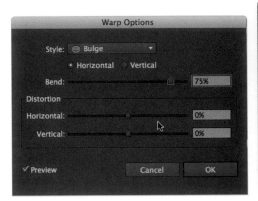 

*The Warp Options dialog box allows you to adjust the effect until you obtain the desired result.*

Now that you've applied the effect to the logo, you will add dimension by applying an image to the text of the logo.

4   Select the NUTZ text. Click the Drawing Modes button (⊞) located at the bottom of the Tools panel and choose the Draw Behind button.

5   Choose File > Place. In the Place dialog box, navigate to the Links folder inside the ai08lessons folder. Select the **sky.jpg** image and choose Place. A small image of a sky at dusk appears on the spread.

6   Reposition the photo behind the NUTZ logo and scale the photo so that it completely covers the logo. Do this by dragging one of the corner handles of the image using the Selection tool (▶) while pressing and holding the Shift key on your keyboard. The Shift key constrains the proportions of the image so that it doesn't become stretched.

7   Press and hold the Shift key and click the *NUTZ* text so that both elements are selected at the same time.

8   Click the Transparency icon (◐) in the dock on the right side of the workspace to open the Transparency panel. There is a preview of the selected items in the Transparency panel. If you do not see a preview, click the Transparency panel menu button (▾≡) and choose Show Options.

**9** Click the Transparency panel menu button and choose Make Opacity Mask. The text of the logo now masks out the photo everywhere except where the type of the logo appears.

*Choose Make Opacity Mask from the Transparency panel menu to make a mask out of the topmost element of your selection.*

**10** Select both the *NUTZ* and *Mixed* text using the Selection tool (k) by pressing and holding the Shift key on your keyboard. Choose Object > Group to group the elements.

**11** While pressing and holding the Alt (Windows) or Option (Mac OS) key on your keyboard, drag the grouped logo up to the top flap of the box. Pressing and holding the Alt/Option key makes a copy of the object that you are dragging. If necessary, increase the page magnification to more clearly see the work you are performing.

**12** Scale down the copied logo by pressing and holding the Shift key on your keyboard while dragging one of the logo's corner handles so that it fits on the left side of the box flap.

*Scale down the copied image.*

**13** Choose File > Save to save your work. Keep the file open.

For more information on how to use effects in Illustrator, see Lesson 11, "Using Effects and Transparency."

## Text in a shape

In addition to the type features that you applied earlier in the lesson, Illustrator gives you the ability to fit type inside various shapes. In the following steps, you will place some text inside a circle on the side of the Nutz box.

**1** Click the Draw Modes button (◉) at the bottom of the Tools panel and select Draw Normal.

**2**    Select the Ellipse tool by clicking and holding the Rectangle tool (□) in the Tools panel and choosing the Ellipse tool (○) from the list of options. You can also access the Ellipse tool by pressing the **L** key on your keyboard.

**3**    Navigate to the lower portion of the side panel, below the ingredients. Click and drag to draw a circle on the side panel of the box. Press and hold the Shift key while you drag to keep the shape proportional.

**4**    With the circle still selected, click and hold the Type tool (T) and choose the Area Type tool () from the list of options that appears. Click the path at the top of the circle to convert the circle to a shape that will accommodate area type.

*Create a circular text area*
*using the Ellipse tool.*

**5**    Your cursor is now inside the circle.

**6**    Choose File > Place and navigate to the Text folder inside the ai08lessons folder. Select the **benefits.txt** file and make sure that the Replace check box is checked, and then click Place. In the resulting Text Import Options dialog box, leave the settings at their defaults and click OK.

**7**    Press Ctrl+A (Windows) or Command+A (Mac OS) to select all the text within the circle. Using the Control panel, change the text Fill color to white.

**8**    Click the Paragraph link in the Control panel. When the Paragraph panel appears, select the Justify all lines button located at the top of the Paragraph panel.

9   At this point, you can adjust the text to fit the circle by changing the tracking values (◫) in the Character panel, as well as by adjusting the leading (⅍) and font size (T) of the type. Sample some of these options, experimenting with different values. Don't worry if it does not exactly fit for this exercise.

*Once you have text in a shape,*
*it can be edited using the Type tool.*

10  Once you've found a look that you like, choose File > Save to save your work. Keep the file open.

## Creating outlines

You might want to modify the character shapes of type itself. Illustrator CC offers two distinct ways you can do this to type that you have already applied to your artwork. One is called Creating Outlines and the other is a new feature called Text Touchup.

In these instances, you can't alter the shape of characters in live text, so you need to convert the characters to outlines. Converting type to outlines converts live text to editable paths in the shape of the original type. This is also useful when you are sending files to someone else and you don't want to include the fonts. Once type is converted to outlines, you no longer need the original font that was used to create the text. Converting text to outlines is generally not recommended with small body text, since it tends to cause the text to look slightly bolder than the original text. In the following steps, you'll see how text can be converted to outlines to create a headline on the front of the box.

1   Press Ctrl+Shift+A (Windows) or Command+Shift+A (Mac OS) to deselect all objects in your document. Click and hold the Area Type tool (▣) from the Tools panel and choose the Type tool (T), then click in an area on the front of the box to create a point type area. If necessary, increase the magnification using the Zoom tool ( ⌕ ) so you can more clearly see your work.

2   Type **A Heart Healthy Snack!**, then press Ctrl+A (Windows) or Command+A (Mac OS) to select all the text. In the Control panel, change the font to Minion Pro Bold Italic, then type **36** into the Size text field. Click the Fill color swatch and choose a red color from the Swatches panel.

**3**   Select the type using the Selection tool (⬆) and choose Type > Create Outlines. This converts all the selected type to outlines (paths).

*After converting the text to outlines, the text reveals the paths that make up the character shapes.*

**4**   When type is converted to outlines, all the text is grouped so that it moves and adjusts as a collective unit. Ungroup the text by choosing Object > Ungroup.

**5**   Using the Selection tool, drag a marquee around the word *Heart* to select only that word. Press the Delete key on your keyboard to remove the word.

In the next steps, you will replace the word *Heart* with a vector drawing of a heart.

**6**   Choose Select > Heart from the menu at the top of your screen. If you do not see the heart image, press Ctrl+(minus) or Command+(minus) twice to zoom out. In the Control panel, click the Fill color swatch and choose a red color from the swatches panel to fill the heart image.

**7**   Drag the drawing of the heart to the empty area of the text outlines where the word *Heart* used to be. Scale and adjust the drawing as you see fit by dragging the corner handle of the object and pressing and holding the Shift key. You might need to zoom in on the remaining text to the right of the heart to close the space and make it look more balanced. Once you finish adjusting the headline, use the Selection tool to select the heart and the text, then group them by pressing Ctrl+G (Windows) or Command+G (Mac OS).

**8**    To add a finishing touch to the headline, select it and choose Effect > Stylize > Drop Shadow. In the Drop Shadow dialog box, type **5 pt** for both the X and Y offsets and **4 pt** for blur. Click OK.

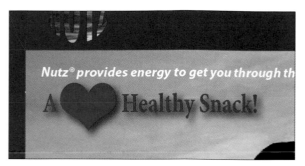

*Apply a drop shadow to the headline.*

## Text Touchup

Text Touchup, a new feature in Illustrator CC, allows you to manipulate individual type characters while still being connected to your font library, and preserving all of the abilities to edit the text afterwards. Individual characters can be rotated, horizontally and vertically scaled, and raised or lowered altering their baseline shift. They cannot, however, be altered by way of manipulating anchor points on a path. Characters still maintain their connection to the font library and would have to be converted to outlines for further alterations.

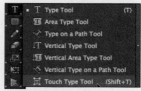

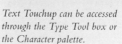

*Text Touchup can be accessed through the Type Tool box or the Character palette.*        *Individual characters can then be manipulated...*        *...and still remain editable.*

## Check spelling

Before you send your project to the client for approval, you should always perform a spell check to verify that there aren't any misspelled words in your document. The Check Spelling command in Adobe Illustrator CC compares the words in your document to a built-in dictionary and alerts you to any misspelled words.

**1**    Press Ctrl+Shift+A (Windows) or Command+Shift+A (Mac OS) to deselect all objects on your page. Choose Edit > Check Spelling to open the Check Spelling dialog box.

**2**   Click the arrow icon in the lower-left corner of the dialog box to display additional options. Leave both checkboxes in the Find section checked, and check the boxes in the Ignore section to ignore words that are all uppercase and words with numbers. This speeds up the process, since the nutrition label contains several of these instances. Click the Start button to begin the spell checking process.

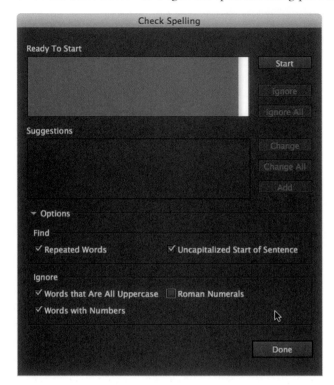

*The Check Spelling dialog box allows you to define the parameters that determine what Illustrator flags as problems.*

After clicking the Start button, the Check Spelling dialog box displays the errors that it finds in your document. Not all errors are necessarily spelling errors; some are repeated words and other miscellaneous errors. Some of these errors can be corrected by choosing an option offered in the Suggestions window in the middle of the dialog box. Illustrator displays the error at the top of the dialog box and also displays suggestions below it for correcting the error. You have the option of choosing Change, which changes the current error to the suggestion shown in the Suggestions window, or Ignore, which skips the currently flagged error.

**3**   Continue through the spell check by choosing either Change or Ignore, depending on the error. There are some misspelled words in the document, so as the spell checker flags them, change them to the correct spelling; other errors can be ignored. Make sure that when Illustrator flags the word *NUTZ*, you ignore it.

Just because a word is not found in the dictionary that Illustrator uses to spell check the document, it doesn't necessarily mean that the word is incorrect. For instance,

Spell Check finds the word *Folate*. Illustrator doesn't recognize this word even though it is correct. One way to handle this situation is to click the Add button on the right side of the Check Spelling dialog box. This adds the current word to the dictionary so that Illustrator will recognize the word from now on, and will no longer flag it as an error. The Add button is useful when dealing with proper nouns and people's names, especially when they appear more than once in a document or range of documents. By adding a word to the dictionary, Illustrator no longer considers it misspelled.

4   When you have completed checking the entire document, click Done.

5   Choose File > Save to save your work.

## Find and Replace

Imagine that this project is due to the client, and at the last minute, you realize that you omitted the ® symbol next to the NUTZ brand name, identifying it as a registered trademark. Fortunately, Illustrator provides the tool needed to fix this problem quickly. Let's see how easily this can be done.

1   Press Ctrl+Shift+A (Windows) or Command+Shift+A (Mac OS) to deselect all objects on your page. Choose Edit > Find and Replace to display the Find and Replace dialog box.

2   In the Find text field, type NUTZ (all caps). In the Replace With text field, type NUTZ (all caps) and then click the arrow to the right of the Replace With text field. From the list of options, choose Registered Trademark Symbol. This inserts an ® next to the word NUTZ in the Replace With text field. This is the character equivalent that Illustrator uses for the registered trademark symbol.

3   Click the Find button once to find the first location where NUTZ appears within your project, then click the Replace All button to replace all occurrences of NUTZ with the new text, including the necessary symbol. Adobe Illustrator notifies you that it made three replacements within your document. Click OK, then click Done.

4   Using the Text tool, remove the additional instance of the registered trademark from the text on the upper-left side of the front of the box.

5   Choose File > Save to save your document.

## Self study

To add a finishing touch to your document, draw a white rectangle encompassing all the text on the back of the box. Send the rectangle backward until it is behind the text. Now choose Effect > Blur > Gaussian Blur, set the radius at 8 pixels and click OK. Next choose Window > Transparancy and change the opacity to about 40 percent. This is a great effect that you can use to subdue the background and allow the type to stand out a little bit. If necessary, change the color of your text to see the effect better.

Practice applying text to various shapes that you draw in Illustrator. Use the Pen tool (◊) or the Pencil tool (✎) to draw a path, and then use your Type on a Path tool (✓) to add type to the shape. You can adjust how type is positioned on a path by dragging the center bracket, using your Selection tool, and moving it left or right along the path. You can even drag the center handle down and flip the text to the other side of the path. In addition, draw some closed shapes and practice placing text inside them to see the different effects that you can achieve.

Add different effects to the NUTZ logo to make it stand out a little more. See Lesson 11, "Using Effects and Transparency," for more on applying effects to objects. Try adding an outer glow to the logo, or even a drop shadow with various intensities. You could also experiment with other effects options in the Effects panel. You might want to remove the existing effect first by deleting it from the Appearance panel.

## Review

### Questions

**1** True or false: Effects can only be applied to type that has been converted to paths.

**2** If you wanted to put text that wrapped inside a given area of your artwork, would you use point type or area type?

**3** Which of Illustrator's features gives you the control needed to maintain consistency and control throughout a range of text in your document?

**4** If a word that Illustrator's dictionary doesn't recognize appears several times in your document, how can you stop Illustrator from flagging each instance of the word?

**5** Which panel in Illustrator shows you all the characters available within a given font?

### Answers

**1** False. Effects can be applied to live type and remain editable even after the effect has been applied.

**2** To put text wrapped inside a given area of your artwork, you would use area type. Point type doesn't wrap within a given area. Point type only wraps if you apply a hard or soft return to the type.

**3** Illustrator's feature that gives you the control needed to maintain consistency and control are character and paragraph styles.

**4** To stop Illustrator from flagging each instance of an unrecognized word, add the word to the dictionary by pressing the Add button in the Check Spelling dialog box. This makes the word a recognized word and prevents Illustrator from earmarking it.

**5** The Glyphs panel is the Illustrator panel that shows all the characters available within a given font.

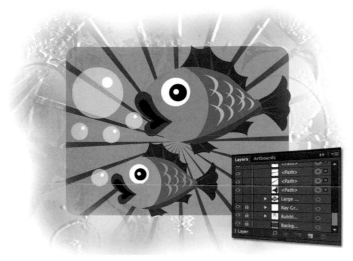

## What you'll learn in this lesson:

- Selecting items on a layer
- Locking and hiding layers
- Creating new layers
- Moving items between layers
- Organizing layers

# Organizing your Illustrations with Layers

*Complex illustrations with many components can make it more difficult to work with and select individual components. In this lesson, you will discover how to use Illustrator CC's Layers panel to organize and manage your illustrations.*

## Starting up

Before starting, make sure that your tools and panels are consistent by resetting your workspace. See "Resetting Adobe Illustrator CC Preferences" in the Starting up section of this book.

You will work with several files from the ai09lessons folder in this lesson. Make sure that you have loaded the ailessons folder onto your hard drive from the included DVD. See "Loading lesson files" in the Starting up section of this book.

### See Lesson 9 in action!

*Use the accompanying video to gain a better understanding of how to use some of the features shown in this lesson. You can find the video tutorial for this lesson on the included DVD.*

## Getting to know the Layers panel

Whether you deliberately work with layers or not, every time you create, import, or paste items in an Illustrator document, you are placing those items on a layer. The default layer that is in every new Illustrator document is called Layer 1. The order in which you add new elements to the document determines their arrangement on Layer 1. The latest additions appear on top of the earlier ones; this is called the stacking order. Just like stacking sheets of paper on your desk, the first one placed appears on the bottom of the stack and the most recent one placed is positioned on the top of the stack. The Layers panel allows you to select an item or items in an illustration, change their stacking order, show or hide them, and lock them. The following exercise will familiarize you with the Layers panel.

1   Launch Adobe Illustrator CC, if it is not already open. Choose File > Open. In the Open dialog box, navigate to the ai09lessons folder and select the **ai0901_done.ai** file. Click Open.

2   Visually, the artboard of this done file will remain the same as your start file, but, if you choose Window > Layers, you see that there are three named layers in this document. You will start with a one-layered document and add additional named layers, as well as take advantage of other layer tips and tricks, throughout this lesson.

3   You can choose to leave this finished document open, or choose File > Close to close it now. If you are asked to save this file, choose No.

4   Choose File > Open. In the Open dialog box, navigate to the ai09lessons folder and select the **ai0901.ai** file. Click Open.

5   Choose File > Save As. In the Save As dialog box, navigate to the ai09lessons folder and type **ai0901_work.ai** in the Name text field. Click Save, then click OK when the Illustrator Options dialog box appears.

6   Click the Layers button (⬛) in the dock on the right side of the workspace to open the Layers panel.

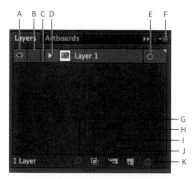

*A. Visibility column. **B.** Edit column. **C.** Selection color column.*
*D. Disclosure triangle. **E.** Target column. **F.** Panel menu.*
*G. Locate Object. **H.** Make/Release Clipping Mask.*
*I. Create New Sublayer. **J.** Create New Layer. **K.** Delete Selection.*

**7**  Click the visibility icon (👁) in the Visibility column to the left of Layer 1; all the items that reside on that layer disappear from the workspace. Click in the box once more to make the pieces visible again.

**8**  Click the empty box to the right of the visibility icon in the Edit column of the Layers panel. The padlock icon (🔒) appears. This locks all the items on the layer, making it impossible to select or edit them. Click the padlock icon again to unlock the items on the layer.

**9**  To the right of the padlock icon is the Selection Color column. The color listed in this column is the color assigned to identify the items on this layer. Each object on the layer will have its frame edges and bounding box appear in the layer color when the item is selected.

*When new layers are created, the layer colors are assigned in sequence down the list of Adobe system colors. There are 27 named colors to choose from, or you can select Other and specify additional color options. Layer colors can help you to visually categorize graphic elements at a glance. You can change the layer colors to fit your own visual system of organizing.*

**10**  To the right of the Selection Color column is the disclosure triangle. Click the disclosure triangle to see all the individual and grouped items (sublayers) that make up the illustration.

*Compound paths, while made up of multiple paths, show up as one item in the Layers panel. Masked items also appear as a sublayer in the Layers panel. The clipping mask and the clipped elements can be revealed by opening the disclosure triangle of the masked group.*

*Click the triangle to see the layers and sublayers.*

## Using layers to organize your illustrations

Now that you've been introduced to the Layers panel, you'll take a look at how you can use these tools to organize the different components of your illustration. This makes it easier to edit the illustration as it becomes more complex. First you will select items, change their stacking order, and then lock, hide, group, and rename them.

1   Make sure that the disclosure triangle next to Layer 1 in the Layers panel faces downward and that all the illustration's paths are displayed. Click the Click to Target icon (**o**) to the far right of any sublayer in the Target column. As you click each item's Target column, notice that the item is selected in your illustration. To select multiple items, press and hold the Shift key on your keyboard as you click in each corresponding Target column. To select non-consecutive items, press and hold the Control key (Windows) or the Command key (Mac OS) as you click in each corresponding Target column Deselect any items you have selected by pressing Ctrl+Shift+A (Windows) or Command+Shift+A (Mac OS).

2   Click the Click to Target icon (**o**) belonging to the sublayer named Bubble Group. This selects all the items on the Bubble Group sublayer and shows the items in the workspace with a light-blue bounding box. The Target column allows you to select items or groups of items directly from your Layers panel. Notice that a color box (**■**) now appears in the active selection column to the right of the Target column. This shows you that these items are selected in the Layers panel and on the artboard.

*The selection color box.*

**3**  With the Bubble Group sublayer still selected, click and drag the Bubble Group sublayer down in the Layers panel until you see a white line appear between the Ray Group and Background sublayers. Once you see the white line that indicates the stacking order position of the layer, release the mouse. The bubbles are now arranged beneath the rays in the illustration, but above the picture's background.

*Move the bubble layer.*

You have now changed the stacking order of those items in the illustration.

## Cloning artwork

If you are looking to replicate objects, try these techniques:

- An Alt/Option drag of a selected item on the artboard will *clone* it, leaving the original and quickly making a copy in the new position where you drag it.

- Press and hold the Alt/Option key and drag within the Layers panel to copy an item in the same X & Y position on the artboard, leaving the original and quickly making a new copy to wherever you drag in the stacking order.

- Choose Edit > Copy and then Edit > Paste in Front to paste the copied artwork exactly on top of the original artwork.

### Using the Layers panel to make selections

Now that you've seen how easy it is to select items in your illustration using the Layers panel Target column, you will use the Edit and Visibility columns to make selections without affecting the locked or hidden sublayers.

**1**  In the Layers panel, click the empty (Toggles Lock) box in the Edit column to the left of the Background, Bubble Group, and Ray Group sublayers to lock each of those layers. Click the visibility icon (👁) in the Visibility column to the far left of the Large Fish Group sublayer to hide the items on that layer.

**2**   Choose Select > All or use the keyboard shortcut Ctrl+A (Windows) or Command+A (Mac OS). Even though you instructed Illustrator to select all the items in the illustration, none of the locked or hidden items are selected.

*Items that are locked or hidden in the Layers panel are unaffected by the Select All action.*

**3**   Choose Object > Group. Notice that all the selected items are now in a new sublayer in the Layers panel, named <Group>. The new Group sublayer has its own disclosure triangle that shows you all the items that make up that group.

**4**   Double-click the <Group> sublayer's thumbnail in the Layers panel. In the Layer Options dialog box that appears, type **Small Fish Group** in the Name text field, then click OK. The Group sublayer is now named Small Fish Group in the Layers panel.

**5**   Click the visibility icon (👁) in the Visibility column of the Large Fish Group sublayer to turn on the layer's visibility, then click the padlock icons for the Background, Bubble Group, and Ray Group sublayers to unlock them.

**6**   Choose File > Save to save your work. Keep the file open for the next exercise.

## Creating new layers and moving items between layers

Now that you have grouped all the small items in your illustration, you will further organize them by creating separate layers for these grouped items. You will rename Layer 1 and create two new layers, one for each fish. You will then select the large and small fish separately, and move them each to their appropriate layer.

**1**   Double-click the thumbnail for *Layer 1* in the Layers panel. In the Layers Options dialog box that appears, type **Background Shape** in the Name text field to rename this layer.

You can also change the layer selection color, convert the layer into a template, lock a layer, show or hide a layer, make a layer non-printing, turn off a layer's preview, or dim a layer in this dialog box.

The Print check box in the Layer Options dialog box controls whether an image is included not just when output to paper, but also when exported to another file format. When this box is unchecked, the image is not included in the printout or export. In some export formats, like PDF, the layer controls are retained in the exported file. Depending on the exported file format, the non-printing graphic might be dropped from the resulting file. You don't want to make any changes now, so click OK.

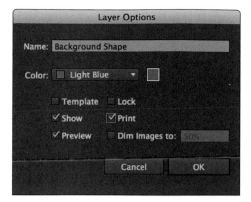

*The Layer Options dialog box.*

*Checking/unchecking the Lock check box in the Layer Options dialog box has the same effect as toggling the Edit column in the Layers panel. Checking/unchecking the Show check box here is the same as clicking in the Visibility column in the Layers panel.*

## Some items should be seen and not printed

Usually, if an item is visible on the artboard it prints, and if an item is NOT visible on the artboard it will NOT print.

So why would someone need to make a layer visible but non-printing? Unchecking the Print box in Layer Options is an opportunity to communicate to the on-screen user of the file without adding to the final artwork.

A great example would be production notes, which can be visual instructions or information about the output of the file that are not actually part of the graphic content. Perhaps there are sizing or positioning constraints established by the corporate graphic standards that should ride along with the company logo. Or, placeholder graphics can give directions about ad placement on a publication page.

**2**   To create a new layer, click the Create New Layer button (⬚) at the bottom of the Layers panel. A new layer named Layer 2 is now situated above the Background Shape layer. Change this default layer name to something more descriptive to keep your layers clearly organized. Double-click the Layer 2 thumbnail, and in the Layer Options dialog box, type **Large Fish** in the Name text field. Click OK.

3    You can avoid the extra step of having to change the default name of the newly-created layer by bringing up the Layer Options dialog box right away. It is more efficient to name your new layers at the same time as they are created. This time, press and hold the Alt (Windows) or Option (Mac OS) key on your keyboard while you click the Create New Layer button. The Layer Options dialog box appears, allowing you to name the layer as it's created. In the Layer Options dialog box, type **Small Fish** in the Name text field, then click OK. The Small Fish layer is listed above the Large Fish layer in the Layers panel.

*In Illustrator CC, you can name a layer directly in the Layers panel, without having to open the Layer Options dialog box: double-click the layer's name in the Layers panel, and when it's highlighted, type in a new name. Then press the Enter or Return key to accept the change.*

When you draw, place, or paste an object onto the Illustrator artboard, a new sublayer is created for it. This new sublayer appears in the active layer and at the very top of the stacking order within the active layer.

Rather than create layers in an arbitrary order and then have to arrange them as desired, you can build the stacking order of your graphics on-the-fly. Position new graphics and groups in the layer sequence as intended by targeting the layer immediately below where you want the new item to appear.

4    Select the Small Fish Group sublayer (listed beneath the Background Shape layer) by clicking the Click to Target icon (**o**) in the Target column. When the color box (**■**) appears in the active selection column, click and drag the square to the Small Fish layer and release the mouse. Once you release the mouse, the selection square and the color of the bounding box change to green to match the selection color of the Small Fish layer.

*Once an item is moved from one layer to another, its active selection square and bounding box color change to the selection color of the new layer.*

5    Click to target the Large Fish Group sublayer (also beneath the Background Shape layer heading), then click and drag its color box to the Large Fish layer. You have now transferred the features of one piece of a containing layer to its own separate layer.

**6** Choose File > Save, then choose File > Close to close the file.

## Suppressing the printing of a graphic

You can suppress the printing of a graphic in several ways:

- Hide the selected item. [Object > Hide > Selection]

- Hide the item's layer. [Click the visibility icon in the Layers panel]

- Uncheck the Print check box in the item's Layer Options. [Double-click the layer thumbnail, or access it through the Layers panel menu]

- Choose Template in the item's Layer Options (this also dims the view to 50% by default, but can be adjusted to 100% to make the item fully visible).

## Using Layers for versioning

Because layers can be selectively controlled, and easily made visible or hidden, they can be utilized to make versions of your artwork.

Show or hide layers to create comps showing optional design directions, or build multi-lingual packaging using different layers per translated language over a common base of artwork.

## Paste remembers layers

A convenient way to keep your layers organized is to use the Paste Remembers Layers option, accessed from the Layers panel menu. With this option, the clipboard holds not just the Illustrator artwork, but also information about the layer it originated on.

The Paste Remembers Layers option determines where artwork is pasted into the layer stack. When unchecked, the pasted artwork lands on whatever layer is active. When checked, artwork is pasted into the same layer it was copied from, no matter which layer is active in the Layers panel.

Having Illustrator keep track of the layers while you move items can let you work a little faster and more loosely, since you don't have to pay as much attention to the active layer while cutting and pasting items.

Where Paste Remembers Layers really gets powerful is working between documents. When pasting into a different file, artwork is automatically placed into a layer of the same name, and creates a new one of the correct name if necessary. It's a great way to transfer your carefully-named layer structure from one file to another, instead of ending up with lots of default-named layers.

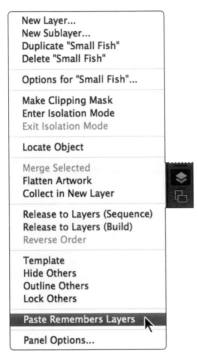

*The Paste Remembers Layers option (accessed via the Layers panel menu) retains information about where the layer artwork originated from.*

## Template layers

Template layers are locked, nonprinting layers that you can use to manually trace images. Template layers can come in handy when you want to trace a raster image by hand or you want to create artwork from the scan of a mock-up design. Template layers are dimmed so that you can easily see any paths you draw over the layer. When that illustration is placed in a layout application, like InDesign or QuarkXPress, the template layer does not show or print. Template layers can be created in two ways:

The most common way to create a template layer is upon import, while placing raster artwork into Illustrator as a template. Select File > Place. In the Place dialog box, select the artwork you want to import and select the Template check box in the lower-left corner; then click Place. The file is placed on a locked layer and is dimmed to 50 percent by default, so that you can clearly see any paths you draw over it.

The second way to create a template layer is to convert an existing artwork layer into a template. Double-click a layer name in the Layers panel. In the Layer Options dialog box that appears, select the Template check box and click OK. The layers icon in the Visibility column changes from the Visibility icon (👁) to a Template icon (🐟), and the layer is automatically locked. If you convert vector artwork to a template layer, it will not be dimmed.

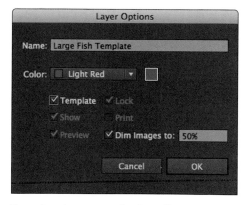

*Converting a layer to a template layer allows you to manually trace an image with ease.*

Try converting the Large Fish layer to a template layer and trace it manually, using any combination of the path and shape drawing tools.

## Self study

Create another layer for another sea creature. Import a raster graphic or scanned image as a template layer, and manually trace over it to build a multi-layered graphic contained within the sea creature layer group. Comp another version of the undersea artwork by hiding the Large Fish layer and showing the sea creature in the same position, so that only one is visible for output.

## Review

### Questions

1   How do you hide a layer?

2   How do you move an item or items from one layer to another?

3   How do you change the selection color for a layer?

### Answers

1   Do the following to hide a layer: in the Layers panel, click the visibility icon (👁) corresponding to the layer you would like to hide.

2   To move items from one layer to another, click or Shift+click the Click to Target icon (o) in the Target column of the items you want to move. Then click and drag the layer's color box to the new layer.

3   To change the selection color for a layer, double-click the layer's thumbnail in the Layers panel. Then, in the Layer Options dialog box, choose a new color from the Color drop-down menu.

## What you'll learn in this lesson:

- Creating and editing symbols
- Importing a symbol library
- Using the symbolism tools
- Editing nested symbols
- Saving symbol libraries

# Working with Symbols

*Symbols make it easy to repeatedly use objects throughout an Illustrator project and even across multiple documents. Symbols can be imported, transformed, colored, and edited with the tools built into the Symbols panel, which you will discover in this lesson.*

## Starting up

Before starting, make sure that your tools and panels are consistent by resetting your workspace. See "Resetting Adobe Illustrator CC Preferences" in the Starting up section of this book.

You will work with several files from the ai10lessons folder in this lesson. Make sure that you have loaded the ailessons folder onto your hard drive from the supplied DVD. See "Loading lesson files" in the Starting up section of this book.

### See Lesson 10 in action!

*Use the accompanying video to gain a better understanding of how to use some of the features shown in this lesson. You can find the video tutorial for this lesson on the included DVD.*

## Cleaning out the symbol library

When you create a new Illustrator document, the Symbols panel is automatically populated with a group of default symbols. These symbols are useful for certain applications, but not for the purposes of this lesson, so you will remove them and import a group of symbols provided in the ai10lessons folder.

1    In Adobe Illustrator CC, choose File > Open. In the Open dialog box, navigate to the ai10lessons folder and select the **ai1001_done.ai** file. Select Open. The completed lesson file appears. You can just take a look at the final project file and choose File > Close, or you can keep it open for reference throughout the lesson.

2    Choose File > Open. In the Open dialog box, select the **ai1001.ai** file, and then click Open. This Illustrator file contains a logo that you will use to create and modify a group of symbols.

3    Once the file opens, click the Symbols button (♣) in the dock on the right side of the workspace to open the Symbols panel. Click to select the first symbol in the panel, a red sphere.

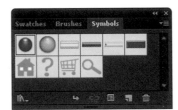

*Select the first symbol in the Symbols panel.*

4    While pressing and holding the Shift key, click the last symbol listed in the panel, a magnifying glass. This also selects all the symbols between the first and last options.

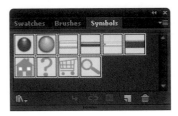

*Shift+clicking the last symbol selects all the symbols between the first and last symbols.*

5    Click the Delete Symbol button (🗑) in the lower-right corner of the Symbols panel to delete the default symbol library. A dialog box appears, asking you to confirm that you want to delete the selected symbols. Click Yes.

6    Choose File > Save As. In the Save As dialog box, name the file **ai1001_work.ai** and click Save. When the Illustrator Options dialog box appears, click OK. Keep the file open for the next part of the lesson.

# Creating symbols

Once you have cleaned out the symbol library, you can begin to populate it with your own creations. You can make symbols from any piece of art that you create in Illustrator, and even from embedded bitmap graphics. The only limitation is that you can't use linked graphics to create symbols. You have to embed them in order to create a symbol from them.

*You can embed a bitmap graphic into an Illustrator file by choosing File > Place, then selecting the image in the Links panel. After selecting the image in the Links panel, choose Embed Image from the Links panel menu.*

1   Use the Selection tool (⬥) to select the Fly Away logo with the double (white/black) outline in the document. Drag and drop it into the now-empty Symbols panel. The Symbol Options dialog box appears.

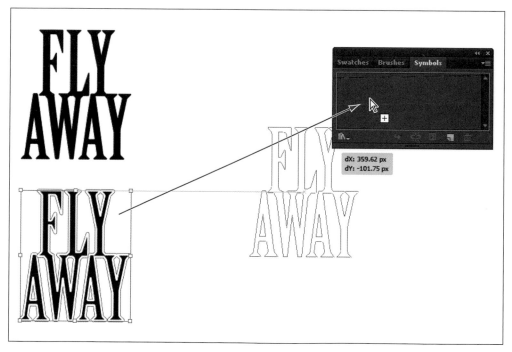

*Turn the Fly Away logo into a symbol by dragging it into the Symbols panel.*

2   In the Symbol Options dialog box, type **Fly Away Logo** in the Name text field. Choose Movie Clip from the Type drop-down menu, and click the center point of the Registration bounding box. Click OK.

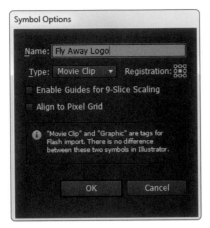

*Determine the settings for the new symbol.*

 *With the exception of the Name text field, the options in this dialog box deal with how the symbol will be treated if imported into Flash.*

The logo is now a symbol in your library, and the occurrence of the logo on the artboard is called a symbol instance. There is a parent-child relationship between the symbol in the library and its instances on the artboard. Any change to the parent, or master, symbol in your library cascades down to the children, or instances, on your artboard.

## Editing symbols

The logo symbol that you have is not bad, but it is a good idea to test out various color combinations before settling on a final one. In order to experiment with variations of the symbol you have created, you will add a new symbol instance to the artboard, make it editable, modify it, and use it to create a new symbol.

1   From the Symbols panel, drag the logo symbol onto the artboard, creating an instance somewhere away from the other graphics that are already in the document.

2   Click the Break Link button located at the top of your screen in the Control panel. This process, called expanding, breaks the link of the instance to the parent and makes the instance fully editable. You can also break a symbol by clicking the Break Link to Symbol button (⊞) at the bottom of the Symbols panel.

*Break the symbol instance's link to the master symbol to make the instance editable.*

**3** With the logo still selected, choose Object > Ungroup. When the symbol was expanded, it was automatically converted to a grouped object; ungrouping it allows you to edit the strokes around the text.

**4** With the logo still selected, click the Appearance button () in the dock to open the Appearance panel, and the double-click the Contents element. The Appearance panel tells you that you are working with a compound path that has a black fill color and two strokes, one white and one black, applied to it.

*The Appearance panel details the selected symbol's components.*

**5** In the Appearance panel, click the first listing, the white, 3-point outside stroke, to edit it. By selecting this listing, you've activated the color panel and stroke setting, both of which you can access and use to implement changes directly from the Appearance panel.

**6** Click the Stroke color swatch next to the Stroke listing, and from the resulting Swatches panel, select the swatch named RGB Yellow.

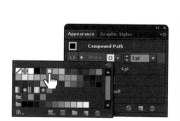

*The Appearance panel updates to reflect the change in the stroke's color.*

*The stroke is now yellow.*

**7** Click the Symbols button (♣) in the dock to reopen the Symbols panel. Using the Selection tool (▶), click and drag the new logo from the artboard to the Symbols panel.

**8**    In the resulting Symbol Options dialog box, type **Fly Away Logo Yellow** in the Name text field. Choose Movie Clip from the Type drop-down menu and select the center of the Registration bounding box. Click OK. You have just created another new symbol.

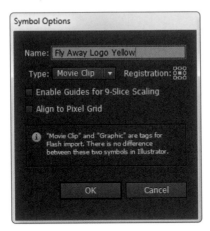

*Name this symbol Fly Away Logo Yellow.*

**9**    Choose File > Save to save your work.

# Importing a symbol library

Symbols can be imported either from dedicated symbol libraries or regular Adobe Illustrator files. This is done from the Symbols panel menu.

**1** In the upper-right corner of the Symbols panel, click the panel menu button (▾≡). From the menu that appears, choose Open Symbol Library > Other Library.

**2** In the Select a Library to Open dialog box, navigate to the ai10lessons folder and select the **butterflies.ai** file. Click Open. A new panel named *butterflies* appears in the workspace.

*A new butterflies panel full of butterfly symbols appears in your document.*

*Symbol libraries are saved in the native .ai format. If you want to edit a library, all you need to do is open the file, add or remove content there, then resave the file over itself. External libraries like the one you just imported are not editable in your local document. For this reason, you must move the library contents into your Symbols panel.*

**3** Make sure that both the butterflies Library panel and the Symbols panel are visible at the same time. In the butterflies Library panel, Shift+click the first and last butterflies to select the panel's entire contents.

*Select all the butterflies in the library.*

**4**   Drag the selected contents from the butterflies Library panel to the Symbols panel. Once they are in the Symbols panel, they are treated exactly like the symbols you created locally.

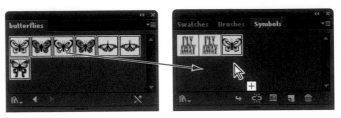

*Drag the symbols from the butterflies panel to the Symbols panel.*

**5**   Close the butterflies Library panel, then choose File > Save to save your work.

## Using the symbolism tools

As you have already seen, you can work with symbols by manually dragging them from the Symbols panel. Once they are on your artboard, you can move, rotate, and scale them individually using tools designed specifically for working with symbols. Now you will use these tools to add and manipulate symbols to create a new logo.

The symbolism tools allow you to create sets of symbol instances and then transform and edit them.

| ICON | TOOL NAME | USE |
|---|---|---|
| | Symbol Sprayer | The Symbol Sprayer tool can place multiple symbol instances, also known as a symbol set, on the artboard at once in a fashion like that of a spray paint can. You can edit symbol sets using the other symbolism tools. |
| | Symbol Shifter | The Symbol Shifter tool moves symbol instances. |
| | Symbol Scruncher | The Symbol Scruncher tool moves instances in a symbol set closer together or farther apart. |
| | Symbol Sizer | The Symbol Sizer tool makes symbols in a set larger or smaller. |
| | Symbol Spinner | The Symbol Spinner tool rotates symbols in a set. |
| | Symbol Stainer | The Symbol Stainer tool colorizes symbols in a set. |
| | Symbol Screener | The Symbol Screener tool adjusts the opacity of symbols. |
| | Symbol Styler | The Symbol Styler tool is used to apply a style from the Graphic Styles panel to symbol instances. |

1   Open the Layers panel by choosing Window > Layers, or clicking the
    Layers button (⬕) in the dock on the right side of the workspace.

2   So far in this lesson, you have been working on Layer 1, the default layer. Click the
    Create New Layer button (⬚) at the bottom of the Layers panel. This creates Layer 2.

*Create a new layer in the Layers panel.*

3   Double-click the thumbnail for Layer 2 in the Layers panel to open the Layer Options
    dialog box. In the Name text field, type **Logo**. Leave all the other settings at their
    defaults and click OK.

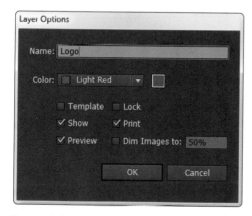

*Rename the layer.*

4   Click the visibility icon (👁) to the left of Layer 1 in the Layers panel to toggle off the
    layer's visibility. The document appears to be empty.

5   Open the Symbols panel by clicking its icon (♣) in the dock. Drag an instance of
    the Fly Away Logo Yellow symbol onto your artboard, then press Ctrl+Shift+A
    (Windows) or Command+Shift+A (Mac OS) to deselect the symbol instance.

*If you are not sure which symbol listed in the Symbols panel is the yellow logo, hold your cursor
over each symbol and a tooltip appears with the symbol's name.*

6    Click and hold the Symbol Sprayer button () in the Tools panel to view all eight available symbolism tools. To the right of the list of symbolism tools is a small tab. Click the tab to tear off these tools and turn them into a floating Symbolism Tools panel.

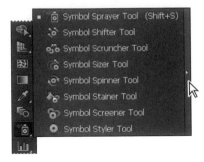

*Click the tearoff tab to the right of the list of symbol tools to turn them into their own floating panel.*

7    Double-click the Symbol Sprayer tool in the floating panel; this opens the Symbolism Tools Options dialog box. Change the intensity value to 3 by typing **3** into the text field. The intensity value specifies the rate at which the symbol sprayer creates symbols. Leave all other values at their defaults and click OK.

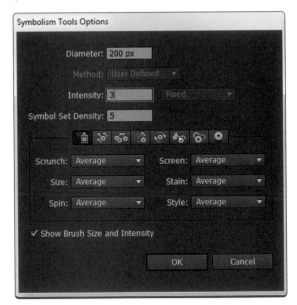

*Set options for your symbolism tools.*

*The symbolism tools all share a common options dialog box. The area at the top of the dialog box allows you to change the overall parameters of the brush that the tools use, while the field at the bottom of the dialog box allows you to view and edit the parameters of each individual tool.*

**8**    In the Symbols panel, select the butterfly symbol named butterfly_03. Notice your cursor, which now resembles a miniature spray paint can with a circular perimeter surrounding it. Click and drag from above and to the right of the logo symbol in a sweeping semi-circle around it. This creates a symbol set of multiple butterflies.

*Use the Symbol Sprayer tool to create a butterfly symbol set.*

*Depending on how long you press and hold your mouse, you might end up with more or fewer symbol instances than you see in the figure above. You can add symbol instances to the artboard by single-clicking where you'd like to add individual instances.*

**9** Double-click the Symbol Shifter tool (≋) in the floating Symbolism Tools panel. In the Symbolism Tools Options dialog box, type **8** in the Intensity value text field. This increases the strength of the tool and allows you to move the symbol instances more easily. Click OK.

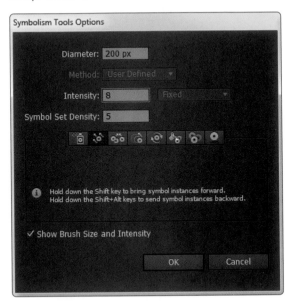

*Set the intensity of the Symbol Shifter tool to 8.*

**10** Use the Symbol Shifter tool to click and drag on the individual symbol instances, positioning the butterflies around the logo.

*Position the butterflies around the logo.*

**11**  Click the Symbol Sizer tool (☉) in the floating Symbolism Tools panel. Press and hold Alt (Windows) or Option (Mac OS) and click some of the butterflies to reduce their size. Keep some of the butterflies big and make some of them small so that each is a different size. The butterflies' size variations, dependent on how long you click and hold with the tool, can add to the overall appearance of the logo.

*Use the Symbol Sizer tool to adjust the butterflies' sizes.*

**12**  Click the Symbol Spinner tool (☉) in the floating Symbolism Tools panel. Click and drag on one of the butterflies. A red arrow appears along its body, demonstrating the angle and direction of the butterfly's readjustment. When you're happy with the butterfly's position, release the mouse. Do the same for the remaining butterflies, positioning them around the logo so that they appear as if they are all flying along the same path around the logo.

*Use the Symbol Spinner tool to set the butterflies flying on the same path around the logo.*

**13** Activate the Symbol Shifter tool again. Click and drag each symbol instance to move all the butterflies closer together. Don't worry if the butterflies overlap the logo.

*Move the butterflies closer together.*

**14** With the Symbol set selected, choose Object > Arrange > Send to Back. This positions the butterflies behind the logo.

**15** Activate the Selection tool (⬉) from the Tools panel and choose Select > All, or use the keyboard shortcut Ctrl+A (Windows) or Command+A (Mac OS).

**16** Click and drag the selected logo and symbol set into the Symbols panel. In the Symbol Options dialog box, type **Logo & Butterflies** into the Name text field and set the center anchor as the Registration point. Click OK. This creates a new symbol. This symbol is a bit different from the ones you have worked with previously, in that it has other symbols nested inside it.

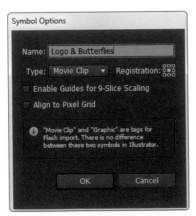

*Edit the symbol options for the logo.*

**17** Choose File > Save to save your work. Keep the file open.

## Editing nested symbols

Nested symbols form whenever you create a symbol using other symbol instances as components, as you did in the previous exercise.

**1** Double-click the butterfly_03 symbol in the Symbols panel. This places a temporary instance of the symbol on the artboard in Symbol Editing Mode. This mode exists to make it easier to edit the content of symbols and groups.

**2** Click the Fill color swatch in the Control panel and choose RGB Yellow, the same color you used to create an alternate version of the logo at the beginning of this lesson.

**3** Select the Eyedropper tool (✐) from the Tools panel. The Eyedropper tool can sample appearance attributes and apply them to other objects.

*The keyboard shortcut for the Eyedropper tool is I.*

**4** Alt+click (Windows) or Option+click (Mac OS) on all the gray-tinted interior parts of the butterfly wings, zooming in on the image if necessary.

*Color part of the butterfly yellow.*

**5** Click the Exit Symbol Editing Mode button (◂) in the gray area at the upper-left corner of the artboard to return to the main artboard area. The butterflies are now also yellow, reflecting the change you just made to the parent symbol.

**6** Choose File > Save to save your work.

## Replacing symbols

Another of Illustrator CC's cool symbol features is the ability to swap an onstage symbol instance with another instance from the Symbols panel.

**1** Switch to the Selection tool (➤) and double-click the instance of the Logo & Butterflies symbol on your artboard. You are now in Symbol Editing Mode.

**2** Select the Fly Away Logo on your artboard. On the right side of the Control panel, click the Replace drop-down menu. Select the first Fly Away logo from the menu. The original Fly Away logo replaces the yellow-bordered symbol instance on the artboard.

*Replace the yellow Fly Away Logo with the original one.*

**3** There is a variation of butterfly symbols in the library that might fit a little better with this new logo. Using the Selection tool, click the butterflies symbol set on the artboard.

**4** Select the butterfly_04 symbol in the Symbols panel. From the Symbols panel menu, select Replace Symbol.

*Replace the yellow butterfly you've used in the logo with another from the Symbols panel.*

**5**   The new symbol replaces the instances of the original butterfly. All transformations that had been made to the original symbols in your set carry over to the new symbol instances. Click the Exit Symbol Editing Mode button (◈) in the upper-left corner of your screen then save the file by choosing File > Save.

*The new butterflies & logo symbol.*

## Saving symbol libraries

You can save symbol libraries for later use in other documents.

**1**   Click the panel menu button (▾≡) in the upper-right corner of the Symbols panel. Select Save Symbol Library from the Symbols panel menu.

**2**   In the Save Symbols as Library dialog box, navigate to the ai10lessons folder and type **MySymbols.ai** into the Save As text field.

**3**   Click Save to save the symbol library.

**4**   Choose File > Save to save your work.

## Self study

Open a new file and import the **butterflies.ai** symbol library into it. Practice editing symbols from the library and creating new symbols from them.

Open the **cartoonbot.ai** file included in the ai10lessons folder. This is a robot character that has been divided into segments—arms, legs, a head, and so on. Practice creating symbols by converting each segment into a symbol.

## Review

### Questions

1. What types of objects can you convert into symbols?

2. Explain the relationship that exists between master symbols in the Symbols panel and their symbol instances on the artboard.

3. In what two places on the Illustrator interface do you have the option to replace one symbol on your artboard with another from the Symbols panel?

### Answers

1. You can convert almost all Illustrator objects—shapes, groups, even embedded bitmap graphics—into symbols. The only limitation is that you can't use linked graphics.

2. There is a parent-child relationship between the symbols in the Symbols panel and the symbol instances on the artboard. Any changes made to the parent object, either by editing it directly in the Symbols panel or by entering Symbol Editing Mode for the instance on the artboard, results in a change to the symbol instance on the artboard.

3. The two places on the Illustrator interface where there is an option to replace one symbol with another are:

   **a.** When a symbol is selected, the Replace option appears in the Control panel.

   **b.** When a symbol is highlighted and you click a new parent symbol in the Symbols panel, the Replace Symbol option is available in the Symbol panel menu.

# Lesson 11

## What you'll learn in this lesson:

- Applying effects using the Appearance panel

- Learning how to edit effects

- Saving graphic styles

- Applying a graphic style to a symbol

- Working with blending modes and opacity

# Using Effects and Transparency

*Using the Appearance panel you can gain more control over properties that are applied to individual components of an object, or the entire object. You can then store combinations of properties as graphic styles, making it easy for you to make updates, or apply the styles to other objects.*

## Starting up

Before starting, make sure that your tools and panels are consistent by resetting your workspace. See "Resetting Adobe Illustrator CC Preferences" in the Starting up section of this book.

You will work with several files from the ai11lessons folder in this lesson. Make sure that you have loaded the ailessons folder onto your hard drive from the included DVD. See "Loading lesson files" in the Starting up section of this book.

**See Lesson 11 in action!**

*Use the accompanying video to gain a better understanding of how to use some of the features shown in this lesson. You can find the video tutorial for this lesson on the included DVD.*

## Working with the Appearance panel and effects

In this exercise, you will work with a series of text logos for the masthead of an imaginary magazine called *Vector Magazine*. You will explore various looks for this logo using Illustrator's effects and working with the Appearance panel and graphic styles.

**1** Open Adobe Illustrator CC, if it is not already open. You will work with a pre-existing file in this exercise.

**2** Choose File > Open. In the Open dialog box, navigate to the ai11lessons folder and select the **ai1101.ai** file. Click Open.

**3** Choose File > Save As. In the Save As dialog box, navigate to the ai11lessons folder and type **ai1101_work.ai** in the Name text field. Click Save. The Illustrator Options dialog box appears. Leave the settings at their defaults and click OK.

You will be applying different effects to the same text in order to compare the results.

*The file contains a few example logos.*

**4**  Choose Window > Appearance or click the Appearance button (⬤) in the dock on the right side of the workspace to open the Appearance panel. The Appearance panel allows you to determine what the attributes of an object, group, or layer are. As your files become more complex, the Appearance panel becomes increasingly useful.

**5**  Choose the Direct Selection tool (⬚) from the Tools panel and select the blue and yellow hexagon to the left of the *Vector Magazine* text at the top of the page. When you select an object, group, or layer, the selection's attributes are listed in the Appearance panel. There are currently three attributes for this object: Stroke, Fill, and Default Opacity.

Attributes affect the look or style of an object but they do not affect the structure. Attributes in Illustrator are strokes, fills, transparency, and effects. The order in which the appearance attributes appear in the panel affects the appearance of the object. For an overview of the Appearance panel, review Lesson 1, "Adobe Illustrator CC Jumpstart."

*Attributes in the Appearance panel.*

**6**  Select the text to the right of the object. The appearance attributes for the text object are Characters and Default opacity.

**7**  Double-click the Characters attribute in the Appearance panel. Stroke and Fill attributes now appear listed in the panel, indicating that they are nested inside.

**8**  Select the Type: No Appearance attribute at the top of the Appearance panel to return to the default view.

## Applying effects

As you saw in the last exercise, the Appearance panel is a convenient location to view and modify the fill and stroke of an object. When you add an effect to an object, the effect name is also listed in the Appearance panel and you are able to modify the effect by double-clicking it.

**1**  Choose the Selection tool (▶) from the Tools panel and select the blue and yellow hexagon to the left of the Vector Magazine text at the top of the page. You will now add an effect to the entire object.

**2** Choose the Effect menu at the top of the workspace, and in the Illustrator Effects portion of the drop-down menu, choose Stylize > Scribble. The Scribble Options dialog box appears. Click and drag the window to the side, if necessary, in order to see the original object.

*Open the Scribble Options dialog box by choosing Effect > Stylize > Scribble.*

**3** Make sure the Preview check box on the left side of the dialog box is selected so you can view any applied effect in real time. The default scribble effect is visible and is currently being applied to the entire object.

**4** Choose Loose from the Settings drop-down menu. The appearance of the shape changes, based on the values of this preset. Click OK.

In the Appearance panel, note the order of the attributes. The top of the panel reads *Path* (which is the path of the hexagon), and listed below are Stroke, Fill, and Scribble. (You might need to extend the panel to see all of the attributes). These three attributes apply to the path. You will now apply the Scribble effect to the fill only.

**5**  In the Appearance panel, click the Scribble effect and drag it on top of the Fill. When you see the Fill attribute highlighted, release the mouse to apply the effect.

*Move the Scribble attribute onto the Fill attribute.*

The Scribble effect is now nested inside the Fill attribute (with the Opacity attribute) and the stroke is unaffected.

**6**  Click the arrow next to the Fill attribute to collapse it. You might find that collapsing these nested attributes makes it easier to understand the hierarchy within the Appearance panel.

**7**  Select the Stroke attribute in the Appearance panel. Click the arrow to the right of the Stroke box in the Control panel and select None (☒) to remove the 4 pt yellow stroke.

In a later exercise, you will learn how reordering effect attributes allows you to create more complex effects.

**8**  Choose File > Save to save your work.

## Editing effects

Once you have added an effect, it is fairly easy to modify it through the Appearance panel.

**1**  In the document window, click the object with the scribble applied to it to select it. If necessary, choose Window > Appearance or click the Appearance button (⬤) in the dock to open the Appearance panel, then click the arrow to the left of the Fill attribute to expand it.

**2**  Double-click the Scribble effect, and the Scribble Options dialog box appears. Any visible effect in the Appearance panel can be modified directly from within the Appearance panel.

**3**  Choose Sketch from the Settings drop-down menu.

**4**  Move the Path Overlap slider to the right, or type **7 pt** into the Path Overlap field. This demonstrates how the shape's original structure, including the anchor points, is constant; only the shape's appearance has been modified. Notice also that when you change one of the values in the Scribble Options dialog box, the Settings drop-down menu changes to Custom.

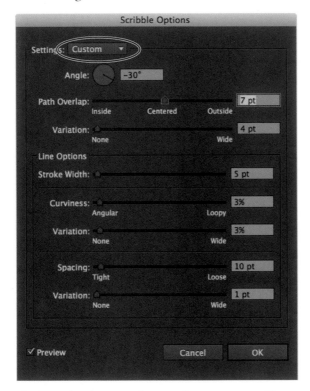

*The Settings drop-down menu changes to Custom once you modify a setting in the Scribble Options dialog box.*

**5** Click OK to close the dialog box and modify the effect.

## Scribble options

**Angle** controls the direction of the scribble lines. You can click any point on the angle icon, drag the angle line around the angle icon, or enter a value between −179 and 180 in the box. If you enter a value that's outside that range, the value is translated to its equivalent in-range value.

**Path Overlap** controls the amount the scribble lines stay within or extend beyond the path boundaries. A negative value constrains the scribble lines within the path boundary, and a positive value extends the scribble lines beyond the path boundary.

**Path Overlap Variation** controls the lengths of the difference in scribble line lengths relative to each other.

**Stroke Width** controls the width of the scribble lines.

**Curviness** controls the amount the scribble lines curve before they reverse direction.

**Curviness Variation** controls how the different scribble line curves are relative to each other.

**Spacing** controls the amount of space between scribble line folds.

**Spacing Variation** controls the amount of space between scribble line folds.

## Using graphic styles

In the previous exercise, you created and modified an effect, but what if you wanted to apply this same effect to different objects? For example, what if you were creating multiple headers in the same style as the first? Or perhaps you would like to use the same effect in another project. In all these cases you would use Illustrator CC's Graphic Styles feature.

Graphic styles allow you to reuse common styles within a single document or between documents. In this exercise, you will add a preset graphic style and then create and save your own.

**1** Using the Selection tool (◣), select the second *Vector Magazine* headline located above the title *Using Graphic Styles* (the second heading from the top of the document).

**2** Click the Graphic Styles button (▱) in the dock or choose Window > Graphic Styles to open the Graphic Styles panel.

**3** Click the panel menu button (▾≡) in the upper-right corner of the Graphic Styles panel and select Open Graphic Style Library, then choose Type Effects. The Type Effects panel appears with a series of thumbnails representing the various type styles. Illustrator CC comes pre-installed with a number of Graphic Style Libraries.

**4** Click the panel menu button of the Type Effects panel and choose Large List View. This allows you to view the names of the graphic styles, as well as the styles' corresponding thumbnails.

**5** Scroll down to select the Shadow style, and the appearance of the type changes to a white fill with a gray shadow. This is an example of a graphic style preset. The original orange color of your text has been overwritten, since the graphic style's fill color was saved as white. Close the Type Effects panel.

**6** Click the Appearance button () in the dock or click the Appearance tab to open the Appearance panel, and scroll down if necessary to see the two fill colors and the Shadow effects that make up the Shadow text style. While many of the preset styles in Illustrator are fairly sophisticated, they often will not match your project. While it is possible to modify graphic styles, it is usually more efficient to create your own. You will now do just that.

*The Appearance panel with updated attributes.*

## Creating and saving graphic styles

Creating your own graphic styles gives you the most flexibility and allows you to easily reuse your own assets. In this exercise, you will add an extra fill and the transform effect to create a custom outline style for your logo.

**1** Select the third Vector Magazine headline (the one above the *Creating and Saving Graphic Styles* title).

**2** Click the panel menu button (≡) in the Appearance panel and choose Add New Fill. By default, the fill is black. Because this new fill is located above the content, it overrides the original orange color. You will now reorder the attributes, placing the new fill below the Characters attribute. Note that there is also a Stroke attribute of *None* that was automatically added in the last step. When you add a new fill, a stroke is necessary as well.

**3**     Click and drag the black fill so that it is below the Characters attribute and the headline's fill reverts to orange. Reordering appearance attributes is very similar to the way you reorder layers in Illustrator. The attributes closer to the top are displayed first. You will now add an effect to this new fill to create an outlined appearance.

*Re-order the attributes in the Appearance panel.*

**4**     Click to the right of the new black fill to select it. From the bottom of the Appearance panel, choose Effect > Path > Offset Path. The Offset Path dialog box appears. The value for the Offset should be 10 pt (which is the default). If it is not, type **10** in the Offset text field. Select the Preview check box to see the effect.

**5**     Choose Round from the Joins drop-down menu and click OK.

**6**     In the Appearance panel, notice the Offset Path effect listed under the Fill attribute. Select the Fill attribute and click the built-in color swatch to see the color options. Select the yellow swatch in the top row, CMYK Yellow.

**7**     Click the Graphic Styles button (⬚) in the dock to open the Graphic Styles panel. Alt+click (Windows) or Option+click (Mac OS) the New Graphic Style button (⬚) at the bottom of the panel. When the Graphic Style Options dialog box appears, type **VM Style Yellow Outline** in the Style Name text field and click OK.

*The Graphic Style Options dialog box.*

**8**     Notice the last thumbnail in the Graphic Styles panel. The style you just created is listed last and is ready to be used on other objects.

## Applying and modifying graphic styles

Now that you have created a graphic style, you can apply that style to objects, groups, and even entire layers. Additionally, you can share graphic styles between documents.

**1** Select the smaller *Vector Magazine* headline, located at the bottom of the document. You will now apply and modify the graphic style you created in the last exercise.

**2** Select the *VM Style Yellow Outline* style in the Graphic Styles panel. For obvious reasons, the effect doesn't work when applied to a smaller object. However, it's easy to modify the size using the Appearance panel.

**3** Click the Appearance button ([icon]) in the dock, or click the Appearance tab, if necessary, to open the Appearance panel. If necessary, click the arrow to the left of the Fill attribute to expand it and double-click the Offset Path effect to open the Offset Path dialog box. Highlight the value in the Offset text field, then type **2 pt**.

*The Offset Path dialog box.*

**4** Click OK to apply the change.

**5** Choose File > Save to save your work.

## Working with object transparency

If you have worked with Illustrator or other image editing applications before you might have worked with transparency (also called opacity). Objects in Illustrator are 100 percent opaque by default, meaning that the fill and stroke of an object cover underlying objects. Reducing the opacity of an object reveals the underlying objects and can be used to create interesting layered effects. As you have seen in this lesson, objects in Illustrator can have multiple attributes in the Appearance panel, such as the extra Fill attributes and the Offset Path effect in the previous exercise. These attributes can be selected and their transparencies independently controlled using the Appearance panel. For this exercise, it might be useful to undock both the Appearance and Transparency panels so they are easily accessible.

**1** Select the *VM* logo at the very bottom of the document. Click the Graphic Styles button ([icon]) in the dock to open the Graphic Styles panel.

**2** Select the *VM Style Yellow Outline* graphic style you created in the previous exercise to apply it to the *VM* logo.

3    Click the Appearance button () in the dock or click the Appearance tab to open the Appearance panel. The attributes from your graphic style have been applied.

4    Choose Window > Transparency or click the Transparency button (●) in the dock to open the Transparency panel. The opacity value is 100 percent.

5    Highlight the value in the Opacity text field, type **30**, then press Enter (Windows) or Return (Mac OS). The entire object is now set to 30 percent opacity. Notice that the colored square behind the type now shows through. Additionally, the opacity value of 30 percent is visible in the Appearance panel.

*Change the opacity in the Transparency panel.*

6    Click inside the Opacity text field and press the up arrow on your keyboard. The opacity value begins to increase by 1 percent increments. Stop when you reach 50 percent. Press and hold the Shift key and press the up arrow; the value now increases by 10 percent. Stop increasing the value when you get to 100 percent, the original opacity.

## Working with multiple opacities

You can also control each of an object's many attributes independently, which gives you precise control over the object's appearance.

1    Select the *VM* logo, if it is not already selected. Open the Appearance panel and double-click the Characters attribute. This expands the characters, allowing you to view and modify the fill and stroke of the text object. Set the Fill color of the text to the first orange swatch in the second row of the Swatches panel.

*Text is different from other Illustrator objects such as shapes. Because a single word is composed of multiple characters, Illustrator nests the Fill, Stroke, and Transparency attributes inside the Characters attribute.*

2    Click once on Opacity (the default attribute at the bottom of the Appearance panel) to open the Transparency panel, then click inside the Opacity field. Press and hold the Shift key and press the down arrow until the value is 50 percent. Press Enter (Windows) or Return (Mac OS).

3    In the Appearance panel, select the Type attribute listed at the top to return to the standard attribute list. The orange fill of the text is set to 50 percent but the yellow fill still has its default 100 percent opacity.

4   Select the Fill attribute in the Appearance panel. Open the Transparency panel, highlight the value in the Opacity text field, type **20**, then press Enter (Windows) or Return (Mac OS). This fades the yellow fill and the offset effect to 20 percent, while the fill of the characters remains at 50 percent.

5   In the Appearance panel, click the arrow to the left of the Fill attribute and scroll down if necessary; notice the opacity is set to 20 percent. Click the arrow again to hide the Fill attributes.

*The Appearance panel reflects the opacity that was set.*

6   Click once on the word Opacity at the bottom of the Appearance panel and notice that the opacity is still set to 100 percent. Change the value to 75%, then press Enter (Windows) or Return (Mac OS). The entire object now fades. There are three levels of opacity in this object: the opacity of the characters themselves, the opacity of the separate yellow fill and effect, and the opacity of the entire object.

7   Choose File > Save to save your work.

## Working with blending modes

Blending modes are another feature you might be familiar with from other applications, particularly Photoshop. Blending modes let you change the ways in which the objects' colors blend with the colors of underlying objects. When a blending mode is applied to an object, the effect of the blending mode is seen on any objects that lie beneath the object's layer or group. Like opacity, you can control the blending modes of the separate attributes in an object.

1   Using the Selection tool, click to select the blue and yellow object in the bottom-right corner of the document. Open the Appearance panel. This object has a yellow stroke of 4 points and a blue fill. You will now apply a blending mode to this object. First, you will magnify your view of the object. This will help you to better understand blending modes.

**2**  Select the Zoom tool (🔍) from the Tools panel and click the object until the magnification is 300 percent. The magnification value is listed in the document's title bar, and in a drop-down menu in the lower-left corner of the workspace.

**3**  Click the Transparency button (◐) to open the Transparency panel. Choose Darken from the Blending mode drop-down menu. The hexagon blends with the background behind it.

*Choose Darken from the Blending mode drop-down menu.*

Understanding blending modes is easier when you use the following terminology: the *blend color* is the original color of an object; in this case, the yellow stroke and blue fill. The *base color* refers to the underlying color(s); in this case, the maroon and gray. The *resulting color* is how it appears to the eye.

For specific details on the various blending modes, refer to the Transparency and Blending Modes section in the Painting section of the Illustrator CC Help Viewer.

**4**  Choose Normal from the Blending mode drop-down menu in the Transparency panel to return the object to its original state.

**5**  Return to the Appearance panel and select the Stroke attribute. Open the Transparency panel again and choose Multiply from the drop-down menu. Notice how the stroke now interacts with not only its background, but also the fill color. This is because it is located above the fill in the hierarchy of the Appearance panel.

**6** In the Appearance panel, click and drag Stroke (in the list) below the Fill. Notice the change in the hexagon's coloring. Since the stroke is now below the fill, it is only blending with the underlying colors.

*Move the Stroke attribute beneath the Fill attribute.*

**7** Select the Fill attribute, and in the Transparency panel, choose Overlay from the Blending Mode drop-down menu. Because the fill is above both the stroke and the underlying colors, it blends with both.

## Saving and importing graphic styles

Earlier in the lesson, you created the *VM Style Yellow Outline* graphic style. You can apply that style to objects, groups, and even entire layers. You will apply the style to groups and layers shortly, but first you will learn how to share graphic styles between documents.

**1** Press Ctrl+Shift+A (Windows) or Command+Shift+A (Mac OS) to deselect everything in the document.

**2** Open the Graphic Styles panel. Ctrl+click (Windows) or Command+click (Mac OS) on all the default graphic styles except the *VM Style Yellow Outline* style.

**3** With the default styles selected, click the Delete Graphic Style button (🗑) at the bottom of the Graphic Styles panel. When the warning message appears, click Yes. You are deleting these styles because you do not want them to be saved as part of your new Graphic Style library.

**4** Click the panel menu button (▾≡) in the upper-right corner of the Graphic Styles panel and choose Save Graphic Style Library.

The Save Graphic Styles as Library dialog box appears. Normally, you are directed to save libraries in your system folder. For this exercise, navigate to the ai11lessons folder. In the Name text field, type **ai1101_styles.ai** and click Save.

**5** Choose File > Save to save your work, then choose File > Close.

**6** Choose File > Open. In the Open dialog box, navigate to the ai11lessons folder and select the **ai1102.ai** file. Click Open.

7    Choose File > Save As. In the Save As dialog box, navigate to the ai11lessons folder
     and type **ai1102_work.ai** in the Name text field. Click Save. When the Illustrator
     Options dialog box appears, leave the settings at their defaults and click OK. You will
     now import the Graphic Style library you just saved.

8    Click the Graphic Styles button in the dock (⧉) to open the Graphic Styles panel.
     Click the panel menu button and choose Open Graphic Style Library > Other Library.
     The Select a library to open dialog box appears. Navigate to the ai11lessons folder,
     select the **ai1101_styles.ai** file, then click OK (Windows) or Open (Mac OS). The
     **ai1101_styles.ai** graphic styles open in a separate panel.

## Applying graphic styles to layers and symbols

In addition to applying graphic styles to a single object, you can also apply them to all
objects in a layer. In this example, there are three different examples of the same logotype,
and you are interested in seeing how the same effect looks on each of them.

1    Click the Layers button (▧) in the dock to open the Layers panel. Click in the empty
     area just to the right of the Click to Target button (○) to the right of the *Three logos*
     layer name to target the entire layer. All three objects on the artboard are on the same
     layer and are automatically selected.

*Click where you see the blue dot to target*
*and thus apply attributes to the entire layer.*

2    Select the VM Style Yellow Outline style from the ai1101_styles panel. All three
     objects now have the same style applied to them.

3    Choose Window > Symbols or click the Symbols button (♣) in the dock to open the
     Symbols panel. From the default group of symbols, click and drag the Cloud symbol
     onto the artboard. Notice that the graphic style is automatically applied to the cloud
     symbol instance you just added to the document. Since you targeted the entire layer,
     all objects on the layer with a graphic style applied inherit the style's properties.

     If you want to add a new object without the graphic style, the best idea is to place it
     on a new layer. In this case, you will remove the graphic style from the layer and then
     reapply it to the three logos as a group.

**4** Open the Appearance panel and select the Layer: VM Style Yellow Outline attribute at the top of the panel to select all the objects on your artboard. At the bottom of the Appearance panel, click the Clear Appearance button (⦸) to remove the graphic style.

*Click the Clear Appearance button.*

**5** Using the Selection tool, click anywhere in the background of the document to deselect the objects. Place your cursor above the three logos, then click and drag downwards making a selection marquee that crosses into them. Release to select them (but not the cloud illustration).

**6** Click the VM Style Yellow Outline graphic style in the ai1101_styles panel to apply it to the group of three logos.

**7** Choose File > Save to save your work, then choose File > Close.

# Self study

You can create unique graphic styles for your projects by combining combinations of effects, fills, strokes, and transparencies. Experiment with the following combinations; when you find ones that you like, be sure to save them into a library for reuse.

**1** Open a new Graphic Style library in the Graphic Style panel. The Image Effects and Artistic Effects libraries are good places to start. Apply a complex graphic style preset to an object and break down the way it was created by looking at the order and properties of the attributes in the Appearance panel. Reverse-engineering the Illustrator CC presets is an excellent way to learn useful combinations for your own projects.

**2** Create a graphic style that uses a gradient as a fill color. Applying this graphic style to rectangles or circles will allow you to make buttons for the Web, for example. Also try applying gradients to text for interesting effects, being sure to save the graphic style.

**3** Create a bull's-eye graphic. Use a basic circle shape with a large stroke. Add multiple strokes using the Appearance panel and apply the Transform effect, increasing the horizontal and vertical scale as necessary.

# Review

## Questions

**1** What are the attributes of an object and where are they located in Illustrator?

**2** After you add an effect to an object, what are the steps you need to take to modify the effect?

**3** What are graphic styles? Name at least one advantage and disadvantage to using preset graphic styles.

**4** True or False: The attributes of an object in Illustrator can have multiple levels of transparency.

**5** How are graphic styles shared between documents?

## Answers

**1** The attributes of an object can be broken down into four categories: Fill attributes, Stroke attributes, Transparency attributes, and Effects attributes. These attributes are editable and are located in the Appearance panel, where they can also be modified.

**2** You can edit an effect by double-clicking the effect name in the Appearance panel. Double-clicking the effect name opens an effect dialog box, allowing you to make changes.

**3** Graphic styles are combinations of attributes that have been saved into a library. An advantage of graphic styles is the ability to quickly apply a complex style to an object or multiple objects. A disadvantage to using preset styles is that the style might not match the design of your project.

**4** True. An object in Illustrator, such as a circle, might have attributes such as a stroke, a fill, and an applied effect. The transparency of these attributes can be controlled independently of each other. Additionally, each of the attributes has a blending mode that can be controlled.

**5** After you create a custom graphic style, you can save it by clicking the panel menu button in the Graphic Styles panel and choosing Save Graphic Style Library. In another document, choose Open Graphic Style Library > Other Library from the Graphic Styles panel menu and select the custom library. Once this library is available in the new document, you can use the graphic styles.

## What you'll learn in this lesson:

- Saving native Illustrator files

- Saving a file in EPS format for use in layout applications

- Saving a file as a PDF for distribution or review

- Saving a file for use on the Web

# Exporting and Saving Files

*In this lesson, you will re-create a logo and then save and export the logo in a variety of different ways for use in print and online. You will save it as an Illustrator file, a PDF, and as a Flash animation.*

## Starting up

Before starting, make sure that your tools and panels are consistent by resetting your workspace. See "Resetting Adobe Illustrator CC Preferences" in the Starting up section of this book.

You will work with several files from the ai12lessons folder in this lesson. Make sure that you have loaded the ailessons folder onto your hard drive from the included DVD. See "Loading lesson files" in the Starting up section of this book.

### See Lesson 12 in action!

*Use the accompanying video to gain a better understanding of how to use some of the features shown in this lesson. You can find the video tutorial for this lesson on the included DVD.*

## Saving using the AI file format

The default Adobe Illustrator file format saves all the data needed to edit and work with your Illustrator documents. Layers, symbols, swatches, and graphic styles are all included when you save a file in the .ai format, and the file's contents remain fully editable.

1   In Illustrator CC, choose File > Open. In the Open dialog box, navigate to the ai12lessons folder, and from the additional_files folder, select **ai1201.jpg**. Click Open. The file that opens is a low resolution JPEG that you will be re-creating. The first thing you should do is save it as a native .ai file, then you can start to modify it.

2   Choose File > Save As. In the Save As dialog box, navigate to the ai12lessons folder and type **ai1201_work.ai** in the Name text field. Click Save. The Illustrator Options dialog box appears.

   The dialog box is divided into four editable sections: Version, Fonts, Options, and Transparency. Make sure that the Version drop-down menu is set to Illustrator CC. This menu allows you to set the version of Illustrator with which your files are compatible. Choosing an older version of Illustrator from this drop-down menu is called saving a legacy file. It is important to remember that legacy files do not support all the features of the current version of Illustrator.

3   Make sure that the Fonts text field is set to 100%. The Fonts area specifies when to embed the entire font as opposed to only the characters that are used in your document. If a font has 1000 characters and you only use 20 of them in your file, it is usually not worth using up the extra file space to include the entire font in your document. This file does not use any text, so leave this option unchanged.

4   Leave the checkboxes in the Options section at their defaults.

| ADJUSTMENT | USE |
| --- | --- |
| Create PDF Compatible File | Saves a PDF representation of the document in the Illustrator file. This option is used to make Illustrator compatible with other Adobe applications. |
| Include Linked Files | Embeds files that are linked to the artwork. If your document does not use any linked files then this option is grayed out. |
| Embed ICC Profiles | Embeds the color profile that Illustrator was using when your file was created and creates a color-managed document. |
| Use Compression | Uses lossless compression to compress the data in the Illustrator file, shrinking the Illustrator file size without sacrificing image quality. |
| Save each artboard to a separate file | Creates a separate Illustrator file for each artboard. If multiple artboards are not used, this option is grayed out. |

*By default, the Create PDF Compatible File and Use Compression options will be selected.*

*The transparency section is grayed out unless you are saving to a version of Illustrator prior to Illustrator 9. When active, this area allows you to determine whether transparent areas of your document are discarded (to preserve the editibility of document paths) or maintained (to preserve the document's appearance).*

**5**   Click OK to save your new Illustrator file. Keep it open for the next part of the lesson.

## Saving an illustration with layers

In this exercise, you will create a logo using the transform effect, then you will make three different versions of the logo on separate layers. Later on, you will generate a PDF that contains layers that you will mail to a fictitious client.

### Making a template layer

The first thing you will do is make a template layer. A template layer automatically locks the layer, and dims the image to 50%. This makes it easier for you to rebuild a new logo over it, because of the color difference and the fact that when the layer is locked, it means that you can't select the logo and move it by accident.

**1**   Open the Layers panel by choosing Window > Layers or by pressing the Layers button (⬛) in the dock on the right side of the workspace.

**2**   Double-click the thumbnail for *Layer 1* in the Layers panel. The Layer Options dialog box appears. In the Name text field, type **template** to rename the layer, then select the Template check box to automatically convert this layer to a template layer. Click OK.

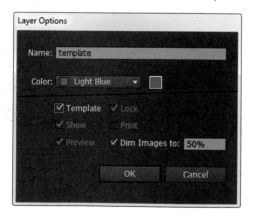

*Converting a layer into a template layer.*

You can now make a new layer on which you can work.

**3**   In the Layers panel, click the panel menu button (•≡) and select New Layer from the list. When the Layer Options dialog box appears, type **working** in the Name text field and click OK.

4    From the Tools panel, select the Ellipse tool (○). The Ellipse tool might be hidden under the Rectangle tool (□). If this is the case, click and hold the Rectangle tool to reveal the other hidden tools and choose the Ellipse tool.

     The first circle you will draw is the bottom-left circle. You will then use the Transform Effect to make all the other circles.

5    In the Control panel at the top of the workspace, choose None (⊘) from the Fill drop-down menu and make sure that the Stroke is set to black.

6    Start by pressing and holding the Alt (Windows) or Option (Mac OS) key to make your reference point centered, then click in the center of the bottom-left circle and drag down and to the right to make the circle bigger. Don't let go of the mouse.

7    While still pressing and holding the Alt/Option key, press and hold the Shift key to make your ellipse a perfect circle.

8    If the circle is not aligned, you can press and hold the spacebar to move the object you are drawing.

9    Now you can let go of the mouse. If necessary, use the Selection tool (▶) from the Tools panel to move the circle into place.

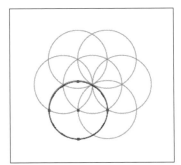

*Drawing the first circle.*

## Using the Transform Effect

Instead of copying and pasting this circle, then manually positioning it, you will use the Transform Effect to do the work for you. The Transform Effect allows you to move, scale, and rotate, while making copies of any given object.

1    Make sure the circle is still selected. If necessary, click the circle using the Selection tool (▶).

2    Open the Appearance panel by choosing Window > Appearance or by pressing the Appearance button (⬤) in the dock on the right side of the workspace. In the Appearance panel, select the stroke.

**3**   Click the Add New Effect button (*fx*) and choose Distort & Transform > Transform.

The Transform Effects dialog box opens. You need to have six circles around the center circle that you have not yet defined. Since you already have 1 circle, you will need 5 more that rotate around the center circle.

**4**   In the Copies text field, type **5**.

**5**   Under Rotate, type **60** in the Angle text field.

**6**   Make sure Preview is checked and drag the Move Horizontal slider to the right. When you release the mouse, you'll see the effect take place. Now type **43 pt** in the Horizontal text field. Click OK.

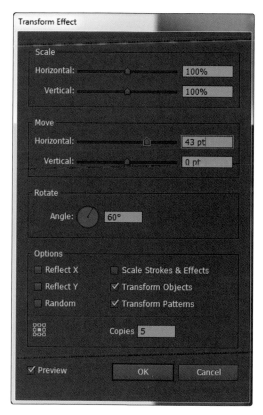

*Choosing the correct settings for the transform.*

## Duplicating a Stroke

You will now duplicate a stroke to make the center circle.

**1**   Make sure the Stroke is selected in the Appearance panel and click the Duplicate Selected Item button (⤵).

**2**   Now that you have a duplicate Stroke, you will change the Transform options for your top Stroke. Click the arrow next to the top Stroke, and click the *Transform* text that appears.

**3** The Transform Effect dialog box appears. In the copies text field, change the number to **1**. In the Move section, change the Horizontal text field to **21 pt** and in the Vertical text field type **–38**. Select the Preview check box to view the change. You should now have the center circle. Click OK.

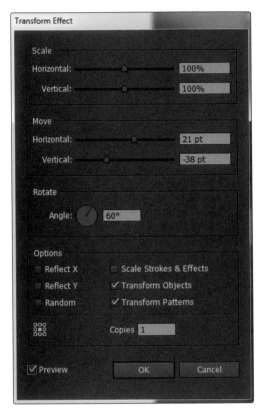

*The settings for the second transform.*

Now that you have the logo completed, you will get the file ready to be made into a layered PDF.

**4** Choose File > Save to save your work.

## Saving different versions of the logo onto separate layers

Now that you have made the logo, it is time to save it onto different layers and colorize it.

### Expanding appearance

The logo itself is just two strokes with Transform applied to each stroke. In order for you to colorize the logo, you will need to reduce the logo down to paths.

**1** Choose View > Outline. Notice that your illustration is just one path.

**2** Choose View > Preview. This takes you back into Preview mode.

### Saving as a graphic style

By saving this illustration as a graphic style, you can create another circle, then apply the graphic style to get this same sort of effect. This effect was based on the size of the original circle, so results may vary; if you draw a circle of the same size, you can get this exact effect with one click. Try it with a square, or any object, and it will apply the same stroke and transform options to the object. See Lesson 11, "Using Effects and Transparency," for more info on graphic styles.

**3** Choose Select > All to make sure your artwork is selected, then choose Object > Expand Appearance.

**4** Choose View > Outline. Notice that the entire illustration appears as paths.

**5** Choose View > Preview. This takes you back into Preview mode.

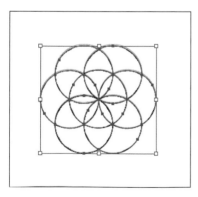

*The artwork expanded.*

## Saving the first version

Now for a little layer management.

1   Open the Layers panel by choosing Window > Layers or by pressing the
    Layers button () in the dock.

2   Select the template layer and drag the layer to the Delete Selection button (🗑) at the
    bottom of the panel. You no longer need the template layer.

    If a dialog box appears stating that the template layer contains artwork and asks if you
    want to delete it, choose Yes.

3   Double-click the text *working* in the Layers panel. When the text appears highlighted,
    type **Version 1** in the text field and press Enter (Windows) or Return (Mac OS).

*Renaming layers.*

4   Click the Layers panel menu button (⋅≡ ) and choose Duplicate "Version 1."

5   Double-click the *Version 1 copy* layer and when the text appears highlighted, type
    **Version 2** in the Name text field. Press Enter/Return.

6   Click the visibility icon (👁) to the left of the Version 1 layer to hide the layer. Now
    that Version 1 is on its own hidden layer, you can change the look of Version 2.

7   Choose File > Save.

## Using Live Paint

The easiest way to colorize all the individual pieces of this logo is to make this logo a Live
Paint Group. You will then be able to colorize this logo with the Live Paint Bucket tool.

1   Make sure the logo is still selected. If necessary, choose Select > All. Select the
    Version 2 layer to make sure you are working on it.

2   Choose Object > Live Paint > Make.

3   From the Tools panel, choose the Live Paint Bucket tool (🖌), which is hidden in the
    Shape Builder tool (🔧).

4   Double-click the Fill color in the Tools panel and choose any color from the Color
    Picker dialog box, then click OK.

5   Randomly click the Live Paint Bucket tool in any section of the logo. You might want
    to color the object symmetrically on corresponding sides for a better overall look.

## Using the Color Guide panel

Since you created this document from a jpeg, there are no colors in the Swatches panel. You will use the color guide to pick colors that are in harmony with your current color, then you can add them to your Swatches panel.

**1** Choose Window > Color Guide or click the Color Guide button (🔲) in the dock to open the Color Guide panel.

**2** If necessary, click the Set Base Color to the Current Color button in the upper-left of the Color Guide panel to display the correct harmony rule colors. Click the Harmony Rules drop-down menu at the top of the panel to view all the Harmony Rules for the initial color you picked. Choose any Harmony Rule from the list.

**3** Click the Color Guide panel menu button (•≡) and choose Save Colors as Swatches. The colors are added to the Swatches panel as a color group.

**4** Make sure the image is deselected by choosing Select > Deselect, then open the Swatches panel by pressing the Swatches button (▦) in the dock. Choose a color from the new color group created in the last step.

**5** Now you can use your left and right arrows on the keyboard, with the Live Paint Bucket tool selected and colorize the artwork any way you would like.

*Your finished Version 2 should look something like this.*

## Saving the third version

**1** Open the Layers panel and with the Version 2 layer still selected, click the Layers panel menu button (•≡) and choose Duplicate 'Version 2.'

**2** Double-click the *Version 2 copy* layer, and when the type appears highlighted, type **Version 3** in the text field and press Enter (Windows) or Return (Mac OS).

**3**    Click the visibility icon (👁) to the left of the Version 2 layer to hide the layer. Now that Version 2 is on its own hidden layer, you can change the look of Version 3.

*Your layers should look something like this.*

**4**    Choose File > Save.

## Using Recolor Artwork

Perhaps you want to apply more one option before you send your illustration off to a client. You will now use Recolor Artwork to change the color.

**1**    Select the Version 3 layer in the Layers panel and choose Select > All.

**2**    Open the Color Guide panel by pressing the Color Guide button (▣) in the dock. In the Color Guide panel, click the Color Guide panel menu button (▾≡) and choose Edit Colors.

**3**    At the top of the dialog box, choose any harmony rule from the drop-down menu. Make sure that Recolor Art is checked in the bottom-left of the dialog box. When you find a color scheme you like, click OK, and if prompted, save any changes to the swatch group.

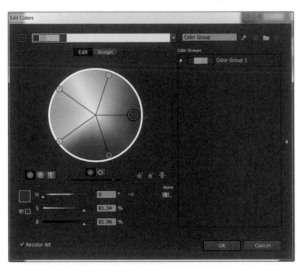 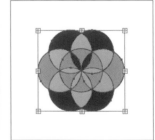

*Recoloring Artwork for the third version.*

**4**    Choose File > Save.

## Saving a layered PDF

Adobe created the Portable Document Format (PDF) as a universal document distribution format. PDF has become the *de facto* standard for the distribution and exchange of forms and electronic documents around the world. Since you created a file with multiple layers, you can export it as a PDF, so that a client can look through the layers within the PDF and choose which illustration they like best.

1   Choose File > Save As. In the Save As dialog box, select Adobe PDF (.pdf) from the Save as type (Windows) or Format (Mac OS) drop-down menu. The Name text field automatically adds the .pdf extension to the existing file name. Click Save. The Save Adobe PDF dialog box appears.

2   Choose [High Quality Print] from the Adobe PDF Preset drop-down menu. This changes the PDF settings to create a file that is optimized for printing on a desktop printer. Unless you have a specific reason for altering the settings of the PDF, it is best to work with one of the provided presets.

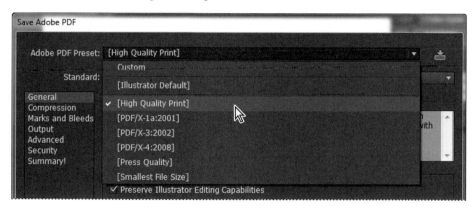

*Choose [High Quality Print] from the Preset drop-down menu.*

3   Choose Acrobat 8 (PDF 1.7) from the Compatibility drop-down menu. The Create Acrobat Layers from Top-Level Layers check box becomes active. Click the check box to enable this option, which allows the PDF file to create PDF layers from your top-level Illustrator layers.

A practical application of creating PDF layers from Illustrator would be a situation where different illustration variations were saved on different layers. You are using it to view separate illustrations. The PDF viewer could then view the different project versions by turning layers on and off.

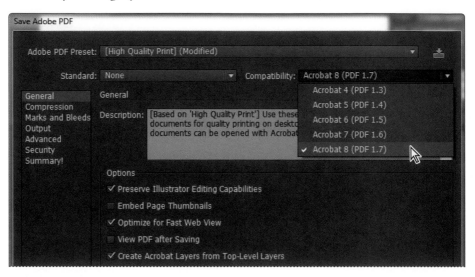

*Choose Acrobat 8 (PDF 1.7) from the Compatibility drop-down menu.*

## Additional PDF options

The Adobe PDF options are divided into categories. Changing any option will cause the name of the preset to change to Custom. The categories are listed on the left side of the Save Adobe PDF dialog box, with the exception of the Standard and Compatibility options, which are at the top of the dialog box.

**Standard** is used to specify a PDF standard for the file.

**Compatibility** specifies with which version of Adobe Acrobat the PDF file will be compatible.

**General** specifies basic file options, such as Illustrator's ability to edit the created PDF file and whether PDF layers are created.

**Compression** specifies whether bitmap artwork should be compressed.

**Marks and Bleeds** specify printer's marks and the bleed and slug areas.

**Output** controls how colors and PDF/X output intent profiles are saved in the PDF file.

**Advanced** controls how fonts, overprinting, and transparency are saved in the PDF file.

**Security** is used to add security (passwords) to the created PDF file.

**Summary** displays a summary of the current PDF settings.

**4**  Click the Save PDF button to save your changes and create your PDF file. Choose File > Close.

Now, when the client opens the PDF, they can view the different layers, even if they only have the free Adobe Reader.

## Integration with other applications

One of the Adobe Creative Suite's greatest strengths is the integration between the individual applications.

### Exporting for Photoshop

Illustrator has two ways of integrating with Adobe Photoshop. The first is Illustrator's ability to export files in the Adobe Photoshop (.psd) format. The second is Photoshop's ability to open and place the native Illustrator file format.

### Integrating with InDesign

There are two ways in which you can use Adobe Illustrator files in Adobe InDesign:

* Illustrator files can be copied in Illustrator and pasted directly into InDesign. When brought into InDesign in this fashion, Illustrator files remain completely editable.

* InDesign also has the ability to import Illustrator files using the Place command.

### Integrating with Flash

Illustrator can export files in the Adobe Flash .swf format for publishing on the Web. Also, Illustrator artwork can be imported or pasted into the Flash authoring environment.

### Integrating with Microsoft Expression Blend (XAML)

Native Adobe Illustrator files can be opened and edited in Expression Blend. In Expression Blend, choose File> Import Abode Illustrator File.

### Integrating with Premiere and After Effects

If you are working with the applications of the Adobe Creative Cloud you can easily import native Illustrator files into both After Effects and Premiere for use in motion graphics and video projects.

## Saving as EPS

Next you will save this logo as an EPS, if you needed to import this logo into an older version of QuarkXPress or another program that can't import native Illustrator files. For this exercise, you can view any one of the three layer versions you created.

The Encapsulated Post Script (EPS) file format is an image format used primarily in the print industry. The EPS format supports both bitmap and vector information, and is ideal for situations in which you have to take artwork from Illustrator into applications, such as Quark, that don't support native Illustrator file import. Virtually all graphic and word processing programs accept imported EPS artwork. Two important facts to note about EPS files: because they are based on the Postscript language, they can contain both bitmap and vector graphics; and they do not support transparency.

In other words, EPS is an outdated and flawed file format (from the early 1990s), fraught with peril and pitfalls for today's workflows with Creative Cloud integration, especially when transparency is involved.

**1**    Choose File > Open. In the Open dialog box, navigate to the ai12lessons folder and select **ai1201_work.ai**. Click Open.

**2**    Choose File > Save As. In the Save As dialog box, select Illustrator EPS (.EPS) from the Save as type (Windows) or Format (Mac OS) drop-down menu. The Name text field automatically adds the .eps extension to the existing file name. Click Save, and the EPS Options dialog box opens.

**3**    Set the Version to Illustrator CS3 EPS. The Version option allows you to specify the version of Illustrator with which you want your new EPS file to be compatible. When you save the EPS file to a legacy version, you lose some editing features.

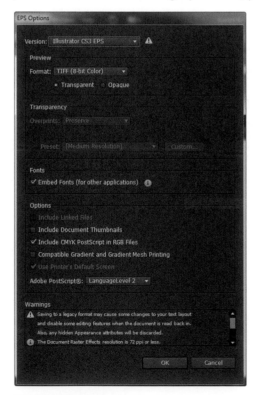

*The EPS Options dialog box.*

**4**   Leave the Preview Format section at its defaults. The Preview Format settings determine the appearance of the preview image that is saved with your EPS file. Preview images are used in applications that cannot display EPS files.

**5**   Leave all other settings at their defaults. Click OK to save your EPS file. Keep it open.

A warning dialog box will appear informing you that saving to a legacy format (CS4 or earlier) might cause some changes in the document. This warning appears whenever you save an Illustrator file to a legacy format. Click OK or Yes to continue.

*The settings in the Save As dialog box are reset to the default configuration every time a new file is created. When a file is opened and re-saved, the settings in the dialog box are based on the previously set options for that file.*

## Additional EPS options

**Embed Fonts (For Other Applications)** to ensure that the original font is displayed and printed if the file is placed into another application, such as Adobe InDesign. Selecting the Embed Fonts option increases the size of your EPS file.

**Include Linked Files** embeds files that are linked to the artwork. This option is grayed out if Illustrator does not detect a linked file.

**Include Document Thumbnails** creates a thumbnail image of the artwork. The thumbnail is displayed in the Illustrator Open and Place dialog boxes. Activating this option increases the file size minutely.

**Include CMYK PostScript In RGB Files** allows RGB color documents to be printed from applications that do not support RGB output.

**Compatible Gradient And Gradient Mesh Printing** enables older printers and PostScript devices to print gradients and gradient meshes by rasterizing gradient objects.

**Adobe PostScript** determines the level of PostScript used to save the artwork.

## Saving for the Web

Illustrator's Save for Web functionality allows you to optimize Illustrator artwork for the Web. Because of the nature of web browsers, only a few file formats can be displayed on the Internet. While you always want to keep your working files in the native Illustrator format, you have to optimize your images before they can be displayed on the Web. In this exercise, you will save a file in the .gif format, which is a good format for limited color artwork like logos and motifs. Since the .gif format supports transparency, you won't get a white box around your logo like you would with a .jpeg.

Keep in mind that the PNG–24 format also supports transparency. If you are planning to use your graphics for UI design elements in a program such as Microsoft's Expression Blend, you will want to save in the PNG format, since Expression Blend does not accept the GIF format.

*For simple graphics, Illustrator CC has a handy "Save for Microsoft Office" command on the File Menu, which will save a PNG-24 file that might be ready to plug & play with Microsoft PowerPoint, Word, etc.*

**1**   With the **ai1201_work.ai** file open, choose File > Save for Web to open the Save for Web dialog box. You can view any one of the three layer versions for this exercise.

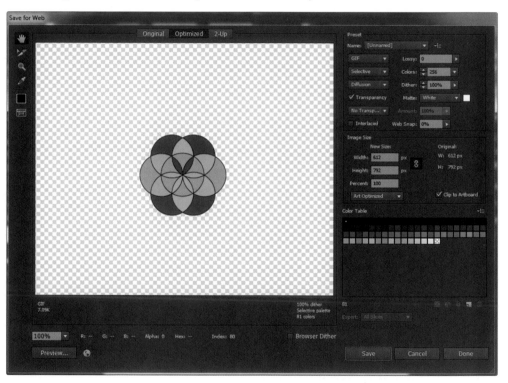

*The Save for Web dialog box.*

**2**   Select GIF from the Optimized file format drop-down menu in the preset area on the right of the dialog box.

**3** In the Colors drop-down menu, select 32. The GIF format allows the image to contain a maximum of 256 colors, which is what makes it unsuitable for saving photographs and other imagery with continuous tones of color. The logo in this example contains a smaller number of colors, so saving the additional color information only adds to the file size without providing any improvement in the appearance of the image. Note that even though the logo contains only 6 colors, if we restrict the GIF too much, the edges of the image will appear blocky and unattractive.

**4** Make sure that the Transparency check box is selected. This will allow your GIF image to have transparent areas. Leave all other settings at their defaults.

**5** Click Save. In the Save dialog box, navigate to the ai12lessons folder and click Save to complete the process.

## Web image formats

**GIF** is an acronym for Graphic Interchange File. The GIF format is usually used on the Web to display logos, motifs, and other limited tone imagery. The GIF format supports a maximum of 256 colors as well as transparency, and is the only one of the three formats listed here that supports built-in animation.

**JPEG** is an acronym for Joint Photographic Experts Group. The JPEG file format has found wide acceptance on the Web as the main format for displaying photographs and other continuous tone imagery. The JPEG format supports a range of millions of colors allowing for the accurate display of a wide range of artwork.

**PNG** is an acronym for Portable Network Graphics. PNG files come in two different varieties: PNG-8 files can support as many as 256 colors (like the GIF format); PNG-24 files can support millions of colors (like the JPEG format). Both PNG varieties can support transparency, and in an improvement on the GIF format, PNG-24 images can actually support varying degrees of transparency.

### Making a Flash animation

You can make basic Flash animations right inside Adobe Illustrator. In this next exercise, you will make your logo rotate, then save it as a Flash .swf file. Illustrator does not have a timeline, so to animate an object, you need to either do it using layers or by using blends. You will use layers to convert the layers into SWF frames.

**1** Make sure you still have the **ai1201_work.ai** file open. You can animate any version of your logo, just make sure none of the other layers are visible. Non-visible layers will not be animated.

**2** Choose the Selection tool (⬏) from the Tools panel and select the image.

**3** Double-click the Rotate tool (○) in the Tools panel. In the Rotate dialog box that appears, type **20** in the Angle text field, then click Copy.

*Rotate the illustration 20 degrees.*

**4** Now you have two copies of the illustration. To animate the rotation 360 degrees, you will need 16 more copies. (18 illustrations × 20 degrees = 360 degrees.)

**5** Instead of using the Rotate tool 16 more times, press and hold the Ctrl key (Windows) or the Command key (Mac OS) and press the **D** key 16 times. This shortcut accesses Object > Transform > Transform Again.

*Use the shortcut key Ctrl+D to create 16 more instances.*

Because Illustrator can animate only top-level layers, you need to release the sublayers in sequence so that they become their own layers. You will then drag them above the top layer, because that layer is really just a holder for all the sublayers. Next, you will delete that holder layer, and you will be ready to animate.

**6**    If necessary, click the arrow to the left of the layer name to expand the sublayers. Select all the sublayers in the Version 3 sublayer by clicking the targeting circle to the immediate right of the Version 3 layer.

**7**    Click the Layers panel menu button (·≡ ) and choose Release to Layers (Sequence).

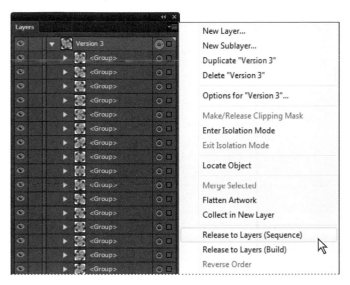

*Releasing Layers to a sequence.*

Now that the layers are released, they should be numbered 4–21. This means you have all 18 versions you need.

**8** Select Layer 4 through Layer 21 by clicking the first one, pressing and holding Shift, and then clicking the last one. Drag these layers above the Version 3 layer.

*Moving the sublayers to top-level layers.*

**9** You can now select the Version 3 layer and click the Delete Selection button (🗑) to delete the layer. The Version 3 layer was a holder layer, which is not needed after you released the layers to sequence.

Now you're ready to animate the illustration.

## Exporting a Flash animation

*Flash files are not supported on Apple iOS devices such as the iPad and iPhone, or most mobile devices. Adobe has discontinued development of Flash support for mobile devices.*

**1** Choose File > Export.

**2** In the Export dialog box, choose Flash (*.SWF) from the Save as type (Windows) or Format (Mac OS) drop-down menu. Navigate to the ai12lessons folder and click Save (Windows) or Export (Mac OS).

**3**    In the SWF Options dialog box, choose AI Layers to SWF Frames from the Export As
drop-down menu.

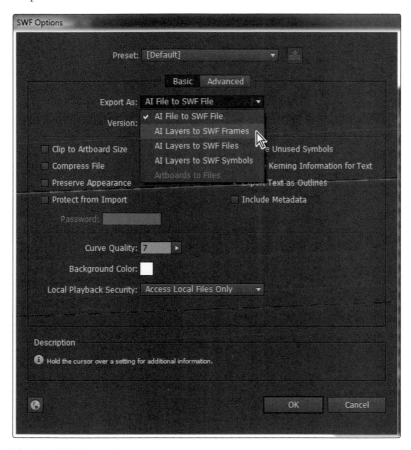

*The Basic SWF Option for export.*

**4**  Click the Advanced button in the top-right of the dialog box and select the Looping check box. This will rotate your logo for infinity.

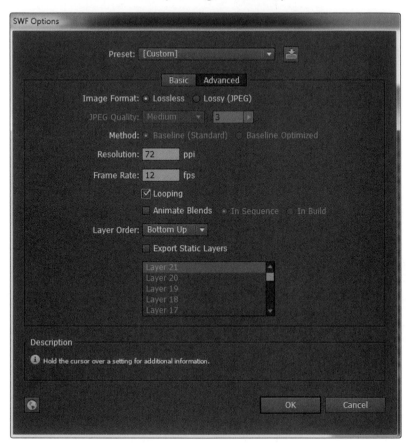

*The Advanced SWF Options.*

**5**  Click OK. Now you can open and play your animation by double-clicking it if you have the Adobe Flash Player. If not, you should be able to open it in any browser window, such as Safari or Internet Explorer, to see your animation.

**6**  Choose File > Close. If asked to save the file, choose No.

| FILE FORMAT | NAME | DESCRIPTION | EXPORT COMMAND |
|---|---|---|---|
| AI | Adobe Illustrator | Illustrator native format, used for representing single-page vector-based drawings. Also available in AIT (Template) format. | File > Save |
| PDF | Portable Document Format | Captures formatting information from a variety of applications, making it possible to send formatted documents and have them appear on the recipient's monitor or printer as they were intended. | File > Save |
| EPS | Encapsulated PostScript | Standard file format for importing and exporting PostScript files. | File > Save |
| FXG | Flash XML Graphics | Format based on a subset of MXML, the XML-based programming language used by the FLEX framework. | File > Save |
| SVG | Scalable Vector Graphics | Vector format that produces high-quality, interactive web graphics. Also offers SVGZ (Compressed) format. | File > Save |
| DWG | AutoCAD Drawing | Standard file format for saving vector graphics created in AutoCAD. | File > Export |
| DXF | AutoCAD Interchange File | Drawing interchange format for exporting AutoCAD drawings to or importing drawings from other applications. | File > Export |
| (W)BMP | Bitmap Picture | Standard Windows image format for low-resolution printing and web applications. | File > Export |
| EMF | Enhanced Metafile | Windows interchange format for exporting vector graphics data. | File > Export |
| SWF | Flash | Vector-based graphics format for creating interactive, animated web graphics. | File > Export |
| JPG | Joint Photographic Experts Group | Standard format for displaying photographic images over the Web. | File > Export, File > Save for Web |
| PCT | (Mac) Picture | Used with Mac OS graphics and page-layout applications to transfer images between applications. | File > Export |
| PSD | Photoshop Document | Standard (native) Photoshop export format. | File > Export |
| PNG | Portable Network Graphics | Lossless compression and display of images on the Web in 8- or 24-bit formats. | File > Export, File > Save for Web |
| TGA | Targa | For use on systems that use the Truevision® video board. | File > Export |
| TXT | Text Format | Exports text in an illustration to a text file. | File > Export |
| TIF | Tagged-Image File Format | Flexible bitmap image format supported by most paint, image-editing, and page-layout applications. | File > Export |
| WMF | Windows Metafile | Exchanges files from 16-bit Windows drawing and layout programs. | File > Export |
| GIF | Graphics Interchange Format | Used for web graphics that allow an image to reference a palette of up to 256 colors from the 24-bit RGB color space. | File > Save for Web |

## Self study

Open one of the Illustrator files you saved from one of the other lessons in this book, and practice saving it as a PDF and EPS file. Try re-coloring the artwork on a saved copy layer. Then view the layers in the PDF.

## Review

### Questions

**1**  What does the Create PDF Compatible File in the Save As Illustrator Options dialog box do?

**2**  What does EPS stand for, and where is it primarily used?

**3**  Which web graphics format is best for saving an image with continuous tones of color, without transparency, and compatible with most web browsers?

**4**  Can you create a Flash animation in Illustrator?

### Answers

**1**  The Create PDF Compatible File option saves a PDF representation of the document in the Illustrator file. This option is used to make Illustrator files compatible with other Adobe applications.

**2**  EPS stands for Encapsulated Post Script. It is a legacy file format used primarily in the print industry.

**3**  The JPEG format is best for continuous tone imagery, does not support transparency, and is compatible with the majority of common web browsers.

**4**  Yes, you can export layer or blend-based SWF files from Illustrator.

## What you'll learn in this lesson:

- Combining objects using the Blend tool
- Applying a gradient mesh
- Creating symbols
- Using the symbolism tools

# Advanced Blending Techniques

*In this lesson, you will explore methods used to blend objects to create realistic appearances and artistic effects. You will use the Blend tool and create advanced gradients using the gradient mesh options, and use symbols to create a surface texture.*

## Starting up

Before starting, make sure that your tools and panels are consistent by resetting your workspace. See "Resetting Adobe Illustrator CC Preferences" in the Starting up section of this book.

You will work with several files from the ai13lessons folder in this lesson. Make sure that you have loaded the ailessons folder onto your hard drive from the included DVD. See "Loading lesson files" in the Starting up section of this book.

### See Lesson 13 in action!

*Use the accompanying video to gain a better understanding of how to use some of the features shown in this lesson. You can find the video tutorial for this lesson on the included DVD.*

## Using the Blend tool

The Blend tool and Make Blend command allow you to create a blend, which is basically a transition between two or more selected objects. Blends are often desirable when there are objects overlapping each other that you might want to have a more combined look instead of appearing more separated, and just kind of sitting on top of one another. To see the blending in action, you'll start by working on the seeds of an apple illustration.

1   In Illustrator CC, choose File > Open. When the Open dialog box appears, navigate to the ai13lessons folder and select the **ai1301.ai** file. Click Open.

2   Select the Zoom tool (🔍) from the Tools panel, then click and drag a marquee around the area of the seeds to zoom in more closely.

*Zoom in on the inner parts of the apple.*

3   Choose the Selection tool (▸) and click the innermost portion of the seed on the upper-left. To see your selected area with more detail, you might want to view the edges of the selected image. To do so, choose View > Show Edges. If you find that you don't like the edges, choose View > Hide Edges.

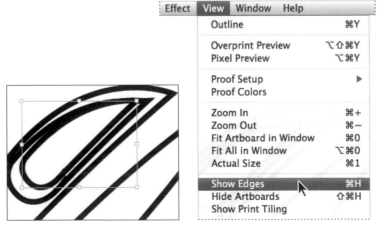

*Select the inner part of the apple's seed, then show the edges.*

**4** With the inner portion of the seed selected, make sure the fill is active in the Tools panel. Open the Swatches panel by clicking the Swatches button (▦) in the dock on the right side of the workspace. Click the Swatches panel menu button (▾≡) in the upper-right corner of the panel and choose Small List View, so that you can see the swatch names to apply as you explore this lesson. Choose the swatch *Inner Seed* from the Swatches panel to apply it to the fill of the seed. Next, you will remove the stroke color.

  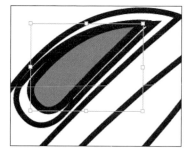

*Make sure the fill is active, then select a color from the Swatches panel to color the seed.*

**5** To remove the stroke, select the Stroke icon (⬚) in the Tools panel. Just below the Stroke icon, click the None button (⬚) to remove the stroke from the seed. Removing the stroke eliminates an adverse effect that can occur on the blend when you combine both objects together depending on the look you're trying to achieve. In the case of the seeds, you want a smooth blending of color rather than harsh edges that the stroke would create.

*Remove the stroke.*

Next you will color the part of the seed located below the area you filled with color and then finish by blending the two together to complete the fill process.

6    Using the Selection tool, select the part of the seed just below the area you just filled.

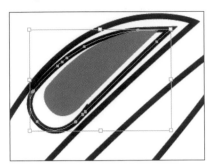

*Select the outer part of the seed.*

7    Make sure the fill is active in the Tools panel and choose the *Outer Seed* swatch from the Swatches panel to apply it to the fill. Once the dark brown is applied, remove the stroke by selecting the Stroke icon, then clicking the None button below it.

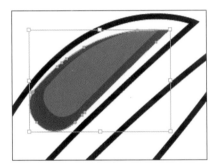

*Color the outer part of the seed.*

Next, you will blend the two together to create a smooth transition of color between both objects.

**8**  Keeping the bottom part of the seed selected, press and hold the Shift key on your keyboard and click the light brown part of the seed with the Selection tool so both parts of the seed are now selected.

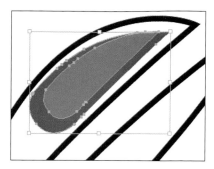

*Select both the inner and outer part of the seed.*

**9**  With both objects selected, choose Object > Blend > Make or use the keyboard shortcut, Ctrl+Alt+B (Windows) or Command+Option+B (Mac OS).

**10**  Deselect both images by choosing Select > Deselect and take note of the transition of color between both objects.

Repeat steps 2-9 for the next seed to the lower right. You'll come back to more blend options with the Blend tool shortly.

*The colored seeds.*

**11**  Choose File > Save As. When the Save As dialog box appears, navigate to the ai13lessons folder and type **ai1301_work.ai** into the Name text field, then click Save. The Illustrator Options dialog box appears, click OK to continue.

## Applying a gradient

Next, you will be applying some gradients to fill in the other shapes that make up the various components of the sliced apple.

1  Select the cutout area just below the top-left seed.

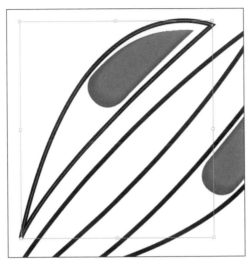

*Select the hollow part of the apple.*

2  At the bottom of the Tools panel, make sure the fill is active and select the Gradient button to apply a gradient fill to the cutout.

*Click the Gradient button to fill the hollow section.*

3  Select the Stroke icon (⊡) in the Tools panel, then click the None button (⊘). Next, you'll change the colors of the gradient to more realistic colors.

4  Open the Gradient panel by choosing Window > Gradient or by clicking the Gradient button (▪) in the dock on the right side of the workspace.

5  In the Gradient panel, undock the panel by clicking and dragging the tab of the panel to separate it from the dock. For more information on altering the workspace, please take a look at Lesson 2, "Getting to Know the Workspace." This makes it easier to use both the Gradient and Swatches panels at the same time.

**6**   Choose Window > Swatches to open the Swatches panel or select the Swatches icon (▦) in the dock.

**7**   With the cutout of the apple still selected, make sure the fill is active in the Tools panel so you can change the gradient color values of the image.

**8**   In the Gradient panel, you'll notice a color ramp at the bottom of the panel and two Gradient Sliders. The Gradient panel has more options that appear in the panel. If you can't see the other options, click the panel menu button (•≡ ) in the upper-right corner of the panel and choose Show Options from the menu that appears.

*Expand the options of the Gradient panel.*

When the gradient is first applied, the colors are set to black-and-white by default. You will be changing the colors in the gradient by using the Gradient panel and the Swatches panel.

**9**   Start by clicking the white Gradient Slider on the left to select it.

**10**   From the Swatches panel menu, you will drag and drop swatches over the color stops in the Gradient panel to create the gradient. Click and hold the swatch *Back of Seed Green* and drop it directly over the White color stop in the Gradient panel.

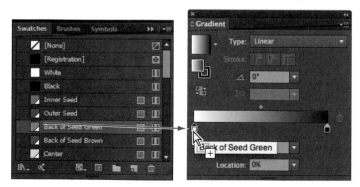

*Drag the color swatch from the Swatches panel onto the white color stop in the Gradient panel.*

**11** Now, click and drag the *Back of Seed Brown* swatch from the Swatches panel over the Black color stop in the Gradient panel.

To create the gradient in the next cutout, you will use a shortcut method with the Eyedropper tool.

**12** Select the cutout to the bottom-right. With the cutout selected, choose the Eyedropper tool (✐) from the Tools panel.

**13** Using the Eyedropper, click the fill of the first cutout. The second cutout should inherit all the color properties from the first one.

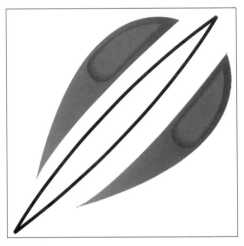

*Use the Eyedropper tool to copy the gradient of the first hollow area to the second.*

The slit in the apple between the seed cutouts will be where you will apply the next gradation.

## Applying radial gradients

You'll now apply a radial gradient instead of the default linear gradient. You can change gradient patterns easily in the Gradient panel.

**1** Choose the Selection tool (▸) from the Tools panel and select the slit between the cutouts.

**2** Apply a gradient fill like you did in step 2 of the last exercise. You'll notice that it applies the gradient using the same color values from the previous gradient that was applied. You will change the colors just like you did before, only this time you'll also change the type of gradient.

*To add another slider, click below the color ramp in the Gradient panel. To remove a slider, click and drag down on the slider.*

3   Click and drag the White color swatch over the left color stop.

4   Click and drag the Center color swatch over the right color stop.

5   To change the pattern of the gradient, choose Radial from the Type drop-down menu just above the color ramp.

*Change the type of gradient to Radial.*

6   Finish the process by setting the stroke value of the object to None. When finished, the image should look similar to the figure below.

*The finished seeds.*

As you can see, there are some nice color and shading options available when you use gradients. For more information about standard gradients, refer to Lesson 4, "Adding Color."

7   Choose File > Save to save your work.

## Applying gradients using Illustrator's Gradient Mesh options

While standard gradients are really nice for shading, they don't offer the flexibility you might need for more complex shading alternatives. With the Gradient Mesh options that are available in Illustrator, you'll find that you can get much more detailed with the shading and color placement of the gradient. You will start by modifying the apple core area with a gradient mesh.

1   Using the Selection tool (⬆), select the apple core area just below the seed cutouts and the slit in the middle. If necessary, choose the Zoom tool (🔍) and zoom out to view the apple core area.

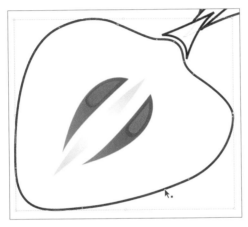

*Select the core of the apple.*

2   Choose Object > Create Gradient Mesh.

3   In the Create Gradient Mesh dialog box, type **3** into the Rows text field and **2** in the Columns text field. Choose Flat from the Appearance drop-down menu and type **100** in the Highlight text field. Select the Preview check box to see the results, then click OK.

*Gradient Mesh settings.*

Once the mesh has been established, you can use different tools to modify it, including the Mesh tool and the Direct Selection tool.

**4**  Choose the Direct Selection tool (⟨⟩) from the Tools panel. You'll notice anchor points on the mesh, click the anchor point at the top of the middle division line. You'll also see that handles for the anchor points appear when you select it with the Direct Selection tool.

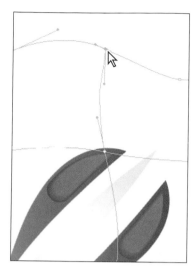

*Select the anchor point to reveal its handles.*

**5**  With the anchor point selected, make sure the Fill icon (⊡) is active in the Tools panel and the Swatches panel is visible. Choose *Inner Apple 1* from the Swatches panel for the Fill color.

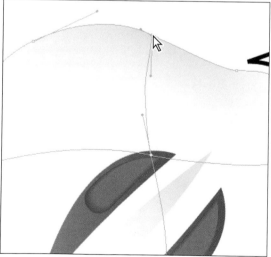

*Select Inner Apple 1 from the Swatches panel to apply it to the anchor point of the apple.*

You can see how the gradient spreads and diffuses from the point of selection. Next, you'll add some more colors to see how they blend together.

6   Click the next anchor point below the top one and select *Inner Apple 2* from the Swatches panel.

 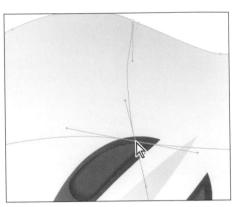

*Select another anchor point in the gradient mesh and choose Inner Apple 2 from the Swatches panel.*

7   Select the next anchor point down and select *Inner Apple 3* from the Swatches panel.

*If you're having trouble selecting the anchor points on the mesh, zoom in more closely with your Zoom tool (*🔍*), as anchor points can be tricky to select at times.*

8   Select the bottom anchor point at the base of the line and choose *Inner Apple 4*.

Clicking one point at a time can take awhile. Sometimes you'll want to apply the same color to multiple points (such as at the edge of the image). You can select multiple points by pressing and holding Shift on your keyboard and clicking the different points using the Selection tool. Another alternative is to use the Lasso tool to click and drag a marquee around the points you'd like to select.

9   Select the Lasso tool (🔎) from the Tools Panel.

10  Click and drag a marquee around the anchor points on the lower-right portion of the apple core. Choose *Inner Apple Edge* from the Swatches panel.

**11** Using the methods you've just discovered, apply *Inner Apple Edge* to the remaining anchor points of the apple core to finish coloring it.

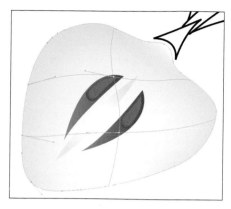

*Add more color to the anchor points of the apple.*

## Adjusting the Mesh

Once you've applied the mesh, you can keep adjusting by using the Direct Selection tool or the Lasso tool to select the points you want and update the color. You can also grab the points and move them to adjust the spread of color.

**1** Using the Direct Selection tool (➤), select the second anchor point on the middle division line. Choose a different shade of color and then drag the anchor point to move it. Notice how the color updates immediately and how the spread of the gradient is affected by moving the anchor point.

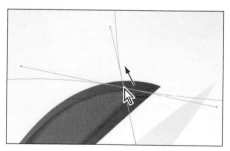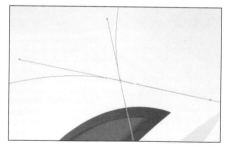

*Select an anchor point and watch as the color updates when you move the anchor point.*

**2** Choose File > Save to save the file.

## Revisiting Blend options

You started the process working with the Blend options. Next, you'll explore how you can control the transition of color between the blended objects using specified steps or smooth color options to help expand the choices you'll have during the process.

**1**  Choose the Selection tool (▶) from the Tools panel and select the triangular shape just above the apple core. From the Swatches panel, choose the *Triangle* swatch for the fill and set the stroke value to None.

*Select, then color the triangle object above the apple's core.*

**2**  Make sure the fill is active and select the stem above the triangular shape. From the Swatches panel, choose the *Stem* swatch. Set the stroke to None.

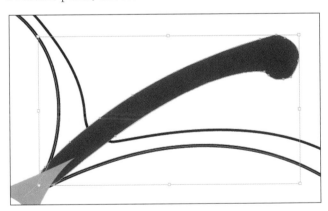

*Select, then color the apple's stem.*

**3**  Choose Select > Deselect.

Last time you used the menu to create the blend; this time you will use the Blend tool and investigate some of the other options available to you.

**4**  Double-click the Blend tool (➴) in the Tools panel. The Blend Options dialog box appears.

**5**  From the Spacing drop-down menu, choose Specified Steps and leave the steps set to the default of 8. Click OK.

*Blend Options.*

**6**  Click once on the triangular shape, then click once on the stem and notice the results of the blend.

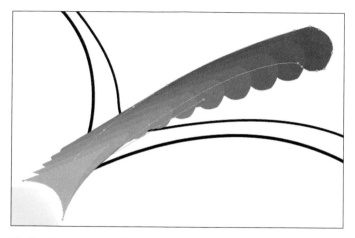

*The blend between the two objects.*

You can see the effect of the specified steps gives the appearance of the blend a kind of morphing effect between the shapes. While this creates a pretty cool and funky way of transitioning between the shapes, this isn't really the desired effect for the apple. Now, you'll try this using a smooth color transition.

**7**  Choose Edit > Undo Make Blend.

*Choose Edit > Undo Make Blend.*

8   Double-click the Blend tool in the Tools panel to open the Blend Options dialog box. Set the Spacing value back to Smooth Color and click OK.

*Choose Smooth Color from the Spacing drop-down menu.*

9   Click once on the triangular shape, then click once on the stem and take note of the difference. You are back to that smooth transition of color again. Another thing you'll see is the way the blend affects the nature of each image, where the images widen a bit to blend the underlying framework of each shape together to form one overall merged image.

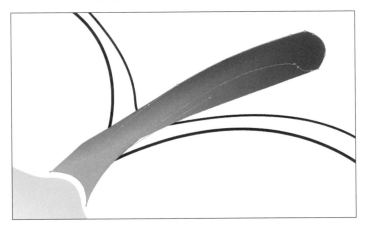

*The two objects blended together.*

*Keep in mind that the Blend tool can distort the underlying framework of the images you're blending. This might have an impact on how you draw images that you're considering blending together.*

As you have seen, the Blend tool doesn't just create smooth color transitions, it can also create new shapes. You'll finish the sliced apple with a bit more gradient mesh work.

## More mesh work

You'll apply another gradient mesh and continue to adjust the mesh by selecting multiple points on the grid at the same time.

**1**  Start by selecting the inner part of the sliced apple with the Selection tool (✶).

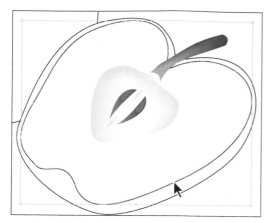

*Select the inner part of the sliced apple.*

**2**  Choose Object > Create Gradient Mesh. In the Create Gradient Mesh dialog box, type **3** in the Rows text field and **3** in the Columns text field. Leave the other settings at their defaults and click OK.

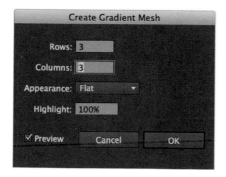

*Set the Rows and Columns for the Gradient Mesh.*

**3**  With the grid still active, choose the Direct Selection tool (▷) from the Tools panel.

**4**  Using the Direct Selection tool, click one of the anchor points that's on the outside edge of the gradient mesh grid. You'll see handles appear on the point once you select it.

**5** Press and hold the Shift key and continue to select the rest of the anchor points on the outside edge of the grid until all the anchor points on the outside edge of the grid are selected.

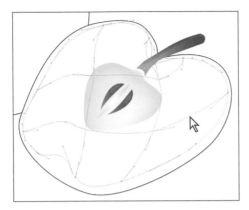

*Select the outer anchor points of the gradient mesh.*

**6** Once they're all selected, make sure the fill is active in the Tools panel then select *Middle Apple* from the Swatches panel.

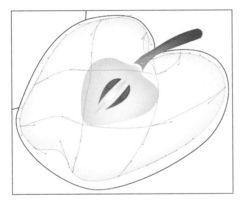

*Select Middle Apple from the Swatches panel to color the apple.*

**7** Choose File > Save to save your work.

Leave the center of the sliced apple set to white; the overall effect of the gradient works well to create some depth. Next, you will wrap up the sliced apple by finishing the outside framework.

# Overlapping images

Overlapping images can make the selection process very difficult when it comes to working with multiple gradient mesh objects. You'll start out this time by locking the inner part of the apple shape.

1   Choose the Selection tool (▸) from the Tools panel and click the inner part of the sliced apple (the part of the apple you just finished with the last grid). Shift+click the apple core, the seeds, and the stem.

2   Choose Object > Lock > Selection. Now the inner part of the apple is locked in place, which is going to make the selection process for the next grid a lot easier.

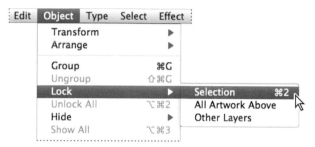

*Lock the selection.*

3   Using the Selection tool, click the outer framework of the sliced apple.

4   Choose Object > Create Gradient Mesh. In the Create Gradient Mesh dialog box, type **6** into the Rows text field and **3** into the Columns text field. Leave the other settings at their defaults and click OK.

*Set the Gradient Mesh options.*

5   Choose the Direct Selection tool (▸) from the Tools panel. Select the anchor points on the right side of the apple's outer framework by Shift+clicking each anchor point as you did before.

**6** Choose *Outer Apple Right* from the Swatches panel.

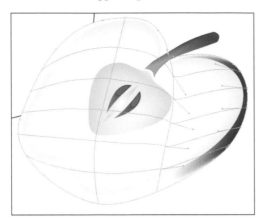

*Choose Outer Apple Right from the Swatches panel to
color the outer part of the apple.*

**7** Using the Direct Selection tool, select the anchor points at the bottom of the shape.

**8** Choose *Outer Apple Bottom* from the Swatches panel.

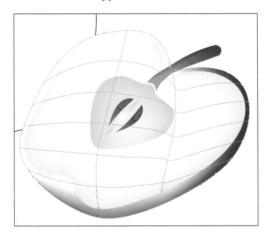

*Choose Outer Apple Bottom from the Swatches panel to
color the outer part of the apple.*

**9**　Select the anchor points on the left side of the apple shape. Choose *Outer Apple Left* from the Swatches panel.

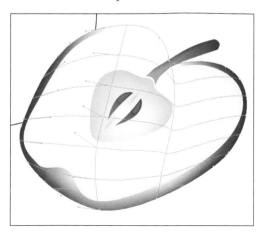

*Choose Outer Apple Left from the Swatches panel to color the outer part of the apple.*

**10**　Select the remaining anchor points at the top of the apple shape and choose *Outer Apple Top* from the Swatches panel.

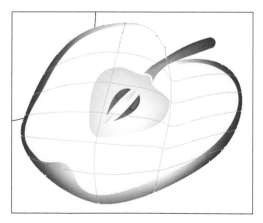

*Choose Outer Apple Top from the Swatches panel to color the outer part of the apple.*

**11**　Choose Select > Deselect, then choose File > Save to save your work.

### Applying a gradient mesh using the Mesh tool

In addition to applying a gradient mesh through the Object menu, there's a more visual way of pointing and clicking to apply the mesh, add grid segments and choose colors using just one tool.

Again, when there are overlapping images that each have grids, it can make the selection and application process a bit tricky. You can temporarily hide images to get them out of your way to ease the process. That's what you'll do to get things rolling—you'll hide the sliced apple and then continue from there.

1   From the Object menu, choose Object > Unlock All to unlock the components of the apple that you locked earlier so you can re-select them.

*You can't select a locked object again unless you unlock it first.*

2   Choose the Selection tool (﹨) from the Tools panel and Shift+click the remaining parts of the sliced apple that you completed earlier.

3   Choose Object > Hide > Selection.

*You can reveal a hidden object at any time by choosing Object > Show All.*

Now that the sliced apple is out of the way, you can turn your attention to the next apple. The last time you applied the gradient mesh, you went through the Object menu, this time, you'll go for the Mesh tool.

4   Select the Mesh tool (▨) from the Tools panel.

**5** Using the Mesh tool, move over the upper-left body of the apple and click it. A grid appears the moment you click with the Mesh tool using the last color used as a fill. If the Gradient Mesh appears with a color, undo this step, press the **D** key on the keyboard to get your default fill of white, then click with the Gradient Mesh tool again.

*Use the Mesh tool on the whole apple.*

**6** Click to the right and a little higher from where you clicked the first time and then to the left and a little lower. You add new segments to the grid each time you click.

*Add more segments to the apple using the Mesh tool.*

*To remove a line segment, press and hold the Alt (Windows) or Option (Mac OS) key and click the segment you want to remove when you see the minus sign next to the Mesh tool.*

Unfortunately, you cannot select multiple anchor points with the Mesh tool to apply color to multiple points at once. You will use something else this time instead of the Direct Selection tool.

**7**    To select multiple points this time, select the Lasso tool (⌕) in the Tools panel.

**8**    Using the Lasso tool, click and drag a marquee around the anchor points on the right side of the grid.

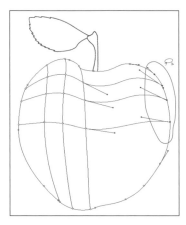

*Make a selection on the right side of the apple.*

**9**    Select *Apple Right* from the Swatches panel. Continue to make selections using the Lasso tool on the bottom, left, and top of the apple, and apply the correct swatches; *Apple Bottom 1*, *Apple Bottom 2*, *Apple Left*, and *Apple Top*. Remember to include the inner anchor points.

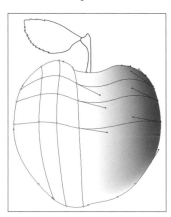 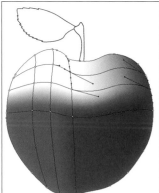 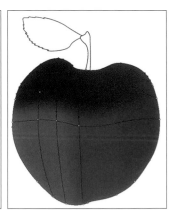

*Apply the swatches to the remainder of the apple.*

**10**    Choose File > Save to save your work.

Next you will fine-tune the gradient mesh with the Mesh tool to modify the shading.

**11**    Select the Mesh tool (⊞) from the Tools panel. With the tool selected, click one of the anchor points toward the left side of the grid and select *Apple Highlight 1*.

*Be careful when making your selection; it's easy to accidentally add a new segment to your grid.*

**12** Now click the anchor point to the right of the one you just selected and choose *Apple Highlight 2* from the Swatches panel.

**13** With the Mesh tool still selected, click and drag on the point that you have currently selected. Notice that you can move the point to adjust the spread of the resulting gradient.

**14** Continue to add additional shading on the apple and use the Mesh tool to click and drag the points until you're happy with the shading.

**15** Choose Select > Deselect to take a look at your shading.

*Finish adding shading to the apple.*

**16** To make further changes to a grid once it's been de-selected, choose the Direct Selection tool (⬚) from the Tool panel and click the object with the grid. The Direct Selection tool will reactivate the grid.

**17** Choose File > Save to save your work.

**Finishing up with the Mesh tool and automatically adding a Highlight**

You'll continue to shade the remaining parts of the apple with the Mesh tool.

1  Select the Zoom tool (🔍) and zoom in on the area of the stem of the apple.

2  Choose the Mesh tool (▦) from the Tool panel and then click the stem of the apple to apply a mesh.

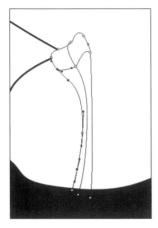

*Apply a mesh to the apple stem.*

3  Using the same methods as you used for the body of the apple, apply the *Stem 2* swatch from the Swatches panel to different anchor points on the stem until you have the stem shaded as you like.

*Don't forget to zoom in and out to make selecting the points on the grid easier to select. Staying zoomed out can make the selection process with the grid much more difficult.*

4  Choose Select > Deselect when finished to take a look at your work.

*The shaded stem.*

To finish the shading process, you'll apply the mesh to the leaf of the apple. This time you'll add one more touch by adding a highlight to the mesh as you apply the gradient mesh.

5  Choose the Selection tool (🔍) from the Tools panel and select the leaf of the apple. Before applying the mesh this time, you'll first fill in the leaf with the *Leaf* swatch.

6  With the leaf selected, select the *Leaf* swatch from the Swatches panel. You'll go back to the menu to apply the mesh this time.

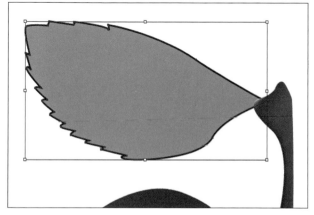

*Set the color of the leaf in the Swatches panel.*

7  Choose Object > Create Gradient Mesh. In the Create Gradient Mesh dialog box, type **8** in both the Rows and Columns text fields.

8  Choose To Center from the Appearance drop-down menu and set the Highlight value to 75%. Click OK.

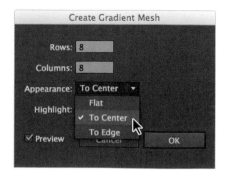

*Set the Gradient Mesh options.*

**9**  Choose Select > Deselect and then save your work.

*To apply a highlight while creating a gradient mesh, you must first fill the object with a fill color other than white before choosing the Highlight option in the Create Gradient Mesh dialog box.*

The apple's shading is done, and you're almost finished. You'll complete the exercise by stylizing the apple's surface a bit using the Symbol tools.

## Using the Symbol tools

Symbols are essentially reuseable art objects that are built into Illustrator. Think of them as your own personal clip art library that comes with the program. You can either use the symbols in Illustrator or you can create your own that can be saved within the program to be used later on. In addition to the symbols themselves, they come with a series of tools that can be used to apply the symbols to your project as well as modify properties of the symbols, such as their size, color, position, rotation, and more.

*For more information about symbols, see Lesson 10, "Working with Symbols."*

You'll start the process by creating the object you want to convert into a symbol and then start to incorporate the symbol tools to apply and modify the symbol to the artwork.

**1**  Choose the Ellipse tool (○) from the Tools panel. If necessary, click and hold the Rectangle tool (□) to reveal the hidden Ellipse tool.

**2**  Using the Ellipse tool, draw a small circle next to the apple (pressing and holding Shift while you draw will produce a perfect circle).

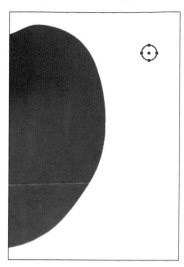

*Using the Ellipse tool, create a small circle next to the apple.*

**3**  Fill the circle with a gradient by clicking the Gradient button (■) at the bottom of the Tools panel.

**4**  The Gradient panel should have opened for you when you applied it to the circle. If not, choose Window > Gradient to open it.

 *You can change the colors of the gradient in the gradient panel by double-clicking the color stop to open its color properties.*

**5**  Double-click the left color stop.

**6** Once the Gradient Slider panel appears, click the panel menu button (⁻▤) in the upper-right corner and choose RGB for the color mode. Type a value of **255, 100, 46** respectively in the R (Red), G (Green), and B (Blue) text fields.

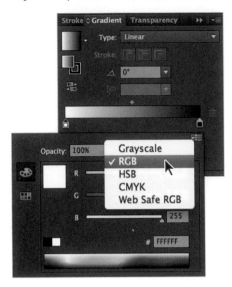

*Gradient Slider color settings.*

**7** Click back on the Gradient panel to close the Gradient Slider panel. Double-click the right Gradient Slider, click the panel menu button in the upper-right corner and choose RGB for the color mode and type values of **158**, **0**, and **0** in the R, G, and B text fields using the same procedure as listed in the previous step.

**8**   In the Gradient panel, choose Radial for the pattern of the gradient.

*Set the gradient to Radial.*

Next you will adjust the gradient to stylize the radial gradient.

**9**   Using the Zoom tool (⌕), zoom in on the gradient and then slide the diamond-shaped Gradient Slider (the one above the other two in the panel) to the left a bit to collapse the radial gradient a little.

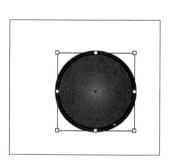 

*Edit the gradient.*

**10**  Finish the image by setting the Stroke value to None.

# Creating a symbol

Next, you'll make the image a symbol, and then start to use it on the artwork to create a texture on the apple.

1    Choose Window > Symbols to open the Symbols panel.

2    Once the panel is open, choose the Selection tool (⬉) from the Tools panel and then select the gradient circle and drag it into the Symbols panel.

3    In the Symbol Options dialog box, type **Gradient Circle** in the Name text field. Leave the other settings at their defaults and click OK.

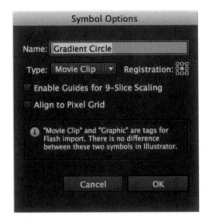

*A Symbol Options dialog box appears when creating a new symbol.*

*Once you've created a symbol, you can then save it to use in other projects. To do so, click the panel menu button (⋅≡) in the upper-right corner of the Symbols panel and choose Save Symbol Library and then name the library. To use the library with your symbols in other projects, choose Open Symbol Library from the panel menu and then navigate to the place where your library is saved to open it.*

4    With the Selection tool (⬉), click the gradient circle on the artboard and delete it. You'll be reapplying it to the artwork in a different way.

5    Zoom out a bit so you can see the whole apple.

6    Select the Symbol Sprayer tool (🖋) from the Tools panel.

Before you apply the symbol, you'll adjust the Symbol Sprayer tool settings.

**7** Double-click the Symbol Sprayer tool to open the Symbolism Tools Options dialog box. Set the Diameter value to approximately **13mm** and click OK.

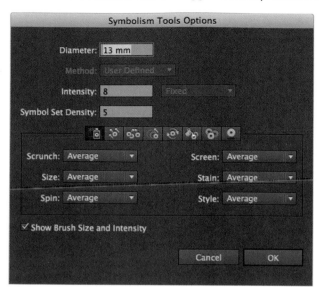

*Symbolism Tools Options.*

**8** Make sure the Gradient Circle is selected in the Symbols panel (you must select the symbol) and then click and drag with the Symbol Sprayer over the surface of the apple to paint the symbol on top of the apple.

*The more you click and drag, the more instances of the symbol are created. Each copy of the symbol on the artboard is referred to as an instance.*

*Paint the Gradient Circle symbols over the apple.*

**9** Choose File > Save to save your work.

## Modifying a symbol's appearance

Next, you'll use a few more symbol tools to adjust the symbol's appearance. You'll find a number of tools that can be used to alter the symbol; you will use tools that will affect size and transparency.

1   Using the Zoom tool (🔍), zoom in on the apple, then choose the Symbol Sizer tool (⊙) from the Tools panel. If necessary, click and hold the Symbol Sprayer tool (🖈) to reveal the hidden Symbolism tools.

*Select the Symbol Sizer tool from the Tools panel.*

*If you click and hold any of the gradient circle symbol instances on the apple, they'll start to enlarge.*

2   Press and hold the Alt (Windows) or Option (Mac OS) key and then click and hold one of the gradient circles on the apple to adjust its size and make it smaller. Let go of the mouse when you're satisfied with size.

**3** Keep re-sizing various instances of the gradient circles to adjust the look of them to your liking.

*Resize the symbols.*

Now you'll work on the transparency a bit.

**4** Select the Symbol Screener tool () from the Tool panel.

*The more you click and hold with the Symbol Screener, the more transparent the image becomes.*

**5** Click the different instances of the gradient circle on the apple to adjust them to varying degrees of transparency. Keep in mind, the longer you hold, the more transparency is applied. To undo some of the transparency, press and hold the Alt/Option key and click the object again.

*Add transparency to the symbols.*

Let's finish up by taking a look at everything together.

**6** Choose Select > Deselect to deactivate the selected symbols.

**7** Zoom out a bit. To reveal the hidden images, choose Object > Show All.

**8**   Choose File > Save to save your work.

*The finished image.*

Now you've gotten the circles to blend in a bit with the apple itself, giving the images a more natural combined appearance.

## Self study

Continue experimenting with the Blend tool by drawing two different objects that are two different colors. Select the Blend tool and try blending them together in different ways. Try this with different shapes, different colors, and different positioning each time.

## Review

### Questions

**1**   How do you access the blend options for the Blend tool?

**2**   How can you apply a gradient mesh?

**3**   How do you turn an image that you've created into a symbol?

### Answers

**1**   To access the blend options for the Blend tool, double-click the Blend tool.

**2**   To apply a gradient mesh, use the Mesh tool from the Tools panel or select an image and choose Object > Create Gradient Mesh.

**3**   To turn an image you've created into a symbol, select the image with the Selection tool and then drag it into the Symbols panel.

## What you'll learn in this lesson:

- Using Multiple Place
- Unembedding images
- Helpful link information
- New Brush features
- Packaging your files
- New CSS and SVG workflows

# Adobe Illustrator CC New Features

*In this lesson, you discover some of the major improvements that have been implemented in Adobe Illustrator CC. Many features are included in this lesson, and you will find more incorporated into the lesson files throughout the rest of this book.*

## Starting up

Before starting, make sure that your tools and panels are consistent by resetting your workspace. See "Resetting Adobe Illustrator CC Preferences" in the Starting up section of this book.

You will work with several files from the ai14lessons folder in this lesson. Make sure that you have loaded the ailessons folder onto your hard drive from the included DVD. See "Loading lesson files" in the Starting up section of this book.

### See Lesson 14 in action!

*Use the accompanying video to gain a better understanding of how to use some of the features shown in this lesson. You can find the video tutorial for this lesson on the included DVD.*

## What makes Adobe Illustrator CC so great?

At first glance, the new features in Adobe Illustrator CC might not be apparent, but once you start working, especially with placed imagery, you will find numerous improvements that save time and frustration. In this lesson, you will have the opportunity to try out some of these great new features.

Note that not all the features included in this lesson's step-by-step exercises are new; many are helpful features that relate to the task at hand. Many shortcuts are included so you can pick up other helpful tips and tricks as you work. In this lesson, you will create a custom oversized luggage tag using several images, the tracing feature, new text controls, image brushes, and more.

### Opening the finished file

You can take a peek at the original file by opening the finished version of this file.

1   Choose File > Browse in Bridge. When Bridge appears, navigate to the ai14lessons folder and open the file named **ai1401_done**. An image of a front and back of a luggage tag appears. This illustration takes advantage of several new image and text features that you will use in this lesson.

2   You can leave this file open for reference or choose File > Close to close it.

### Creating the luggage tag

In this part of the lesson, you will create the luggage tag outline and assign a Pantone color to the tag.

1   In Illustrator, choose File > New, or use the keyboard shortcut Ctrl+N (Windows) or Command+N (Mac OS). The New Document dialog box appears.

**2**  If they are not already selected, choose Print from the New Document Profile drop-down menu and Inches from the Units drop-down menu. When you change the units to inches, the New Document Profile setting changes to [Custom]. You can always change the Document Profile and the units of measurement after creating the file. Leave all other settings at their defaults and click OK.

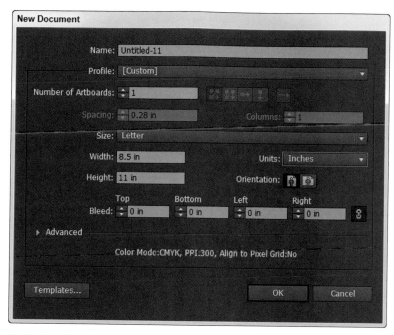

*Specify the settings of your new Illustrator document.*

You will start this illustration by building the outline for the luggage tags.

**3**  Click and hold the Rectangle tool to select the hidden Rounded Rectangle tool.

**4**  With the Rounded Rectangle tool selected, click once anywhere on the artboard. A rounded Rectangle dialog box appears.

5 To create a rounded rectangle in the correct dimensions for your tag, enter **2.75** for the Width, **5** for the Height, and **.3** for the corner radius. Click OK; the rounded rectangle is created to the size of a typical oversized luggage tag. You will now apply a Pantone color to the luggage tag.

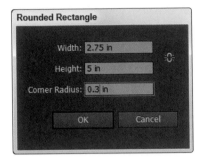

Create the rounded rectangle to size.

6 Make sure the Swatches panel is visible. If it is not, select Windows > Swatches.

7 Make sure that the rounded rectangle shape is selected, and then select the Swatch Libraries menu icon ( ) from the lower-left area of the Swatches panel. A list of available color libraries is visible; select the one named Color Books, and then select the color book named Pantone+ Solid Coated. A separate Pantone+ Solid Coated panel appears, and it contains most of the colors from the Pantone Color library (PMS colors).

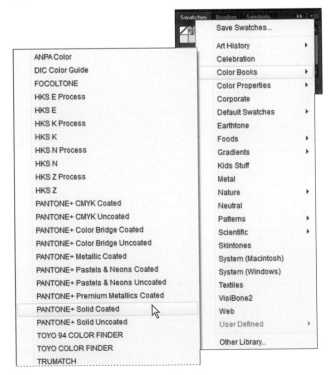

Select to view the Pantone+Solid Coated panel.

**8**   Click the panel menu in the upper-right area of the Pantone+ Solid Coated Panel to display the panel menu, and then select to view the PMS colors in the Small List View. Your colors now appear in a detail list.

**9**   From that same panel menu, select Show Find Field; a Find text box appears. Use this text box to type the PMS color you want to locate.

**10**  Type **2925** into the Find text box; the Pantone 2925 C swatch appears.

*Type a PMS number into the Find text box.*

**11**  Click the 2925 color swatch to fill the selected Rounded Rectangle box with the color and add the color to the Swatches panel.

**12**  Press Ctrl+S (Windows) or Command+S (Mac OS); the Save dialog box appears. Type **ai1401_work** into the File name text field. Keep the Save as type set to Adobe Illustrator. Navigate to the ai14lessons folder and click Save. If you receive a dialog box warning about spot colors, click Continue.

**13**  When the Illustrator Options dialog box appears, click OK to keep the default and save the file. Keep this file open for the next part of this lesson.

## Punching out the strap holder

In this next exercise, you will create the hold that is needed for the strap.

1   Select the Rounded Rectangle tool and click once on the artboard; the Rounded Rectangle dialog box appears.

2   Type **.85** into the Width text box and **.2** into the Height text box; leave the Corner Radius value at .3 and then click OK. The rectangle is created.

3   With the small Rounded Rectangle selected, position the cut mark for the strap so that it is approximately in the center and relatively close to the top. Don't worry about exact position, since you will adjust that shortly.

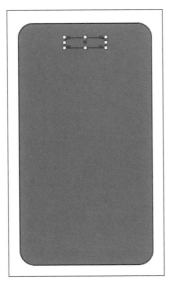

*Position the hold for the strap on the tag.*

4   Using the Selection tool, Shift+Click to add the large luggage tag to the selection. You now have both the hold for the strap and the large tag selected.

**5**  Choose Window > Align, and then select the Horizontal Align Center button.

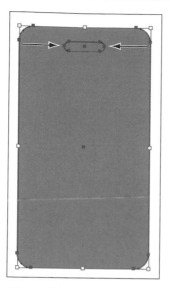

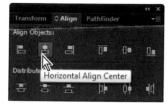

*Select Horizontal Align Center.*          *The strap hole is now centered horizontally.*

**6**  With both the strap hole and the large tag selected, press Ctrl+8 (Windows) or Command+8 (Mac OS). (You can also choose Object > Compound Path > Make). This essentially punches out the small strap shape that was on top of the large tag.

**7**  Press Ctrl+S (Windows) or Command+S (Mac OS) to save this file. Keep it open for the next part of this lesson.

## Cloning the tag

Since you are creating a front and back of a luggage tag, you will clone the artwork that you just created.

**1**  Make sure that you still have the luggage tag selected and that the Selection tool is active.

**2**  Press and hold the Alt (Windows) or Option (Mac OS) key; a double arrow cursor appears, indicating that you are about to clone the selected artwork.

**3**  While pressing and holding the Alt/Option key, press and hold the Shift key and drag to the right. By pressing and holding the combination of Alt+Shift (Windows) or Option+Shift (Mac OS), you can clone and keep the cloned artwork constrained to the same horizontal position. When you have positioned your cloned artwork off to the right, release the mouse first, and then the modifier keys.

*If you release the Shift or Alt/Option keys before releasing the mouse, the clone will not be successful, and the cloned shape can "bump" out of position.*

You now have a front and back for your luggage tag. In the next part of this lesson, you will start taking advantage of some of the new features in Illustrator CC.

## Placing multiple images

In Illustrator CC, you can select multiple files to place at one time. In this section, you will place the two images that you will use for this tag.

**1**   Choose File > Place; the Place dialog box appears.

**2**   Navigate to the ai14lessons folder and select the image named **ai1402**. Then, Shift+click the image file named **ai1403**. Verify that when you select these images, the Link check box, located in the lower portion of the Place dialog box, becomes selected. This indicates that the images are not going to be embedded into this Illustrator file, but will be linked to the original files. You will find out how this affects your workflow later in this lesson.

*When placing these files, make sure that the Link check box is selected.*

**3**  Choose Place. If an embedded profile message appears, click OK. A loaded cursor appears with a small thumbnail of the first image that you are about to place.

*A loaded cursor appears when you choose to place multiple images.*

**4**  Click once anywhere on your artboard to place the first image (a person on a motorcycle); your cursor "loads-up" with the second image. Click again on your artboard to place the second image (a small .png of a motorcycle).

**5**  Press Ctrl+S (Windows) or Command+S (Mac OS) to save this file. Keep it open for the next part of this lesson.

## Converting an image to vector art

You will now quickly convert the artwork of the woman on the motorcycle to vector art to create the effect of pen and ink. If you want more details about how to use the Tracing features in Adobe Illustrator, read Lesson 5, "Working with Drawing Tools."

**1**  Using your Selection tool, select only the image of the person on the bike.

**2**  Click the Tracing Presets downward pointing arrow to the right of Image Trace in the Control panel at the top of your artboard. Select Sketched Art from the drop-down list that appears. The image changes into a black and white sketchy Image.

*Select Sketched Art for a tracing preset.*

## Investigating the improved Links panel

In this section, you will have the opportunity of investigating the new Links panel. In Illustrator CC, the Links panel offers additional information and capabilities.

1.   If the Links panel is not visible, select Window > Links.

When the Links panel appears, you see your two place images listed in the panel. Using the Links panel, you can discover details about the images and other placed files you are using in your Illustrator file.

2.   Double-click the file named **ai1402** that is listed in the Links panel. The information about the image appears in the lower portion of the Links panel, and it includes details such as the fact that the file is a 300 ppi, PSD file that is at 100% scale.

In the Links panel for Illustrator CC, you can now locate the Color Space, PPI (Pixels per inch), Dimensions, and transparency information. You can also find helpful tools to help you locate your placed file in your Illustrator file, and edit the original file.

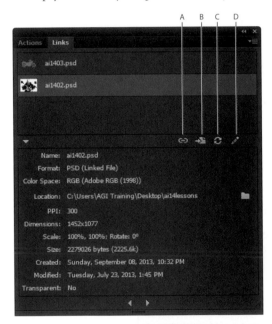

*Find the details about placed files in the Links panel.*

**A.** *Relink.* **B.** *Go To Link.* **C.** *Update Link.* **D.** *Edit Original.*

3.   With the **ai1402** image still selected in the Links panel, click Edit Original () in the Links panel. Photoshop launches and the **ai1402** image is opened in Photoshop. You will make some simple editing changes in this image, and then return to Illustrator.

*If you do not have Adobe Photoshop installed, you can launch Creative cloud to download and install Photoshop as a part of your subscription or as a trial.*

**4**    In Photoshop, select the Eraser tool, and then erase the mirrors on either side of the bike. Don't worry about doing a perfect job, since this is just an exercise of workflow.

*Use the Eraser tools to remove the side mirrors.*

**5**    Once you are finished removing the mirrors, choose File > Save and then File > Close.

**6**    Return to Illustrator. Since your placed file is linked to the original, you will receive a message indicating that some files are missing or modified. Click Yes to indicate that you would like to update those files now. The traced file is updated and the mirrors are removed.

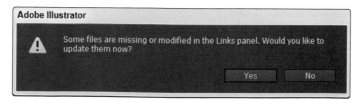

*Adobe Illustrator notes that the placed file has been updated.*

7    With the **ai1402.psd** image still selected, double-click the Scale tool (⬛); the Scale dialog box appears. Type **60** into the Uniform text field, and then click OK. The image is scaled down in size. Note that the Links panel documents this scaled size.

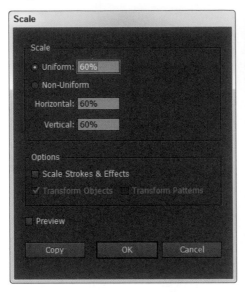
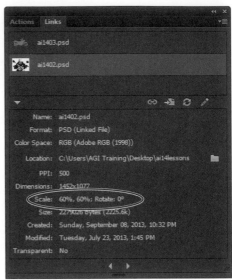

*Scale the image down to 60% The Links panel tracks the scaled size.*

8    Using the Selection tool, click and drag to position the traced image into the lower portion of the luggage tag.

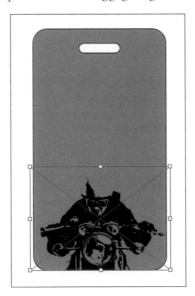

*Position the image in the lower portion of the tag.*

9    Press Ctrl+S (Windows) or Command+S (Mac OS) to save this file. Keep it open for the next part of this lesson.

# Adding text

In this next section, you will add text to your tag and take advantage of the new Touch Type tool.

**1** Select the Type tool (T), and then click and drag a text area across the luggage tag with the image.

**2** Type **Don't touch the bike** using any typeface and size.

**3** Press Ctrl+A (Windows) or Command+A (Mac OS) to select all the text.

**4** Press Ctrl+T (Windows) or Command+T (Mac OS) to see the Character panel, or choose Window > Type > Character.

**5** Choose Myriad Pro (as in our example), or any other typeface.

**6** To set the size, with your text still selected, press Ctrl+Shift+> (Greater Than) or Command+Shift+> (Greater Than) repeatedly to increase your type in 2 point increments. Do this until you are happy with the text size.

*Select a typeface and then select a size.*

**7** Select White from Fill in the Control panel across the top; the text is now white.

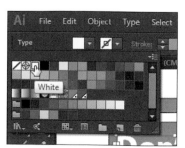

*Change the Fill of the text to white.*

**8** Press Ctrl+S (Windows) or Command+S (Mac OS) to save this file. Keep it open for the next part of this lesson.

## Using the new Touch Type tool

In Illustrator CC, you can now take advantage of several tools built for touch. An example is the Touch Type tool that allows you to modify the properties of characters using the cursor or touch controls. In this exercise, you will use your mouse and cursor.

**1** Make sure that your text from the previous part of this lesson is still selected.

**2** Click and hold the Type tool (T) and select the new Touch Type tool (▦).

**3** Click the letter "D" to see handles appear around it. Click and drag down to change the position of just the letter "D".

**4** Using the Character panel, change other attributes of the letter "D" including the font and size.

*Using the Touch Type tool, you can customize an individual character's properties.*

**5** Click other letters and click and drag up or down to change their alignment. There are no specific settings for the arrangement of your characters; just have fun and experiment with this creative tool.

*Experiment with different type properties to create a unique text effect.*

**6** Press Ctrl+S (Windows) or Command+S (Mac OS) to save this file. Keep it open for the next part of this lesson.

## Embedding an image

In this next section, you will embed your small motorcycle image into the Illustrator file.

There are many benefits to embedding an image file. Most users will make this selection if they want to ensure that the image file travels with the illustrator file when sending the file to their printer, or to someone else who might be working on a different computer. You also need to embed an image file that you plan to use as a symbol (see Lesson 10, "Working with Symbols") or for the new Image Brush feature. You will take advantage of the new Image brush feature later in this lesson.

**1** In the Links panel, click to select the image named **ai1403.psd**.

**2** From the Links panel menu, choose Embed Image(s). If you receive a Photoshop Import Options dialog box, click OK to flatten the layers in this .psd file into a single image.

Notice that the image is no longer named **ai1403.psd**, and that it now has an icon to the right of the image thumbnail indicating it is embedded in this file.

*In Illustrator CC, you can now unembed an image so you can access your file for further editing work. Access Unembed using the Links panel panel menu. When selected, you will be directed to save the unembedded file in your system.*

## Creating an image brush

In this part of the lesson, you will create a custom brush using your embedded motorcycle image. Now in Illustrator CC, you can create a brush from an embedded image.

**1** Using the Selection tool, select the motorcycle on the Illustrator artboard.

**2** Choose Window > Transparency to see the Transparency panel. You will change the blending mode of the motorcycle so that the blue motorcycle appears on the blue background of the luggage tag.

**3** With the motorcycle image selected, choose Multiply from the Blending mode drop-down menu. Multiply is a blending mode that will make the motorcycle art blend as though it were created with a magic marker, darkening the blue of the image.

*Change the blending mode to Multiply.*

**4**    If your Brushes panel is not visible, choose Windows > Brushes.

**5**    Click and drag the motorcycle art directly into the Brushes panel. When you see the cursor with the plus sign, release the mouse; the New Brush dialog box appears.

**6**    Select Pattern Brush and click OK; the Pattern Brush Options dialog box appears. Now in Illustrator CC, you have more advanced controls for creating pattern brushes.

**7**    In the Pattern Brush Options dialog box, type **bike pattern** into the Name text field.

**8**    Click the Outer corner tile to see your options for creating a pattern for your pattern brush. For this example, select Auto-Centered.

*Select a method for corner creation.*

**9**    From the fit section, choose Add space to fit. Using this method will not distort the motorcycle image.

**10** For Colorization, leave this set at None and click OK. The new image brush has been added to your brushes panel.

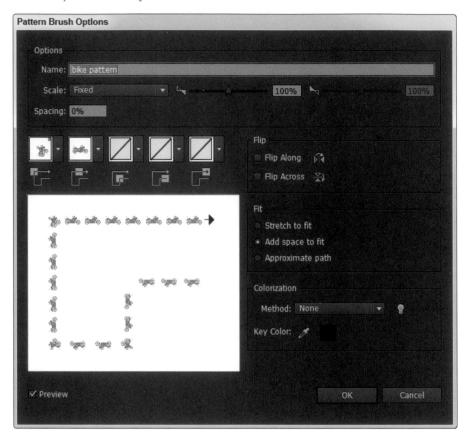

*The settings for your image pattern brush.*

**11** Press Ctrl+S (Windows) or Command+S (Mac OS) to save this file. Keep it open for the next part of this lesson.

## Applying the image brush to a stroke

You will now create a shape and use your motorcycle brush as a border.

**1** Select the Rounded Rectangle tool, and click and drag a rounded rectangle on the second side (blank) of your luggage tag. Don't worry about an exact size, but make it slightly smaller in width and height. In our example, the rectangle is approximately 2.375 in width and 3.85 in height.

**2** Press **D** on your keyboard to put the rounded rectangle back to the default foreground and background color of white for the fill and black for the stroke.

**3** Using the Selection tool, select both the luggage tag (under your new rounded rectangle) and the rounded rectangle shape.

**4**  Choose Window > Align. Before selecting an alignment method, click once on
the luggage tag behind the rounded rectangle shape. A selection of the luggage tag
becomes bolder. This indicates that this shape is locked in position and will only allow
the newly created rounded rectangle to reposition when aligning.

**5**  Choose Horizontal Align Center from the Align panel.

**6**  Choose Select > Deselect to deactivate any selections.

**7**  Click once on the newly created rounded rectangle shape you created, and then click
the new motorcycle brush you created in the Brushes panel. The motorcycle is now
used as the border for the shape.

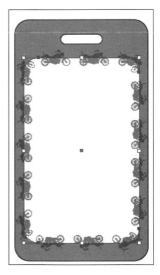

*The new motorcycle stroke creates the border.*

**8**  Press Ctrl+S (Windows) or Command+S (Mac OS) to save this file. Keep it open for
the next part of this lesson.

## Packaging a file

In this last section of your lesson, you will package your file. You can package a file to
keep a back up of an important illustration, or to easily send all components to another
person who might be working on this file.

**1**  Press Ctrl+S (Windows) or Command+S (Mac OS) to save your file.

**2**  Select File > Package. The Package dialog box appears.

**3**  For location, select the ai14lessons folder; you can leave the folder name at the default
of ai1401_work_Folder.

4   Under Options, leave all selected. As you can see, by using the new Package feature you can now easily collect the fonts and images used in your Illustrator file. Click Package.

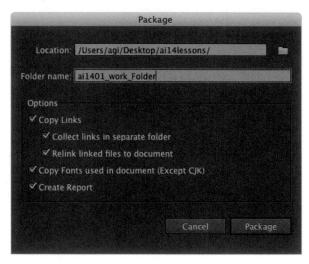

*The new Package feature allows you to collect fonts and images.*

5   A warning dialog box appears indication font restrictions. Read the message and click OK.

6   When the Adobe Illustrator dialog box appears indicating that your file is packaged, click Show Package. You are directed to your folder, which contains Fonts, Links and your Illustrator file and a report.

*Note that unlike the Adobe InDesign Package with Document Fonts feature, fonts packaged from Illustrator are not automatically activated when the recipient opens the Illustrator file from the package. They will need appropriate rights to manually install any appropriate fonts. Consider converting fonts to outlines as a workaround, or syncing fonts using Adobe TypeKit, which will not be packaged.*

In this lesson, you discovered some of the new features available to you in Adobe Illustrator CC. There are plenty more scattered throughout other lessons in this book, and they are best explained in context with their functionality.

# INDEX

# John Wiley & Sons, Inc.
# End-User License Agreement

**READ THIS**. You should carefully read these terms and conditions before opening the software packet(s) included with this book "Book". This is a license agreement "Agreement" between you and John Wiley & Sons, Inc. "WILEY". By opening the accompanying software packet(s), you acknowledge that you have read and accept the following terms and conditions. If you do not agree and do not want to be bound by such terms and conditions, promptly return the Book and the unopened software packet(s) to the place you obtained them for a full refund.

1. **License Grant**. WILEY grants to you (either an individual or entity) a nonexclusive license to use one copy of the enclosed software program(s) (collectively, the "Software") solely for your own personal or business purposes on a single computer (whether a standard computer or a workstation component of a multi-user network). The Software is in use on a computer when it is loaded into temporary memory (RAM) or installed into permanent memory (hard disk, CD-ROM, or other storage device). WILEY reserves all rights not expressly granted herein.

2. **Ownership.** WILEY is the owner of all right, title, and interest, including copyright, in and to the compilation of the Software recorded on the physical packet included with this Book "Software Media". Copyright to the individual programs recorded on the Software Media is owned by the author or other authorized copyright owner of each program. Ownership of the Software and all proprietary rights relating thereto remain with WILEY and its licensers.

3. **Restrictions on Use and Transfer.**

   **(a)** You may only (i) make one copy of the Software for backup or archival purposes, or (ii) transfer the Software to a single hard disk, provided that you keep the original for backup or archival purposes. You may not (i) rent or lease the Software, (ii) copy or reproduce the Software through a LAN or other network system or through any computer subscriber system or bulletin-board system, or (iii) modify, adapt, or create derivative works based on the Software.

   **(b)** You may not reverse engineer, decompile, or disassemble the Software. You may transfer the Software and user documentation on a permanent basis, provided that the transferee agrees to accept the terms and conditions of this Agreement and you retain no copies. If the Software is an update or has been updated, any transfer must include the most recent update and all prior versions.

**4. Restrictions on Use of Individual Programs.** You must follow the individual requirements and restrictions detailed for each individual program in the "About the CD" appendix of this Book or on the Software Media. These limitations are also contained in the individual license agreements recorded on the Software Media. These limitations may include a requirement that after using the program for a specified period of time, the user must pay a registration fee or discontinue use. By opening the Software packet(s), you agree to abide by the licenses and restrictions for these individual programs that are detailed in the "About the CD" appendix and/or on the Software Media. None of the material on this Software Media or listed in this Book may ever be redistributed, in original or modified form, for commercial purposes.

**5. Limited Warranty.**

**(a)** WILEY warrants that the Software and Software Media are free from defects in materials and workmanship under normal use for a period of sixty (60) days from the date of purchase of this Book. If WILEY receives notification within the warranty period of defects in materials or workmanship, WILEY will replace the defective Software Media.

**(b)** WILEY AND THE AUTHOR(S) OF THE BOOK DISCLAIM ALL OTHER WARRANTIES, EXPRESS OR IMPLIED, INCLUDING WITHOUT LIMITATION IMPLIED WARRANTIES OF MERCHANTABILITY AND FITNESS FOR A PARTICULAR PURPOSE, WITH RESPECT TO THE SOFTWARE, THE PROGRAMS, THE SOURCE CODE CONTAINED THEREIN, AND/ OR THE TECHNIQUES DESCRIBED IN THIS BOOK. WILEY DOES NOT WARRANT THAT THE FUNCTIONS CONTAINED IN THE SOFTWARE WILL MEET YOUR REQUIREMENTS OR THAT THE OPERATION OF THE SOFTWARE WILL BE ERROR FREE.

**(c)** This limited warranty gives you specific legal rights, and you may have other rights that vary from jurisdiction to jurisdiction.

**6. Remedies.**

**(a)** WILEY's entire liability and your exclusive remedy for defects in materials and workmanship shall be limited to replacement of the Software Media, which may be returned to WILEY with a copy of your receipt at the following address: Software Media Fulfillment Department, Attn.: *Adobe Illustrator CC Digital Classroom*, John Wiley & Sons, Inc., 10475 Crosspoint Blvd., Indianapolis, IN 46256, or call 1-800-762-2974. Please allow four to six weeks for delivery. This Limited Warranty is void if failure of the Software Media has resulted from accident, abuse, or misapplication. Any replacement Software Media will be warranted for the remainder of the original warranty period or thirty (30) days, whichever is longer.

**(b)** In no event shall WILEY or the author be liable for any damages whatsoever (including without limitation damages for loss of business profits, business interruption, loss of business information, or any other pecuniary loss) arising from the use of or inability to use the Book or the Software, even if WILEY has been advised of the possibility of such damages.

**(c)** Because some jurisdictions do not allow the exclusion or limitation of liability for consequential or incidental damages, the above limitation or exclusion may not apply to you.

7. **U.S. Government Restricted Rights.** Use, duplication, or disclosure of the Software for or on behalf of the United States of America, its agencies and/or instrumentalities "U.S. Government" is subject to restrictions as stated in paragraph (c)(1)(ii) of the Rights in Technical Data and Computer Software clause of DFARS 252.227-7013, or subparagraphs (c) (1) and (2) of the Commercial Computer Software - Restricted Rights clause at FAR 52.227-19, and in similar clauses in the NASA FAR supplement, as applicable.

8. **General.** This Agreement constitutes the entire understanding of the parties and revokes and supersedes all prior agreements, oral or written, between them and may not be modified or amended except in a writing signed by both parties hereto that specifically refers to this Agreement. This Agreement shall take precedence over any other documents that may be in conflict herewith. If any one or more provisions contained in this Agreement are held by any court or tribunal to be invalid, illegal, or otherwise unenforceable, each and every other provision shall remain in full force and effect.

# Register your Digital Classroom book for exclusive benefits

Registered owners receive access to:

 The most current lesson files

 Technical resources and customer support

 Notifications of updates

 Online access to video tutorials

 Downloadable lesson files

 Samples from other Digital Classroom books

**Register at** *DigitalClassroomBooks.com/CC/Illustrator*

# DigitalClassroom

**Register your book today at**
**DigitalClassroomBooks.com/CC/Illustrator**